# 30 YEARS
## A LIFE LIVED EVERY DAY

# 30 YEARS
## A LIFE LIVED EVERY DAY
### CORY ALEXANDER MCLEOD

First published 2023 by DB Publishing, an imprint of JMD Media Ltd,

Nottingham, United Kingdom.

ISBN 9781780916521

Printed in the UK

# CONTENTS

## 26    (13 September 2017 – 12 September 2018)                                    220

## 27    (13 September 2018 – 12 September 2019)                                    245

# THE REAL-LIFE TRUMAN SHOW

6 MILLION. This is the number of people in the world who watched me grow up from birth to age 21. For a while, it felt like I was living my own version of *The Truman Show*.

In 2012, my father and I released a film project on YouTube, called '21 Years' on my dad's channel, 'cloddyclips'. The video went viral and saw us do interviews around the world, including ITV, CBS America and the BBC. As I continued the project, taking the photos myself whilst living and travelling abroad, the idea came to me to write a book, mainly so there were some stories to accompany the photos. In the various backdrops you can see places I have visited, such as Patagonia, Machu Picchu and Mount Everest. You can see family, friends and girlfriends, each with their own story of how they wound up in my life and what they mean to me.

I've loved, I've hated, I've bullied and been bullied. I broke down in tears at the age of 13 and never cried again. I've excelled and been expelled. I've suffered with anxiety but battled it and won. I've reached out for help and been the one people go to for help. I've tried to make the most of my adult life and do more with each day. I've tried not to take life too seriously but hope I have made my parents proud along the way.

This is not your usual autobiography or memoir. I'm not a movie star, footballer or a TV personality, I'm just like you, trying to navigate my way through everyday life.

My name is Cory Alexander McLeod, I am from a town called Harrogate in the UK and I recently turned 30. This is a true story of what an everyday person's life looks like.

I hope you enjoy the book, as well as the latest video '30 Years: A Photo of Cory Every Day' which is out now.

## DISCLAIMER

Some of my friends' names in the book have been altered so their parents or employers don't find out all the illegal stuff they've done.

# LIFE BEFORE LIFE

## My cheeky, loveable Dad

To reach the point of arriving into this crazy world, I had a fairly unusual path. On my dad's side, my great, great grandad (Allan Milne McLeod) emigrated to Australia from Scotland in the 1880s. He settled in Queensland where there was a lot of resentment towards the government. Allan became a staunch socialist and associated with a newspaper publisher, Mr William Lane – a committed left-winger. News was received in 1890 that the Paraguayan government was granting large areas of forest, for free, to any group who would sell and market the timber. The world was crying out for quality timber and Paraguay needed to export. Mr Lane set the wheels in motion, and through his newspaper was able to interest and enlist a large number of disgruntled people – around 600 in all – to agree to this scheme. Everyone was to receive equal pay, religion was banned and the rules of behaviour would be strict. With the sales of everyone's possessions, the 'Royal Tar' sailing vessel was purchased and in July 1893 set sail from Sydney on her first 1300-mile voyage around Cape Horn to Asunción. The colony was named New Australia, founded in October 1893. My great grandad (John McLeod) was born on 3 March 1894. Life on the commune became extremely difficult. Money and food were in short supply and communication with the outside world could only be established on horseback. Alcohol was not permitted and it was against the rules for men to fraternise with natives. The question of pay also became an issue as hard-working lumberjacks received the same pay as tally clerks. Within a few short years, several families (including the McLeod's) decided to leave and form a new colony, which they named Cosme.

My grandad (Ronald 'Ronnie' George McLeod) was born on 27 January 1921. He grew up happily in Cosme, where he found a love for cricket, and later was given the job of delivering milk daily, on horseback, to various families living in the area. By 1929, trouble was brewing between Bolivia and Paraguay, which would later lead to the Chaco War.

Without the knowledge of his father, Ronnie was hastily bundled onto a train to Buenos Aires. After almost two days of travelling, he was met by his mother (Lily Ryan) at Lacroze Station. His mother was a talented dressmaker and had recently found suitable work in the patterns department at Harrods Buenos Aires. One of her first tasks was to find him a pair of shoes as he had never worn a pair before!

Ronnie was enrolled as a boarder at St Alban's College. It was a private school run by an Anglican priest, the Rev. George Henry Knight-Clarke. The college motto was 'Philomathes Polymathes' (If thou art fond of learning thou wilt be very learned). Ronnie went from not being able to read or write to becoming the best in his class for many of the exams. However, on the whole, his eight years as a boarder was a sad time in his life. Unlike the other boarders, he didn't have much pocket money and his allowance could only afford him one apple on a Wednesday afternoon and five boiled sweets on a Saturday. There was little or no money for clothes, so 'cast-offs' kept him going. Ronnie was always hungry, and the butler, a man called Eladio, would occasionally slip him some buttered bread.

In 1932, at the ripe old age of 11, Ronnie discovered that he had been posted as a 'deserter' by the Paraguayan authorities for failing to answer the 'call-up' to fight in the war that was raging in the Chaco. His uncle (Herbert Ryan), who was still living in Paraguay, warned him that he would be liable for four years' imprisonment with hard labour if he returned.

By the age of 21, World War Two was well underway and, along with his friends, he volunteered for service. Grandad Ronnie boarded the Highland Princess from Montevideo to Belfast on 24 October 1942. The non-stop voyage took 28 days. Early one morning, whilst on night watch, Ronnie developed an acute attack of appendicitis. The ship's doctor was sent for but they discovered him face down in his cabin suffering from delirium tremens. Ronnie was placed in the ship's hospital and taken care of by the Royal Air Force surgeon. There were no suitable means of carrying out an operation so the inflammation was controlled by May & Baker pills, plus a strict diet. As he lay in his hospital bed, he felt apprehensive at the thought of having to join the Tank Corps, so on one of his visits to the toilet he tore up the papers and flushed them down the middle of the Atlantic.

When they were greeted by representatives from the Forces and Ministry of Defence, they were asked for their documents and split up into the Navy, Army and Air Force. Ronnie was asked by an official which service he wished to join. 'Royal Air Force, Sir.' 'And where is your certificate from the British Consulate?' 'I haven't one, Sir.' (This was true in one sense). That resolved the matter and he was grouped with the batch destined for the Brylcreem Boys (RAF).

Some years later, whilst on a post in Scotland, he was having a drink outside a bar. A lady approached him and said, 'Hola, Argentino,' after noticing his Argentinian flag on his uniform. That lady was Cecilia McLean, who would later become my grandmother. Grandad said, 'That was the luckiest and most wonderful meeting of my whole life!' Cecilia was also living in South America, but in Chile, and volunteered for the Women's Auxiliary Air Force. Ronnie fell in love instantly and invited Cecilia for lunch the following day … and every day after that! In fact, they got engaged six weeks after meeting. By January 1946, Ronnie was eagerly pressing Cecilia to settle on a date for their wedding. One evening they went to the local cinema to watch the film Enchanted Cottage, featuring Robert Young and Dorothy Maguire. The story was about an amorous encounter during World War One, on 6 April 1917. Ronnie turned to Cecilia during the interval and suggested they get married on 6 April. She looked at him and said, 'Okay, provided it's a Saturday.' He took out his diary, and it was!

On 10 April 1956, my dad, Ian, was born in the port city of Antofagasta, northern Chile. He was a cheeky but lovable kid – a bit like his son. After only two years, Cecilia and Ronnie made the decision to take the kids (Margaret, Lis and Ian) to the UK so they could reunite with family and be educated in a British school. They boarded the Reina del Pacifico ocean liner – which turned out to be the last journey it ever took. During the six-week journey, my dad found a gap on the top deck and tried to jump off the ship. One of the crew noticed and ran over, grabbing him at the last second. I wouldn't be here today if it wasn't for that man. This must also be where my adventure and adrenalin junkie characteristics originated.

Ian started his first few years on UK soil in Glasgow and Aberdeen, before moving to Yeadon in Leeds. By the age of ten, Ian and the family had moved to Harrogate and my dad became a pupil at Western Primary School on Cold Bath Road before later joining the Harrogate Grammar School. From the stories I've been told, my dad was a bright kid, but mischievous. Before the days of Facebook, there was a site called Friends Reunited.

You could sign up and fill in all your details: where you grew up, what school you went to, and start chatting to old school friends you may have lost touch with. Ian signed up in the early 2000s and there were several stories about 'Clod' already on there. Clod was my dad's nickname growing up. He was very artistic and creative and made two logos out of his nickname. One was a face using the letters and one was the sole of a shoe. One of the website users said he engraved his nickname into every wooden desk in the school. We were at one of his friend's parties (three decades later) and his daughter said she saw his name on some of the desks. Another story on the website said he changed the clocktower school flag to a pirate flag. He was never a bad person, just enjoyed some harmless humour and being cheeky.

Being cheeky did get him into trouble on one occasion though. When he was only in Year 7, he decided to tease the biggest guy in school, who was in the sixth form. The boy who was twice the height and size of him didn't hesitate before punching him to the ground. Lesson learnt. Us McLeod's, we learn the hard way. Ian enjoyed a bit of fishing on a weekend, but he wasn't so much the sporty type. In Rugby, he was always flatlined due to being small, but one day he managed to score a try. It was his greatest sporting achievement as a kid. Unfortunately, the referee disallowed it so it never counted.

In his mid-teens, he started following Leeds United and travelled to many of the games, home and away. This was during the hooliganism days and wearing a Leeds shirt in any city other than Leeds made you a human target. One day, in Nottingham, he was boarding the coach after the game and bricks were flying through the bus windows, with one hitting the driver, Keith Murgatroyd of Murgatroyd Coaches, and splitting his head open. He saw one lad get chased by a gang down a one-way street and get stabbed. That guy ended up coming to his 40th birthday years later. Other Leeds fans were forced to swim across the

River Trent, whilst bricks and bottles were thrown at them from the bridge. 'All good fun on a dark evening,' my dad said. 'It even made the front page of the national newspapers!'

Cecilia and Ronnie moved back to the warmth of Chile, whilst Ian and his sisters (Margaret and Lis) stayed in the UK. Margaret was in the Women's Royal Navy Service and met RAF officer Dave. They fell in love and bought a house together in Doncaster. Lis worked for the Ministry of Defence in the office and was a proud Mod, with a Lambretta scooter for transport. My dad made use of his artistic ability and moved to Cambridge to study at art college, where he met my mum, Karen.

## My wonderful, most beautiful and caring mother

My wonderful, most beautiful and caring mother, Karen, was born in Saltburn (near Middlesbrough) on 28 October 1963. Mum was the middle child of five – three brothers (Martin, Sean and David) and one sister (Mandy). Her parents were brought up in the North East. Her dad, Bill, was from Redcar, the son of Welsh parents. His father had died in his early 30s in a work accident. He had moved from South Wales to Redcar for work. He left eight children, seven of them boys, to be brought up by his wife Katie. Katie's only daughter died aged 21. The family were very close and a great support for each other throughout their lives. My grandad, Bill, died in 1999. I still remember the moment my mum found out on the phone, it still haunts me. There were only three of the seven brothers remaining in 1999 and they all died within a few weeks of each other. Although I was young when he died, I have fond memories of Grandad Bill. He was the joker in our family and always had a mischievous grin as if he was up to something. Often, he would sit all the grandkids down on the carpet by his chair and tell us a new joke he'd written. He would say they were his … but maybe they were just from the back of a Penguin wrapper!

Nana Mavis/Mum's 'mam' (as they say in the 'Boro') was born in Guisborough and lived in South Bank. She was the granddaughter of Irish and German immigrants. There were many Irish Catholics in the North East who had left their native homes to look for work in the iron and steel industry. Nana went to St Peter's Catholic School and enjoyed

her time there, making many friends and having lots of fun. She said if she had worked harder at school instead of having a good time she wouldn't have had to catch up later in life. Following school, Nana attended sixth form college, but halfway through was advised by the art teacher to enrol at Cleveland College of Art and Design. This she says was the best decision she ever made.

You could see Nana's influence on my mother as she excelled in art class and later went to art college. She was also a half-decent footballer and the boys used to call her 'Wilfie' (Wilfred James Mannion) when she kicked the ball back to them, as it was always a perfect long-distance pass. Mum and her siblings spent most of their time 'playing out' but would always stick together. The Boro can be a rough place and on one evening, some of the girls were picking on Mandy at the local field. My mum went over and shouted at them to scare them off and took a distraught Mandy home to Bill and Mavis. That's the type of family they were, they always had each other's back – and still do to this day!

The words below were sent to me by my mum after I asked what she remembered from her childhood. I thought it was nice and better to leave it as it was:

*The first few years of my life, I lived in South Bank, Middlesbrough (although I was born in Saltburn). I am curious about memories and nostalgia. I am curious about what I remember and what I don't remember.*

*In South Bank, I remember the streets, the chimneys, the women sitting outside in the sun – there were no gardens. I remember the back yard, the cobbles, the wash house, the smell of dinner cooking, the steaming pans. I remember the stairs, the flamingo wallpaper in the bathroom. I remember being ill and I couldn't lift my head off the pillow. I remember one of my brothers breaking my doll's eye with a screwdriver … but I don't remember all the details. I remember Bells the butchers, the shoe shop, the market, and the Post Office. I remember my grandad's brothers, my nana's friends, the ticking of the Big Ben alarm clock. I remember going to Church, the priests, the nuns, going to infant school, wetting myself laughing, wooden dolls, my doll's house and BIG windows I couldn't see out of.*

*I remember my Dad taking us to Redcar on the bus, walks to our cousin's house, cousin envy – they had more than we did but I still loved spending time with them. We had ice cream and played on the beach. We would go to the cemetery to pay respects to my dad's mother. I still go to this day. I pay respect to his mother, to him and his brothers. I like graveyards. I have found his mother's mother and father's unmarked graves and in Eston I have found my mother's great grandfather's grave, and the Germans. I'm nostalgic about them.*

*Ever since I was a kid, I have loved storytelling. I dream practically every night … epic stories. I make up stories about people I pass in the street. For example, today I saw three men walking in different directions. They all knew each other and looked surprised but happy to see one another. Instantly, I decided that two of them had met at university, and the third was a former boss of theirs. I didn't take it any further this time, but usually I do. When I talk to friends about incidents at work, I use far too many words, creating a story to entertain them. I get a lot of pleasure out of it.*

*I studied illustration at college, my pictures tell stories. I love having stories told to me and I love reading stories to children. I would like to write children's stories. My favourite books are fiction, but I also like non-fiction … if it's a good story.*

*Friends and family are very special to me. I've always wanted to paint or illustrate them – Carole with her fashionable clothes and chairs, Helen with her dog, Roxy etc.*

## How I met your mother

Mum said she saw Dad across the room in art class and his T-shirt had an image of an ant that said, 'I'm so happy I could shit.' The ant had its head in its hand looking depressed and apparently Dad was doing exactly the same pose, and she asked herself, 'Who on earth is that guy!?'

## Sorry Mr Coppola

Dad was easily influenced back in those days. One night, they were going to pick up some weed from The Midland Pub, where they met two Rastas. One of them asked Dad if he had a house. He replied, 'Yes,' with no idea of the repercussions those three letters would cause. They asked if they could come over on the Thursday and play some music. Dad loved his music so he allowed them to. What he wasn't expecting was hundreds of people showing up from all over the country to party. It was only a small house, but it was overflowing onto the streets. The police showed up, but there were so many people that they couldn't do anything. Whilst it may have been a bit of fun at first, Mum said they disregarded them as owners of the house and treated it as their own. The following morning, Dad's landlord, who was part of the local Italian mafia, came to the house with a hammer and threatened to kill him. As he was tapping the hammer in the palm of his hands, Dad said, 'Sorry Mr. Coppola, it won't happen again.'

During my parents' time in Cambridge in 1987 or 1988 (Dad's memory isn't the best), they were both invited to their friend Barry Kamen's art exhibition and party, where Stephen Fry was also present. They bring it up every time we watch QI. My parents both passed the art course with flying colours (excuse the pun) and moved back to Harrogate, getting a flat together on Harlow Moor Drive.

## My parents' influence

Besides their love for art, they shared a similar passion for music. Mum was into her disco and Dad was into his rave and dance music, but they both loved a lot of the same bands, such as Little Feat, Radiohead, Oasis and singers such as Tim Buckley, Jeff Buckley and Elliot Smith. By the age of 12, Dad had records by The Kinks, The Beatles, Bob Dylan, Donovan, The Beach Boys, Joe South, Marvin Gaye and Stevie Wonder, to name a few. On his ninth birthday, he received some money and went to buy Dylan's 'The Times They Are a-Changin'' and Donovan's 'Catch the Wind'. He saw Donovan on his father's 36th birthday and had the single signed.

It's safe to say, I have been heavily influenced by my parents in terms of my music taste. All their favourite bands and singers growing up are my favourites now. In 1995, they met Jeff Buckley and got his autograph after his show in Leeds, which I am extremely jealous of. Thankfully, in 1996, they took me to see Oasis at Loch Lomond, which made up for it. I listen to Radiohead, Oasis, Jeff Buckley and Elliot Smith on an almost daily basis. My parents were also very sociable people and their house was usually the place to go to on a weekend. They were known for booking DJs for their house parties and installing lights, lasers and even smoke machines. I've been passed the baton when it comes to organising parties. It's usually down to me to organise nights out and events for me and my friends.

## Quiet heroes

My parents are quiet heroes. They are genuine, easy-going people who I look up to a lot. They don't like stress in their life – although sometimes there is no hiding from it due to pressures from work and money. They're people you can talk to, people you can have fun with and people you can take advice from. They've taught me from a young age to value my friends and not to take life too seriously so you don't enjoy it. My friends say I'm similar to my parents, which I'm proud of. They've given me that laidback freedom to do what I want with my life and not be pressured into settling down too early or following a specific path.

An example of what type of people my parents are is when my mum became close friends with Mrs Hinchcliffe, an elderly lady who lived next door to our house on St. George's Road, Harrogate. Her family didn't live close by, so my mum would go and check up on her each day and make her tea. They both became fond of each other and my mum enjoyed hearing all the stories from Mrs Hinchcliffe's earlier years. Mrs. Hinchcliffe offered to give her cottage in the Lake District to my mum in her will. Despite the cottage being worth a lot of money, my mum graciously declined the offer. She later told me she wouldn't want Mrs. Hinchcliffe's family thinking she was only friends with her for that reason.

## Laidback family traits

My Aunty Lis told me where this laidback trait came from in our family. She believes it goes back generations. Grandad Ronnie's dad used to be very militant and strict with him. He was always brought back in line and had to do as he was told or he would be punished. When Ronnie had Margaret, Lis and Ian, he promised himself he would take a more laidback approach and give them more freedom. Dad has carried that on to me and never been too strict – although I was a little shit growing up so he shouted at me when he had to!

## Havana bad time in Cuba

Before they even thought about bringing someone into the world, both my parents had some more travelling to get out of their system. Dad and Lis had always dreamed of visiting Machu Picchu so they spent a month in South America backpacking. My mum joined her best friend, Ruth, working as crew on a millionaire's yacht. They spent a lot of time around the Caribbean, Mexico and North America. She had the time of her life, but had no idea how badly it was going to go wrong. On one of their trips the captain accidently crossed international waters into Cuban territory. This didn't go down well with the Cuban authority and they surrounded the yacht and starting firing shots at it. The captain took Ruth, my mum and the rest of the crew below deck for safety. Mum said it was a terrifying experience and she thought she was going to die. The whole ordeal made the news back home and a photo of Ruth and Mum was published in the national papers. My dad didn't even know anything about it until the Daily Mail were at his door. He was in such a state of shock and not thinking straight. When they asked for a photo of Mum, he handed them the first photo he could find. It was a photo of her hungover after she had just thrown up.

# 0

## (13 September 1991 – 12 September 1992)

### Unlucky for some

I was born in Harrogate Hospital on Friday the 13th, on the 13th hour, on the 13th minute of September 1991 (unlucky for some), weighing in at 6 pounds and 15 ounces. Dad, being Dad, was sat at home watching Crimewatch with a bag of fish and chips when he received the call to rush back to the hospital. Apparently, as I came out of the womb, my dad was standing at the end of the bed with a scary Joker and Batman T-shirt on. It wasn't the arrival into the world I was expecting. Funny really, the only nightmare I remember having as a kid was Batman burgling our house.

After months of going back and forth on names, they decided it would be Cory if I was a boy and Rosie if I was a girl. Jokingly, Dad suggested calling me Rupert (incredibly posh name in England) so they could both shout 'Rupert! Rupert!' whenever they needed my attention. We weren't a posh family so it would've been funny.

Other than the baby scan, this would be the first day I would have a photo taken for our daily photo project on YouTube. Over a glass of wine, my dad had the idea to take a photo of me every day of my life and turn it into a flick book – obviously there was no YouTube back then! It was just an idea that came to him randomly and two decades later we released a time-lapse film online called 21 Years which received over six million views and had us doing TV and radio interviews all around the world.

It wasn't long before all our family and friends were cramming into the hospital ward to get their first glimpse of me. I received three teddy bears as gifts. The teddies weren't granted a name until much later when I could eventually speak. When my parents asked me what I wanted their names to be, I said, 'Big Ted, Little Ted and…' I couldn't think of another name. Mum pushed me for an answer: 'Go on! What would you like the third teddy's name to be?' I replied 'Name!' and so it stuck. Big Ted, Little Ted and Name became residents at the McLeod household and still exist to this day – although Little Ted only has one eye now.

I was fortunate to be born in the beautiful spa town of Harrogate. 'The happiest place to live in the UK' is home to The Stray, Valley Gardens and the Harlow Carr botanical gardens, as well as the infamous Betty's Tea Room. Harrogate is great for kids and elderly people as it's a safe town with lots of things to do. There is no university in Harrogate, so many young people leave for other cities to study, only returning to live once they have found a partner to settle down with. The town is very community driven and you can't walk more than 30 seconds without bumping into someone you know.

During my first three months, I developed a severe allergy. I was in immense pain with my skin ravaged by rashes. I'd spend the entire night writhing in bed, rubbing the skin from my face and scratching my thighs with my toenails. My parents were distraught seeing me suffer and had many sleepless nights. The early sign was after leaving the laundrette to do our weekly washing. My parents dressed me after and my skin became red all the way up to my neck. Mum and Dad decided to do their own washing after that, using a product kinder on the skin. Much to their (and my) disappointment, the change in product didn't cure it. Mum continued to breastfeed me and my skin became so bad that I looked like what my dad described as 'a sad old man'. If Mum fed me, it would make matters worse as I was often sick.

The doctors couldn't work out what it was and there was some confusion as I would have the rash at home, but by the time I reached the hospital it would recover. This happened a few times and so the doctors didn't take it as seriously as they maybe should have. It was one doctor who was only in the Harrogate Hospital temporarily to cover a

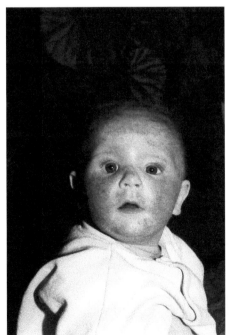 

*Photos taken one month apart.*

shortage of staff who noticed I had an issue and sent me to a specialist. Thankfully, they made the decision to keep me in the hospital over a few days and study how I reacted to a variety of different foods. They concluded it was an allergy to dairy passing through breast milk, so recommended that my parents switch to powdered soya milk and avoid dairy altogether. My parents were given creams and bandages to help my skin and the smile on my face soon returned.

The change from sad baby with itchy skin to happy baby with healthy skin is really noticeable in the daily photo project.

Still to this day, I'm not sure if I was planned or not – I daren't ask! My parents were in between jobs, before my dad eventually settled on a picture framing job he secured through a friend and my mum was a part-time cleaner. Mum would take me to the houses and place me in front of the TV whilst she cleaned.

# 1
## (13 September 1992 – 12 September 1993)

### My 1st birthday!

My first birthday was a joyous one. The rents took me to Saltburn to play on the beach and then I had a caterpillar birthday cake to celebrate with my mum's family. Like my dad (at a similar age), when he tried to jump into the North Atlantic Ocean, I was attracted by the water at first sight. In the split second my family turned away, I began to run towards the sea, to reach the water. Unfortunately, my little legs could only go so fast and my dad caught up with me.

Despite spending my first year in England, my first word was in Spanish. I waved to my parents' friends and said, 'Hola!'

## Young backpacker

In December 1992, my parents decided to take me backpacking with them in Chile. Grandad Ronnie, Granny Cecilia, Aunty Lis and her kids were all living in Viña del Mar, on the west coast of Chile, so we stayed with them before boarding a train south towards Patagonia. Before embarking on our travels, I had the privilege of meeting my great grandmother, Karen (pronounced 'Kahn' as she was Danish). At the time of our only meeting, Karen was 100 years old and I was one.

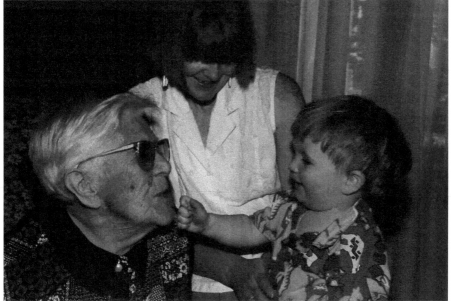

My dad said I was 'quite the star' when I went to Chile for the first time. After being there a few months, my hair had turned blond and people were approaching me saying 'Precioso!' Some of the locals had never seen a blond baby before. One shopkeeper even asked if they could take a photo of me to put in their shop window.

# 2

## (13 September 1993 – 12 September 1994)

### Early memories

Whilst writing this book, I looked through old family photos and videos to refresh my memory. There were some videos I'd never even seen before. Although me and my dad love each other we're not very affectionate these days and rarely embrace each other with a hug. I was surprised by some of the footage; hours and hours of my dad playing with me, and I looked so happy. We had press-up competitions, pretended to play in a band (whilst I was dressed as Batman) and he even built me a giant swing that would send me high above the hedges so all the neighbours could see me. I guess I've always taken my upbringing for

granted and not appreciated how lucky I have been to have loving parents.

When I wasn't having fun at the house, I would be at the local fields kicking a ball around. My dad wasn't much of a footballer so he used to let me run around with the ball myself. I was happy as Larry, and because I had no one to play with it's probably the reason I became a good dribbler. My coaches would say I dribble too much though …

When my dad was at work, I would beg my mum to play

football with me. She never liked doing it because I would always make her go in goal. Mum preferred rainy days so she could give me one-to-one art classes instead. Each time we would do a different style. It could be painting, watercolour, fine art or even stencil drawing. By the time I started school, I was beyond my years when it came to any art-related projects.

There was rarely a day that went by when we didn't have guests at the house. My parents had many friends and a big family. Summers were incredibly busy. We had family flying in from Chile, friends from London visiting for the weekend and my cousins would often come to visit from Middlesbrough. On a weekend it was normal for there to be 20 to 30 people in the house. I enjoyed wandering around and meeting new people. Despite the age difference, I became close with my parents' friends. They would always make time for me and even if they were having a party, I would be involved. Sarah, Helen and Carole were three of my mum's earliest friends in Harrogate and we still see them on a regular basis. It's more fun now as I can actually have a drink with them.

# 3

## (13 September 1994 – 12 September 1995)

### I spy with my little eye

One day, we were in hospital as Grandad Bill was having trouble with his eye. I was being my usual mischievous self in the waiting room of the eye ward. All the seats were taken in the waiting room, with each patient having either one or two patches on their eyes while they waited to be seen (unintentional pun). I paraded around the floor, screaming and shouting. After growing tired of shushing, Mum announced a brilliant idea to distract me. 'I know! Cory, let's play a game!' 'A game! I love games!' Meanwhile, Nana was thanking the heavens. 'So what game would you like to play?' 'Ooo, ooo! Erm, tig!' 'Noo, we can't play tig in a hospital Cory!'

I shouted, 'I know! I spy!' Nana shook her head and Mum put her hand over her face to hide the embarrassment. 'I Spy' is the best and most efficient game to keep the kids busy… unless you're in an eye ward of a hospital. My mum, noticing the huge beaming smile on my face, tried to think of an alternative. You could tell all the patients in the ward were willing my mum on to think of something. 'Okay, okay, we can play it. But… we have to call it by another name. We will call it Something beginning with.' Mum mistakenly suggested for me to start. What she should have done was … go first, pick something difficult and I could've been guessing for hours until the operation was over. Unfortunately for her, she lost this particular duel.

'Mini-me' began to think: 'Okay, something beginning with …' whilst looking around the room for a good object. Several minutes passed. 'Something beginning with … B!' Nana was dropping off, so my mum gave her a nudge. 'Away mam, help us out with the guessing!' Nana looked for all the objects beginning with B: 'Is it Bin?' 'No! Guess again!' 'Is itttt Box?' 'Is it Bench?' 'Noooo!' This went on and on until they couldn't think of anything else. By this point Nana was becoming frustrated. 'Well go on! What is it?' Apparently, I turned, pointed towards the window and shouted at the top of my voice …

'Blind!!' (meaning window blinds). The whole room gasped. The shock on their faces was priceless. You can call it naivety and youthful exuberance or you can call it what I'd call it … comedy genius!

# 4

## (13 September 1995 – 12 September 1996)

### Nursery

In September 1995, I joined the local nursery at St Mark's Church on Leeds Road. This would be where I would make some of my friends for life, including Sam Hodson and Chris Hooper. I don't remember this time so well and it's a bit blurry, but my parents tell me I loved my time there. I was a fun, bubbly kid and always looked forward to 'play time'. Apparently, I used to always come home and tell them about a new friend I had made. This was the foundation of me being a sociable person who loves meeting new people.

My obsession with football continued, and every day after nursery I would play football until it was dark. I would get upset when I had to go home, so my dad invested in a soft ball so I could play inside the house. I used the radiator as a goal and scattered all my teddy bears on the carpet so I could dribble past them and score. It must have been easy for my parents bringing me up as I entertained myself!

### Rock 'N' roll star

I asked my dad about the Oasis concert we went to at Loch Lomond on 3 August, 1996. We (myself included) were huge fans, so we travelled up to Scotland to see them on the (What's the Story) Morning Glory? tour. Five per cent of the UK population applied for tickets for the two record-breaking shows at Knebworth … to give some scale and context of how big this tour was. Noel Gallagher famously said, 'It was the last great gathering of people before the birth of the internet.' Being on my dad's shoulders at the Loch Lomond gig was one of my first memories. Here's what he said about the trip:

'*We went up for the weekend. Our friends had tickets for the Saturday. We went exploring the west, passing through Inveraray, Mum and you having a go on the dodgems, then onto Kilmartin and saw the 15th-century carved grave slabs and visited a stone circle. Then on Sunday – OASIS. The atmosphere was great. The bottles flying over everybody's heads were, hopefully, plastic. What they contained I will leave to your imagination. You spent a lot of your time on my shoulders, clapping away to the music. I was hoping you didn't get smacked on the head by a bottle of piss. The crowd were enjoying the occasion. As it became darker, I thought it would be a good idea to make our way further back. It would've been easy to lose you in the crush when the gig finished. We found a spot well back, overlooking the stage, and enjoyed the rest of the show.'*

Typically, children didn't go to Oasis gigs, so the only T-shirt my dad could buy for me as a souvenir was a small women's size.

You can find footage from that gig on my dad's YouTube channel – 'cloddyclips'.

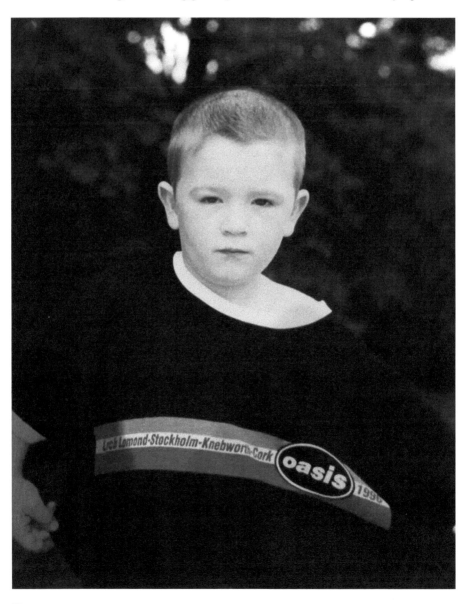

# 5

## (13 September 1996 – 12 September 1997)

### First day at school

It was September 1996 and I was excited for my first day at Oatlands Infant School. The highly regarded school was, and still is, on Hookstone Road, a ten-minute walk from my first house. Some of my friends from St Mark's Nursery were also attending the school, including my best friend, Chris Hooper. This made it easier to settle into my new environment quickly. The uniform was a white shirt, light grey jumper and dark grey shorts, accompanied by my beloved Star Wars lunch box. It was a proud moment for my teary-eyed parents as they waved me off at the gate.

My Reception teacher was a lovely Irish lady named Mrs. Arthur. I was obsessed with Power Rangers at the time and I was a cheeky kid, so when she asked our names for the register, I told her it wasn't Cory, but Tommy (the white Power Ranger). Surprisingly, she believed me and changed my

*Carly (Ruth's daughter) and I, on our first day at school.*

name. Everyone in the school addressed me as Tommy for an entire month until a parents' evening when my mum, who was flabbergasted, had to explain the mix up. From that day, Mrs Arthur and my mum's friendship blossomed. Mrs Arthur and the Year 1 teacher, Mrs Conway discovered what a talented artist my mum was and invited her to do some art classes for the kids. Mum was only doing a few hours a week, but the class was so popular with the kids that she was offered a full-time job as an assistant teacher and art director for the school.

I don't remember any of the lessons at school. I spent the whole time looking forward to the lunch break. There was a long shed in the playground that had two goal posts painted on the bricks. Each week one year group would be allowed to use it. One week it was the Reception, the next the Year 1 group and then the Year 2 group. It was frustrating as I loved playing football. My friends and I got a detention once because we were playing football with a stone, whilst one of the other year groups had access to the shed and football. It didn't take long before I started finding some female friends. They introduced me to a game called 'Kissy Catch' – we started young I know. It was similar to the game 'Tag', but you had to catch a person and kiss them so that they become 'it'. I always let myself get caught. By the end of the first term I had been kissed by every girl in the year. I was friends with a kid called Jasper and we used to swap jackets and pretend we were the other person. This also meant we had the other person's girlfriend for the time we were wearing the jacket. Kids ey!

I have only fond memories of infant school. I made some great friends, I was enjoying learning, the teachers were nice and playtime was the best thing in the world. I became close friends with a boy called Dave Hall. His mum also worked at Oatlands and we used to hang around after school every day. If we weren't playing football outside, we'd be bouncing down the school corridors on big inflatable exercise balls. To fuel our after-school activities, we would buy pick & mix sweets from the shop across the road. We never had any money so we would go to Dave's mum and beg for fifty pence each, saying that my mum didn't have any spare change. Then we would go to my mum and say Dave's mum didn't have any spare change and get 50 pence each from her. One pound each on sweets was a lot. We'd do that every day, and because our mums were busy they wouldn't bat an eyelid. I built up a strong friendship with Dave. When he used to come to my house for a sleepover, he would purposely leave one of his belongings at my house. Once his parents had picked him up and taken him home, I would ring and say he needs to come back and collect his things so we could play out some more.

## Passion for football

There was Dave Hall, Craig Ramplin and I, who were the standout football players in the year. Every night after school we would play on the fields until dark. Pannal Ash, the local junior football team, were training on the same field. Their manager, Cliff Trotter (who would later go on to become the Mayor of Harrogate) invited us to join a training session one evening. We impressed and joined their weekly training sessions. Dave and I practised every single day. Even when the sun went down, we would move inside the house and play with a soft ball. We were obsessed, and we became outstanding players for our age. Luke Garbutt, who went on to captain England Under 21s and play for Everton, was in our team and we used to win almost every game – although we had a fierce rivalry with Harrogate Railway.

Dave and I also became big Liverpool fans from an early age. We were watching an England game and a lot of the players played for Liverpool, so we decided to support them. Michael Owen and Steven Gerrard became our idols and we used to pretend to be them. I was given a few hand-me-down retro Liverpool kits, but the first new one I received (for my eighth birthday) was the green away 1999-2000 kit, and it had 'Owen' on the back.

## An eye for the arts

Thanks to my parents, art became a passion of mine from a young age. There was an art competition that every pupil in the school took part in. I was only in Reception but ended up winning first prize for my painting of a bumblebee. Not all my artwork won prizes though. My 'sad angel', which I designed for the Christmas project, wasn't well received. Although, it does still have a place on our Christmas tree every year.

Another thing that stayed with me from an early age, was the number 64. Whether it would be the number given to me for a game at school or my result in a test, it would consistently show up. It soon became my lucky number.

# 6

## (13 September 1997 – 12 September 1998)

### My first home

I only lived at St George's Road until the age of nine, but I witnessed some crazy parties. It was a big flat considering we only had the middle floor. My parents must have struck a deal with the landlord (maybe he was invited to the parties for cheaper rent). One night, my dad invited a DJ from the Haçienda club in Manchester to play the music for his house party. He installed lasers, smoke machines, the lot. The house was packed and they couldn't afford a babysitter at the time so I was running around with my rave stick.

It was usually disco, house or 90s rave music for our parties – the best kind. By the early hours it had progressed into thumping techno, which disappointed their Latina friend. She demanded Spanish songs she could salsa dance to and it reached the point where she was screaming at my mum, with tears running down her face, shouting, 'Change this fucking music, it's shit!' She's a legend … but it was 4am, peak time in the rave, and everyone else was loving it. It wasn't the time or place for Buena Vista Social Club (as good as it is).

It wasn't many tracks later that two figures appeared through the smoke dressed in yellow colours. This wasn't too conspicuous considering they are go-to rave colours. One of the men questioned my unassuming father: 'Is your name Ian McLeod?' Dad replied, 'Yes, nice to meet …' Before he got to the 'you' he noticed two police badges. Now this could have been fancy dress, but judging by the tone of their voice it was fair to say they weren't there looking for ecstasy. 'Sir, you need to shut this party down now or we will have to arrest you and everyone in here.' Dad tried his luck, 'Are you sure I couldn't offer you a drink?'

Apparently, the police were driving past the house and saw puffs of smoke escaping out the window – in sync with the bass of the subwoofer. Dad said it looked like the house was having a fag. Inventively, he had gathered every mattress in the house to board up the windows and soundproof the party.

*Toy Story wall with Dave.*

It wasn't all parties though. I was a big Toy Story fan (who wasn't at age six?), and I remember my loving father painting my walls light blue, with white Toy Story clouds painted over the top.

*My creative father also made a giant clock out of the house, which he named 'CloddyClox'.*

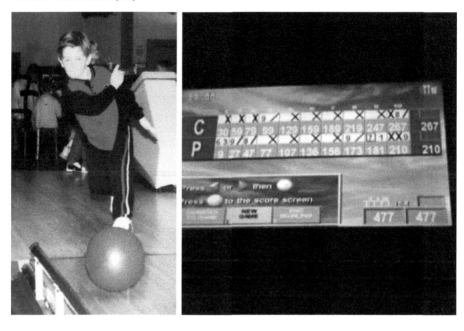

## Bowling maniac

My dad was flicking through the paper and noticed an advertisement inviting kids to come down to a new ten-pin bowling league on Tower Street. He was probably sick of me being a nuisance and looking for ways to get rid of me for a few hours on a weekend. I've no idea why he thought I'd enjoy bowling but I was hooked early on and became good for my age.

Murray was the coach of the YBC (Young Bowlers Club) and was like the Roy Keane of ten-pin bowling. I shat myself every time he came near me. He bollocked me on numerous occasions. I was always messing about, endangering me and the kids around me doing stupid things with bowling balls. I have memories of trying to hit the roof with a ball, trying to bowl backwards (which I eventually mastered) and trying to slide down the lane on my knees.

Every Saturday morning my dad would drop me off and I would play for a four-man team. The team names were chosen by kids so you would end up with ridiculous names. I played for 'Bowling Maniacs' and '3 and a Half Men' – I was the half, as the other three were all tall 17-year-olds. I began entering competitions around the country. In a competition held in Newcastle, I won an Under-16 competition, aged just ten.

Around this time, I started having football training on Saturday mornings and it was always difficult balancing both. I enjoyed both sports but prioritised football. My career in ten-pin bowling started to fizzle out as I approached my mid-teens. The highest possible score is 300, and although I was good for my age, I rarely got over 200. Fifteen years later, I was playing in Leeds with my friend Paul Worsnop and managed a score of 267, not missing a single pin and getting 9 strikes.

## 90s kid!

I used to love Saturdays. I would jump out of bed in my Spiderman pyjamas, pour myself a bowl of Nesquik chocolate cereal and watch Live & Kicking, presented by Zoe Ball and Jamie Theakston. By 9am, I was at ten-pin bowling or football, then we'd go out for the day with my parents' friends and their kids. We would alternate between hiking, cycling and camping. I was close to Cal and Georgie Bolton and Neil and Kira Lauber. Our parents had been good friends for years, so we spent a lot of time together growing up. This was before the days of phones and laptops, so we used to enjoy being in the outdoors, making up games and exploring nature. Wow, I sound old.

# 7

## (13 September 1998 – 12 September 1999)

### Scouted

Besides playing for our local football team, Pannal Ash, Dave and I used to play in coaching courses run by Leeds United FC, Middlesbrough FC and the FA. The coaches used to give us separate drills, as the main group drills were too basic for us. We were both skilful footballers, but Dave had lightning quick pace and was invited down to Middlesbrough first by one of their scouts. Despite some slight jealously, I was proud and happy for Dave. He was my best mate so I wanted to see him do well. To show my support, I went to watch his first match with his dad, Jon.

As the teams were in the dressing room, Jon overheard the coaches mentioning a few of the players hadn't turned up. He jumped in to say, 'David's friend Cory can play. He's good, give him a shot!' They discussed it between themselves before calling me over. I couldn't believe it. I was in a shirt and jeans with no expectation of playing that day. By that age, my feet had already grown in size to that of an adult so I was struggling to find any boots that fit. Dave had spares but they were a few sizes too small. With no other option, Jon grabbed them out of the car and held them in my face. 'You have to make them fit!' I ripped the skin off both heels forcing them in. My toes were curled up against the leather, but I had to take the opportunity and ignore the pain.

I started on the bench. Dave was having a good game on the right wing and was involved in the first goal. I wasn't sure if I would even come on, but the chief scout, Terry, waved me over at half-time and put me on as an attacking midfielder. I took a few deep breaths and the whistle blew. Before I knew it, I was just playing my game and forgot about the pressures of playing for Middlesbrough FC. I scored two goals from outside the box and we won the game 3-1. Jon came over and gave me a big hug. I was invited to join up with their development squads the following week.

## Smello!

As Mum's friend Ruth was now living in Nice, France, we used to go over every summer. It was great as her daughter, Carly, was around the same age so we used to play out whilst they drank wine. We spent all day playing with the local kids in the swimming pool outside the apartment block. Every day we would have a race up to the apartment to decide who could use the shower first. Usually it was a race up the stairs, but this time I cheated and opted for the lift. Every floor is identical, so when you press the wrong number and you're in the middle of a race, you aren't going to realise when you step out of the lift. The doors opened on the floor below Ruth's. I sprinted out of the lift, across the corridor and arrived at the door which was identical to Ruth's. I knocked as hard as I could and a middle-aged French lady answered the door. I assumed it was one of Ruth's friends and shouted 'Smello!' (I'd been watching a lot of The Simpsons), barging past her and straight into the bathroom. I locked the door so Carly couldn't get in and started the shower. In an attempt to wind Carly up even further, I took the longest shower I've ever taken so she would have to wait. After 20 minutes, the bangs on the door became more aggressive. I dried off, smugly exiting the bathroom. When I opened the door and looked up, I saw four people I'd never seen in my life staring at me. It was at that moment I realised what I had done and screamed, 'Pardon! Pardon!' running out of the house and up the stairs. Ruth, Carly and my parents were in hysterics and now, every time Ruth sees me, she says 'Smello!'

# 8

## (13 September 1999 – 12 September 2000)

### Crab football

One of the main reasons I was looking forward to starting in Year 4 was that Mr Coates organised a 'crab football' competition every Friday (open to Years 4, 5 and 6). It was like five-a-side football, but you had to sit on your bums in the school hall and kick the soft ball in between two orange cones. We had some talented players in our year, so even the Year 6's were afraid of us. Three teams from Year 4 entered the competition, including our team 'Miniature Heroes', which consisted of Dave, Chris, Pete, Mike and myself. We finished our first year in the competition as runners-up and the following two years we claimed first prize.

### School hero

Thanks to my parents meeting at Cambridge Art College, I won a national art competition and became a hero at school. The competition ran during EURO 2000 and kids across the country were asked to draw their favourite footballer. I chose Michael Owen. Out of thousands of entries, I won and was awarded a football kit and sports equipment for my school. Our school had never even had a football team in their entire history so this gave Mr Coates the idea to start one – with me as captain!

I bumped into Owen once in a Dubai bar with my friend Bash. He took a seat next to us to watch the Liverpool game. It was surreal.

### Aspirations

During a 'career day' in school, we discussed our aspirations in life and had to pick our top three jobs we would like to do when we were older. Everyone picked three answers: fireman, scientist, teacher etc., but I only wrote down one answer – 'footballer'. It was the only thing I had in my mind. Football was going well and I was having trials with Middlesbrough FC and Leeds United FC at their academies. I was regularly playing games

*Me and Sam Hodson wearing the new kit.*

next to the first team squads at Thorp Arch, Leeds, and Rockliffe Park, Darlington (where Middlesbrough trained).

I never had much luck with the trials. One winter trial with Leeds, I arrived without my boots. I thought they were in my football bag but they must have been taken out to be washed after my last game. My dad was devastated. He ran around the complex trying to find some boots, but no luck. I had to play on a frozen pitch with trainers and I was slipping and sliding all over. It was embarrassing; the coaches and scouts weren't impressed. In one Middlesbrough trial match we were playing a team from France. I went up for a header and the goalkeeper punched me in the head. I couldn't continue the game because I was so dizzy. As a young kid I was always one of the better players wherever I went. Unfortunately, my attitude let me down at times. At Leeds United training sessions, I remember always messing about and showing off. One day, I went to the Chinese takeaway on the way to football and I did the first few drills whilst having a bag of chips in my hand. I didn't deserve to make it as a footballer with that behaviour.

# 9

## (13 September 2000 – 12 September 2001)

### Sick day

Usually my mum would stay at home to look after me when I was sick, but due to work commitments she couldn't on this particular day. It wasn't often I would get a full day alone with my dad, so I thought I would ask him some man-to-man questions. I was a young, curious, nine-year-old child with many questions about how the world worked. The following question taught me that some things aren't worth knowing. After asking him some fairly mild questions, I stepped it up a notch. I asked, 'When was the last time you had sex?' – expecting him to say 1993 or something. He replied, 'Thursday.' Safe to say, that shut me up and I went back to watching Star Wars.

### Right little shit!

During these years, I could be a right little shit. On Christmas Day 2000 my parents bought me a bicycle and some clothes. As good as that was, everyone at school had been talking about the new PlayStation 2 coming out and I had a tantrum, balling my eyes out. They let me calm down before sending me to their bedroom, where there was a big box laying on the bed. I tore all the wrapping paper off, ripped open the box to find a brand-new PlayStation 2. I went from devastation to ecstasy in a split second. This was one of my first lessons on how not to be a little ungrateful brat.

A few months later, my dad came home with three PlayStation 2 games for me. I still managed to have a tantrum that they weren't a top-ten game. Looking back now, I still feel terrible at how ungrateful I was. As a father, he was looking forward to giving me those games he had bought using his hard-earned money and I practically threw them back in his face.

My mum once asked my dad what he wants to achieve in life. His response was, 'I want to leave this world knowing I have set my son on the right path.'

Mum put matters into her own hands (quite literally) when it came to me being a spoilt little brat. One day, we were on a countryside walk with her friend Carole. Halfway through, the skies opened. We were walking through farmland and with every step my wellies were sinking into the mud. I hated it, crying and moaning the entire time. I was driving them mad. There was a giant puddle ahead and Mum saw that as the perfect opportunity to silence me. As we approached it, she pushed me in – face first! I was drenched head-to-toe and couldn't believe my own mother would do that to me. Carole was a children's social worker and even she agreed the push was warranted. We laugh about it now but at the time I was livid!

## Village people

After nine memorable years at St George's Road, we had to relocate due to the landlord selling the property. We weren't having much luck in finding a new place, until my parents spotted an advertisement in the local paper. A rich couple in the village of Killinghall were looking for a gardener and cleaner for their lavish country estate. In return, they would provide one section of the house to live in for free. It sounded great – for me, anyway. I got to run around the mansion grounds, which boasted a giant lawn, river, table tennis table and tennis court! Of course, for my parents they had to do the work around the house and garden in their free time (whilst having their full-time jobs). Despite this, we did live the high life for a while – especially when the couple went on holiday!

It was like the English version of the Korean film Parasite.

Once we had settled in, that was when things started going wrong. The couple abused their power to the point Mum was having breakdowns. The lady was so strict, complaining about the smallest bits of dirt. If there was a fingerprint on the window or a hair on the floor she would notice and call for it to be cleaned up.

My parents knew we couldn't stay there forever, so started house-hunting around Harrogate. Houses were becoming more expensive in the centre, so we had to look at the outer suburb areas of Bilton and Starbeck. One of the houses in Bilton had human blood splashed over the walls so we stopped looking in that area. It was one terraced house in Starbeck that stood out for us. It was away from the high street, down a small private road, and had a field, swimming baths and bowling green opposite. After signing the contract, we had six months to wait until we could move in, so we stayed on the top floor of our friend Murray's place on Kings Road. It was being renovated and we had to climb step ladders to reach our floor. This house was where I witnessed one of the worst days in the modern era unfold on television.

## The day that changed the world forever

11 September 2001. I was buying pick & mix with Dave at the shop opposite Oatlands Infant School when I heard the news. Two planes had crashed into the World Trade Centre in New York. It was one of those events that are so catastrophic and unprecedented that

you remember it so vividly. It didn't make sense to me. How could something like that happen? All the people in the shop huddled up to listen to the shopkeeper's radio. I ran back to the school to tell my mum, who was as equally shocked as I was, and we went back home, watching the news until we went to bed. Everything changed after that. Stricter security in airports, more CCTV in the streets, more hate crimes and everyone became nervous flyers in the months after. The world didn't seem like a safe place anymore. We could see Menwith Hill from the top floor of Murray's and Mum was nervous there could be attacks close to home. The site is the NSA's largest surveillance base outside of the US.

# first 10 years

| likes | dislikes |
|---|---|
| oasis | milk     Asthma |
| football | cats |
| friends | egg! |
| art     Beyblades | manchester United |
| Pokemon | Batman |
| spice girls | daily photos |
| School | Mummy nagging |
| Michael Owen | |

# 10

## (13 September 2001 – 12 September 2002)

### Bend it like Beckham

One of my final memories from staying in Murray's place involved David Beckham. On 6 October 2001, 'Golden Balls' scored one of the most iconic goals in football history. England were trailing 2-1 to Greece and needed a goal to send them to the 2002 World Cup. It was the 93rd minute, when England were awarded a free-kick in a dangerous area, and I remember thinking if we didn't score my summer was going to be ruined. It wouldn't be the same watching the World Cup without having a team to support. Our captain, David Beckham, placed the ball down carefully and the whole country held its breath.

In true bend-it-like-Beckham style, the ball flew over the wall and curved into the top corner. The stadium erupted and the streets in England went into pandemonium. I sprinted down the stairs and out the back door to celebrate with the neighbouring kids. We spent the rest of the day trying to recreate the free-kick.

### Skint

Despite spending my first nine years on St George's Road in central Harrogate, I spent the majority of my time after that in Starbeck, 'The Bronx of Harrogate'. This is how people in the more affluent areas view it, but really, for the people living there, it's fine. There may be more Ford Mondeos than Range Rovers, but at least the people are down to earth. Starbeck is blessed with a KFC, chavs and KFC litter. My childhood friend's mum once warned my friend not to play outside my house when he comes to visit because it's too dangerous. She must have been worried one of the chavs outside KFC might throw some popcorn chicken at him or stab him with a wooden fork.

Although they don't like to admit it, most of my friends are well-off and have huge houses in Harrogate. They always had the latest phone, the latest toys and I was always a few thousand quid behind. I received hand-me-down clothes from my older family friend Cal. He was a lot bigger than me so I looked like I belonged in Death Row Records with my baggie jeans and knee-long T-shirts. For school lunch, I used to have home-made sandwiches to save money. I was thankful but jealous of the other kids having hot meals.

Despite our new house in Starbeck being derelict, we were proud of it being our first home. There was no kitchen sink, only two taps coming out of the wall. My dad made a temporary kitchen from a camping stove and a microwave, and we washed up in the bath until we had the kitchen fitted properly. Only one of the bedrooms was liveable so we shared one room and had a portable radiator to keep us warm at night. I thought I was in luck as there were five kids next door who played football, but we discovered they were moving into a bigger house.

*Our late friend Mike Hine was a big supporter of Starbeck and put a lot of time and effort into helping improve the quality of life in the area. He was part of 'Starbeck in Bloom', a community-led team that raises money through fundraisers to plant flowers all down the high street every year. RIP 'Mr. Harrogate'.*

# 11

## (13 September 2002 – 12 September 2003)

### The hunt for the whale bone

In Year 6, we headed to East Barnby on the north-east coast for a school trip. We stayed in army-like huts in rows of bunk beds. We would do activities with the teachers in the day and as soon as they went to bed it would be chaos. Girls sneaking into boys' rooms, pillow fights, even some kids smoking out of the windows.

On one of the day trips to Whitby, we were set the task of finding a whale bone. We had to pair up and explore the nearby area. 'Nearby', meaning – in sight. Me and Chris, being the class clowns that we were, decided to turn around and head to the beach (which was a mile away). We told ourselves we had more chance of finding a whale bone by the sea. We covered the entire beach and didn't find any bones. After two hours, it was becoming dark and we decided to head back. We didn't want to return empty handed, so we bought a toy whale from a souvenir shop. As we walked back up the hill, two teachers came sprinting down, 'Where have you been!? We have been looking everywhere for you!' The whale bone should've taken a few minutes to find. We arrived back two hours later.

After one muddy session orienteering in the local forest, we came back to use the showers. Chris realised his cubicle had control of everyone's water temperature. Oblivious, Jasper entered his cubicle and screamed as his water jumped between scolding hot and freezing. He leaped out of the shower, slipping and smashing through the door in the process. Jasper was simultaneously laughing and crying as his knee gushed with blood.

Kids can be cruel at times. Whether you realise it or not, most people have been on both ends of bullying. I know I bullied others and got bullied back, but I guess that's how you learn to become a good person. You learn how it feels to see someone you've hurt and you discover what it's like to be on the receiving end of it.

One of my worst experiences at school was watching Jesus Christ Superstar. We were doing an exercise where we had to read passages from the film. For whatever reason, I had

*Sam, Dave, Leo, Pete, Chris and Me at Oatlands Junior School.*

the tune in my head and couldn't read it out loud without singing it. It sounds stupid, but I couldn't stop myself and the whole class was laughing at me because I couldn't read it normally. I burst into tears and rushed to the bathroom to hide from the embarrassment. My classmates teased me for weeks.

## Farewell Oatlands

For our last hoorah, we worked on an 'End of Year Pantomime Show' to present to our parents on the final day. I auditioned for the lead role as Special Agent. The character would wear a cool suit, black shades and all the girls would fancy him. My audition went terribly and I lost the role to my classmate, Leo. As the other roles were already filled, I ended up in a non-speaking role as the back end of the cow. Of course, it was my fellow class clown, Chris Hooper, who was in the front. I say non-speaking role, but we did 'Moo' a few times. Aside from that stellar performance, I also helped out on some of the art design.

My time at Oatlands went so fast and I was sad to be leaving. I'd made friends for life, friends who I still talk to every day. Unfortunately, I didn't have enough 'church points' to get into the same school as all of my friends – St Aidan's Church of England High School. I can't believe in my lifetime 'church points' were required to gain access to a good education. To attain church points, you had to attend Sunday School, Scouts and other church-related activities. St Aidan's was one of the best schools in the country, so any other school you got into in Harrogate was well below that standard. My second choice was the Harrogate Grammar School (Dad's old school). Unfortunately, I didn't get into that school either as I lived on the wrong side of the train tracks, meaning I was out of the catchment area. I ended up at my third choice, Rossett School. It had a reputation as a rough school, but it was also known for having excellent sports facilities, so I wasn't too disheartened.

I'm proud of my parents. They never forced me to go to church despite the expectation society puts on you that you should associate yourself with a religion. My friends' parents (who weren't religious) would send their children to church every Sunday to get them the points required. You can't blame them but how messed up is the system where that is what you have to do.

# 12

## (13 September 2003 – 12 September 2004)

### First day at secondary school

I didn't realise what a spoilt little shit I'd become spending my school years at Oatlands.

So, as I wasn't willing to say, 'I believe in God' and sing hymns every Sunday morning, I ended up at the rough school. A rough school in Harrogate doesn't compare to a rough school anywhere else, but there were still fights every day. Five of us from Oatlands arrived at Rossett, whilst the other 60 went to St Aidan's, the Grammar School or St John Fishers. Rossett was a bit of a shithole, but I was keen to start with an open mind and make new friends.

We were asked to congregate in the main courtyard whilst our names were read out, establishing which classes we'd be placed into. I was fortunate as I ended up in a class with six lads I recognised from the local football leagues. One I knew by name, Josh Briggs, was the top scorer in a recent tournament. I was a goal behind him so we laughed about that and soon became friends. I thought, maybe Rossett isn't so bad after all!

I was decent at football so I gained respect from my new classmates early on. In the first few PE lessons it was clear who were the better players and we gravitated towards each other. When the football trials came to decide who would make the first team, it consisted mainly of players from Killinghall Nomads. Aside from them, there was Dan Rayiru from Pannal Sports and myself from Pannal Ash. After making the first team, Dan and I were constantly pressured into joining Killinghall – mainly by the captain, Stuart Williamson. We lasted three months before both joining.

### The hustle of being a dickhead

Despite only being 10-to-15 years old, school was a hustle and we were constantly fighting to get to the top in terms of respect and popularity. This was my downfall. I was always a cheeky kid and making jokes at Oatlands, but I took it to another level at Rossett. I was renowned for being the class clown and always doing my best to disrupt the class

– to impress my peers. In the short-term, it worked but in the long-term it counted for nothing.

In Year 8 Art class, I must have had a reputation by this point because I genuinely didn't mean to disrupt the class. I knocked over a big box of coloured pencils from the table which scattered across the floor. The teacher lost his patience and ordered me to leave the classroom. He followed me out into the corridor and gave me a stern bollocking in front of passing teachers and pupils. He lost his cool and shouted in my face, 'You dickhead!' I was 12 years old and it was only a box of pencils! He was in a state of shock, realising what had just come out of his mouth. He apologised repeatedly. I wasn't even that bothered, but he owes me one since I didn't complain to the headteacher or my parents. He could have been fired. Teachers need to understand, kids aren't trying to be little cunts, we're just hustling.

Innit.

Talking of cunts.

Apologies for the language, but it is relevant. I don't think I ever swore until I got to Rossett. Cursing was common practice in the corridors, classrooms and playground. You picked things up from the older kids who were in sixth form. I bumped into this older girl once and she screamed, 'You cunt!' Now I never really learned what that word actually was until I was 17, but I proceeded to take it home.

'Mum, what's a cunt?'

'Cory! You cannot say that word!' This was the start of the end for my time at Rossett.

## Bullying

The best quality I learnt from secondary school was to take the piss out of myself. Nothing really offends me anymore, but it took years to reach that point. I was one of the popular kids at Oatlands. Maybe not in terms of personality, but because I was this aspiring wonder kid at football. When I arrived at Rossett, I wasn't the only good footballer, there were lots of us. So whilst I may have been higher up the hustling scale in terms of popularity, I still had people above me who could put me in my place.

You'd hear rumours of potential fights brewing in class and you'd know something was going to boil over into lunch time. There were some huge brawls on the field. It's funny looking back. At the time you thought you were watching men fighting, but in reality they were only little kids. I'd never been hit in my life. Those things didn't happen in my previous 'upper-class' school. There was one occasion in the playground at junior school when I saw Jasper arguing with a kid younger than him. The younger kid happened to be the younger brother of Louise, a girl I was friends with, so I stepped in and shoved Jasper and we wrestled on the ground. Mr Coates dragged us by the ears and took us to the headteacher's office. Me and Jasper were mates so whilst we were being dragged we started giggling and apologised for our behaviour.

Fast forward to the playground at Rossett and one of the kids called me fat. If there was anything that upset me the most back then it was being called fat. It was my fault I was

fat, but still, it always hurt every time someone said it. He said it repeatedly and eventually I had enough and pushed him. Without hesitation, he swung and struck my cheekbone, knocking me to the ground.

This was the most embarrassing thing to ever happen to me (aside from Jesus Christ Superstar). The whole playground stopped, then saw me burst into tears and leave the playground crying. I was the laughing stock of lunch time and instantly went from football legend to complete softy. Because I let it affect me so much, it made me more of a target for bullies and more people started making fun of me. I wasn't even that fat, I was just a bit chubby for someone who was on the football team.

If you can learn anything from these experiences when you're growing up as a young kid, it is to remember that whilst it feels like the end of the world at the time, it's not. I'm now mates with the guy who hit me.

## Tough guy

I believe that day when I was hit changed me. I knew I had to be more streetwise and fit in with the crowd. From that day forward, I was even more cheeky in class, always showing off in front of the tough kids and becoming more of a 'dickhead'. My first isolation came on a non-school-uniform day. It was always one of the best days of the year, where students get to do fun activities and don't have to do any studying. I was buzzing for this particular one as there was a DJ coming into the school to give lessons. I was overly hyper when I arrived, excited for the day ahead. We were all messing about and just as the teacher arrived I grabbed my friend's cap and threw it across the classroom, landing on his desk. The teacher lost his shit (way over the top for throwing a flimsy cap). The veins in his forehead were bursting as he shouted. He sent me to the headteacher and they decided my punishment was isolation for the entire day, missing the DJ lessons and all the fun activities. I had to sit in a room without windows all day and write lines.

The only good thing to come from that day was that I got in with the naughty kids. I received more respect after that, so started doing everything I could to get isolation. Stupid really. I never started any fights or lit the school on fire, but I would always be naughty in class and try to make everyone laugh.

During a counselling session with my head of year, they asked me what my aspirations were. I said to work for MI5. They said I wasn't intelligent enough.

## Furry companion

I was forever jealous of my friends having pets. All I ever had as a young boy was stick insects, but you can't really pet them, they're just twigs with eyes. Eventually, after years of begging, my mum allowed me to have a furry companion. Before my parents made any rash decisions, I looked after Sarah's (Mum's friend) rabbit for a week. Unfortunately, I didn't pass the 'responsible owner test', so we downgraded and bought a hamster. The night before picking it up we went out for a curry with Ruth, who was visiting from France. It was a disaster! The service was terrible, they kept getting our orders wrong and the food was two hours late. The waiter kept asking if we wanted more wine and beer (me Coca-Cola) to distract us, but six pints later we were (pissed) even more angry. We managed to see the funny side and brainstormed names for the hamster.

The following morning we welcomed Poppadom into the McLeod household.

# 13

## (13 September 2004 – 12 September 2005)

### Rejection

I never gave up my dream of becoming a footballer. I'd been playing at junior level with Middlesbrough FC and Leeds United FC for almost five years, and being anything other than a footballer was never an option. A letter arrived from Middlesbrough whilst I was at school. My parents came up to my bedroom with the letter and asked me to open it. It was a letter signed by Terry, saying, with regret, I had been released by the club and they would not be inviting me back for the upcoming season. I cried and cried and cried. It was the worst feeling in the world. It was like all your dreams in life being crushed in an instant. My parents were upset too and gave me a big hug. One thing this experience did for me, though, was toughen me up. That was the last time I cried. I shed enough tears for a lifetime.

Developing a thicker skin has helped me in life whether it be confronting bullies at school, dealing with rejection or facing tough work situations. Initially, I held back on telling people at school I'd been released. I was too embarrassed, but as the months went by, more of my friends were released and it became clear how difficult the path to stardom would be. Even Dave was released, and I was positive he'd make it.

### Champions of Europe

Following Liverpool FC during my youth had been a rollercoaster. I was born a year after their 1990 First Division win and there wasn't too much to follow until the early 2000s. Rafa Benítez took over in 2004 and gave me one of the best nights of my life. We had qualified for the UEFA Champions League, but no one in their right mind believed we would go on to win it.

We narrowly advanced into the knockout stages thanks to a late Gerrard screamer against Olympiakos – you know the one, 'Ohhhh, ya beauty! What a hit son. What a hit!'

We went on to beat Bayer Leverkusen, Juventus and Chelsea en route to the final in Istanbul. Awaiting us was one of the greatest teams in history, AC Milan, who had a squad of world-class players. No one gave us a chance. I was always optimistic, so I invited Dave over to watch it. We wore our Liverpool shirts and waved scarves in the air as if we were there. Unfortunately, things didn't go to plan in the first half and before we knew it we were 3-0 down. The team looked shell-shocked.

We were too, so we headed outside to kick a football about and discuss what had just happened. Dave saw no way back and said he was going to ask his mum to come and pick him up. Even some people in the stadium left the game. It was virtually impossible for us to recover the deficit against such a great team. I'm not sure where it came from but I said to Dave, 'We can still win this.' It took some persuasion, but Dave eventually agreed to stay.

We came back into the house and could hear the Liverpool fans singing on the TV. The fans didn't give up and, because of this, neither did the players. Liverpool scored three goals in quick succession, sending the game to extra time. Dudek then pulled off the best save in football history, point blank from Shevchenko. It felt like it was destiny for Liverpool to win the cup. The game was decided on penalties – the most nerve-wracking experience of my life. We hid behind the sofa, with our eyes peeping over the top. I don't know how we did it, but we won the shoot-out and danced around the house in ecstasy. I had fun at school the following day boasting to the Manchester United fans.

## The greatest goal ever scored

To round off the season with Killinghall Nomads we applied to represent England in the Gothia Youth World Cup in Sweden. To raise funds for our flights and accommodation, we volunteered at the local supermarkets every weekend packing bags. The managers, Steve and Billy, used some of the funds to order a brand new kit, which looked exactly like the Brazil home kit. I was given the number-nine shirt, which pleased me as it was an important number, and an indication I would be starting the games. The competition took place in Malmö and we shared accommodation with the Bosnia team. It was a small school, with two classrooms and 20 beds crammed inside each room.

In the first two games against Paraguay and Cameroon I'd only played ten minutes. We had a striker called Kev, who was built like a 30-year-old man, so with the first two games tight, they didn't want to take him off. I spent a lot of the trip sulking. It wasn't nice travelling that far and not being involved. Another person in our squad who was in the same boat as me was James 'Smiley' Thorp. He was a shy lad who had a bit of a tough childhood, but everyone loved him as he never stopped smiling. He was a boy of few words, but I managed to get some out of him occasionally and we talked about how we would love to help the team more on the pitch.

In the third and final group game, we needed a win against Sweden to progress into the next round. Again, it reached the second half and we were still on the bench, yet to be called upon. Steve and Billy went for broke. There was five minutes left and nothing to lose with the game level at 1-1, so they threw me and Smiley on. I won a challenge in midfield, the ball fell at my feet, and from that moment everything went in slow motion. I could see Smiley free in space, running towards the goal. There was only one option. I played a long-range pass over his head. Everyone gasped as he ran onto it. Usually his touch can be a bit dodgy, but he controlled it perfectly, opened his body and placed the ball in the bottom corner.

The place erupted. Our entire team ran across the pitch and jumped on Smiley. We had tears in our eyes as we lifted him onto our shoulders. This was his first ever goal. We had a strong squad so it was rare he would get any minutes, but he would always show up every weekend and support the team.

With a McLeod assist and Smiley goal, we progressed into the knockout stages. In the last 16 we faced a Finland team who all seemed to be 6ft tall. We battled hard in the rain, but they were too strong for us and we lost 3-1.

At the time, I showed animosity towards the two coaches, I felt like I deserved more minutes on the pitch. Growing up now, I realise how difficult a job that was taking 16 kids to Sweden. They weren't just coaches, they had to parent us and try their best to keep us all happy. It wasn't an easy job. I'm still good friends with their sons Scott and Nathan. Nathan's dad, Billy, went on to work with Manchester United as an academy coach. The Sweden trip brought us all together and we became close mates. Every weekend we would do something as a team, whether it was playing out in the street, going paintballing or going to theme parks.

Our school friend, Rachel Daly, who now plays for England Women, used to play with us at Killinghall Nomads. Rachel was one of the best players in the team, but from the age of 12 girls were no longer allowed to play with the boys in official matches.

## The most underrated sport in the world

Aside from football, I'd tried tennis, golf, cricket and rugby. None of them interested me. Opposite our terraced house in Starbeck was a bowling green. Not flat green bowling that you see on television, but Crown Green. The most underrated sport in the world. The game is plagued by an unfortunate stereotype of being 'an old man's game' and only exists in the north of England.

The bowling club advertised an open day in the local paper, so Mum and I signed up. Sue Green was one of the top women bowlers in the area and our coach for the session. To score points you have to roll your bowls closer to the 'jack' than your opponent. The bowls have two biases (finger and thumb) which can make them turn left or right. What I love about crown green is that each bowling club has a different size green with different gradients. This provides an advantage for home bowlers and variety in where you can throw the jack. Think of it like a putting green in golf. When you see Tiger Woods play off the bank and it rolls around, into the hole. We get that same buzz in crown green bowling.

Sue was impressed by how quickly I'd picked it up and invited me to come back. Some of the local kids turned up that day which gave Sue the idea to create a local junior league. Sue and Phil Mason dedicated a lot of time keeping the kids interested, training them so they could be ready for leagues and competitions. Five of the kids who came in that first year still play today and are among the best players in the area.

Every Saturday morning, Sue and Phil would put targets on the green for us to aim at, which would help us with accuracy and length. If we hit the targets, we'd win prizes – which would usually be chocolates (probably the reason for me becoming fat). After two months, I was selected to play in my first league game, representing Starbeck. By chance, I was drawn to play against another junior, Jason Worsnop, who also played ten-pin bowling with me. He was playing for Bilton Dragon, our rivals in the league.

We were the last pair to go on, so all the pressure was on us. 21 points are required to win the game, and after an epic battle the game was tied at 20-20. It was all down to the last end. I remember there being a big crowd for a Division Five game – maybe it was refreshing to see two youngsters competing. I held the final bowl in my hands and assessed my options. I was shaking from the nerves but managed to settle down before releasing the bowl. Using home advantage, I managed to find another route in and my bowl nestled on the jack to win the game 21-20. There was a round of applause from both sets of 'fans'. They weren't clapping for me winning, it was more in appreciation of two juniors enjoying the game and a promising sign for the future of the sport.

# 14

## January transfer window

Twenty or so isolations later, my mum had had enough. I was turning into a complete and utter little shitebag. I'd surpassed the meaning of dickhead. This was not how my parents had brought me up. In a bid to save me from self-destruction, my mum had an idea (which turned out to be a masterstroke). With the help of her good friend Linda, she began constructing the most well-written letter you're ever likely to see. I should've asked them to help me write this book. It was a plea to the headteacher at St Aidan's – the best school in Harrogate, to allow me to transfer and finally get back on track and receive the best available education, in the best environment I possibly could.

It wasn't just the fact I was turning into a complete and utter little shitebag, I was genuinely having a tough time in school. I had a lot of friends there, especially from the football team, but I was still having trouble with certain kids. During school hours, I would do my best not to react or get upset, but by doing this I was only making it worse. All the name-calling would build up over the day and, by the time I arrived home, I would be depressed wondering why people were horrible to me. My parents could see the effect the school was having on me and knew something had to change.

It was Christmas Day at Nana's and I had no idea what was about to happen. When we were opening presents around the tree, I had two envelopes to open. I was an ungrateful kid growing up, so I was never too excited about opening envelopes. It was usually the giant cardboard boxes I was more eager to open. This day was different. I opened it and began to read the letter. It was the letter Linda and my mum had been working on for months, the letter that would be my entry into St Aidan's. My teary eyed mother waited anxiously for my reaction. 'They've accepted you in Cory, you're transferring after the new year!' I couldn't believe it and gave her a big hug. 'This is the best Christmas present ever!'

The second envelope contained two concert tickets to see The Strokes in Nottingham at the end of January. They were my favourite band at the time. I thanked my parents once again, but my mum interrupted: 'The second ticket is for a new friend at St Aidan's that you make. It can't be one of your friends from Oatlands.' This was a smart move, as I made a conscious effort to make some new friends.

## A new chapter

One of my very first classes was Art and Design. Now, I was never going to all of a sudden, become an angel (despite moving to a Church of England school). I made the whole class laugh in the first few seconds as the teacher walked in: 'Hi, I'm Cory,' whilst waving my hand with a big grin. The teacher snapped back instantly, 'Yes, I know who you are.'

Not a great start.

Thankfully, in that class, my art ability saved me. The teacher became fond of me as I achieved maximum scores with every piece of homework. I also received extra bonus points when she spotted me at a Rufus Wainwright gig in Harrogate. She told me she was impressed by my taste in music.

The best part of joining the new school was that I was finally reunited with all my old school mates from infant and primary school. They were a big part of my life growing up, so it was challenging when I was separated from them. I was assigned to the form that had most of the Oatlands kids in. Chris, Dave, Pete, Sam, Tom, Ryan and Gerry made me feel at home immediately, and it was like I'd never been away. Outside the form, I had to start all over again making new friends. This was daunting as I arrived in the middle of the year, so everyone knew me as the 'new kid'. I soon became close with Alex 'Lills' Lilley in one of my science lessons. He had a good sense of humour, similar music taste and was amazing at almost every sport. Lills went on to represent Yorkshire and England at cricket. He soon became the number-one candidate for the second concert ticket. I was nervous asking him because we hadn't known each other long and I wasn't sure what his parents would think. To my relief, once I had plucked up the courage to ask, Alex said yes. My mum was proud of me and it gave her some comfort knowing I was making new friends.

Aside from friends, I was also hoping to find a girlfriend at the new school. Soon after I joined there was a party everybody was talking about. Sam and I wanted to impress some of the girls so we went clothes shopping in York. I was clearly going through a phase as I ended up with white and gold jeans, a red T-shirt and a black waistcoat. It's safe to say I didn't kiss any girls that night.

Dave and Chris told the teachers running the football team that I was semi-decent so I was given a free pass into the first team without any kind of trial. I was selected for their upcoming game, away against Leeds Grammar School. They were a bunch of posh, private-school boys so I was keen to make an impression. The coaches started me on the bench, but with 60 minutes gone in the match and the score tied at 1-1, I was thrown on upfront to try and get a late winner. With my first touch, I ran onto a long through ball and slotted the ball home into the far corner. The whole team ran over to me and gave me a pat on the back. Within a split second of me hitting that shot and the ball finding the back of the net, I went from being the 'new kid' to feeling like I was now part of the team and part of the school. The headteacher spoke about the game in assembly and announced me as 'the best ever January transfer window signing'.

## Chile with my new best mate

After moving to St Aidan's, I'd become close with Sam Hodson. We used to play out after school every day together. My parents and I were heading to Chile with the rest of the family as Grandad Ronnie had passed away. My parents were concerned I wouldn't be able to enjoy my holiday because it was a sad time and there would be a lot of family commitments, so they asked if I wanted to bring a friend, and Sam seemed like the obvious choice. Sam's parents were big travellers when they were younger, spending a lot of time in Asia. Sam was born in Hong Kong, before they moved back to the UK. They were keen for Sam to experience a new part of the world and a few weeks later we were packing our bags and on our way!

Ronnie was one of the nicest men to ever live and was loved by everyone he knew. So many people showed up for his funeral service. Despite it being an incredibly sad time, our family, being our family, managed to find humour in the darkest of times. We scattered Ronnie's ashes in the South Pacific Ocean, off the coast of Valparaíso. Right before they

*Sam, Me, Cousin Danny, Aunty Lis, Cousin Benji and Cousin Mark.*

were scattered, my dad ran up and said, 'Actually, can I get one more photo with me dad.' He posed for a photo, holding the clay pot, and the whole family laughed whilst wiping tears from their eyes. It was amazing to see how brave my dad was in that moment and he lifted the spirits of everyone there.

I saw Ricky Gervais on TV talking about a similar scenario while at his mother's funeral. Ricky and his brother both came prepared with practical jokes to play on the family to lighten the mood. Ricky handed out tissues to all of the women at the service, but the tissues read things like 'snivelling bitch' or 'snotty pig'. They also gave the vicar fake names so when he said, 'She leaves behind four devoted children …' the family would start laughing as they'd be completely made-up names. Apparently, the vicar said he had never got laughs at a funeral before and it was brilliant! Maybe Ricky's version is a bit extreme, but I think that's a great way to handle such a sad time.

Whilst on the trip, my dad entered the Santiago Marathon at the age of 50. A marathon is hard enough, but at that time Santiago's oxygen levels were below safety levels due to pollution in the city. The race should have been cancelled. From watching Casey Neistat's early YouTube videos, I've always lived by his motto: 'Do More'. I thought I got that from him, but looking back that belief to Do More actually came from my dad. When he finished the race, his legs were spasming and he couldn't even speak to us because he was so exhausted. The medics noticed his state and gave him medical treatment. Despite running a marathon in hazardous conditions, he dragged us up to Cerro San Cristóbal, known for having the best view of the city. My dad's grit and determination has shaped who I am today and some of the things I have achieved in later life has been down to his influence.

If you need some inspiration, follow David Goggins or Cam Hanes. They truly know how to make the most of their day. They'll either be doing 1,000 pull-ups before breakfast or racing 200 miles across the desert – for fun. Through following Goggins I came across the book, Living with a Seal: 31 Days Training with the Toughest Man on the Planet, which documents entrepreneur Jesse Itzler training with Goggins every day for an entire month. In 2020 my friend was battling Crohn's disease. I bought him the book as a gift, to motivate him while he was in hospital. Less than a year later he completed his first 100km ultramarathon. That's the power of Goggins, and now my friend is inspiring other people with Crohn's disease who have been struggling to find light at the end of the tunnel.

Me and Sam had an amazing time in Chile and it would be the first of many travels we would embark on together. Unfortunately, in the final few days, Sam developed an illness and was placed on a drip in hospital. Sam's mum had gone on holiday so my parents were in two minds on whether to tell her. They decided to leave her in peace and thankfully the doctors were able to get him back to his best before the flight home.

Sam had a history of being ill around my parents. One night, we were at Helen's (Mum's friend) party in Knaresborough. We stole a few Bacardi Breezers out of the fridge and got quite drunk. My mum called a taxi to take us home. In the time it took for the taxi to arrive, we shot five tequilas each. Mum was sat in the front of the car escorting us home, with Sam, Tom and I in the back. Tom couldn't stop laughing and being giddy in the right, I was screaming and being weird in the left and Sam was silent in the middle seat. Mum spent the whole journey telling me and Tom to shut up. Sam was silent, but just as we were about to get out, he turned to me and threw up all over my jeans and the car seat. The taxi driver flipped and demanded my mum pay £80 to cover the cleaning cost. The poor guy was about to go home after he dropped us off. I was covered in sick, Tom was stumbling everywhere and Sam was in tears because he had let my mum down. The last memory I have from that night is Sam dropping to his knees and shouting down the street, 'Karen! Forgive me! I'm sorry!'

## The youngest winner

I was into my second season of crown green bowling and winning most of my games. One of the biggest competitions in the calendar year is the Len Tipling Trophy, which is held at Starbeck. With 90 per cent of competitors coming from Division One, Sue said it would be great experience for me to enter. Nobody knew who I was at the start of that day. I ended up dismantling five first division bowlers on my way to the trophy. Steve Cochrane, who was a big supporter of mine, wrote a brilliant piece in the Harrogate Advertiser explaining how the crowd got to their feet and were in awe of what they witnessed. I was the youngest winner of a senior Harrogate competition, and 15 years on I still hold this record!

For the next few years I won a host of junior competitions around the country and worked my way up to playing in the Starbeck first team, as well as representing the North Yorkshire senior team. Due to the success of the juniors in the area, a Harrogate junior team was established to compete against other counties in Yorkshire.

*Playing against Wayne Ditchfield in the Federation Junior Merit semi-final in Bolton.*

## CROWN GREEN BOWLS with Steve Cochrane

# McLeod the youngest winner of Len Tipling Cup

WITH some of the big names missing, the Len Tipling cup was up for grabs, and 40 players turned up at Starbeck on what turned out to be a glorious day.

As the rounds progressed some familiar names were making their way into the last 16, Chaz Charleton, Angela Spilsbury, Phil Hill, Chris Olding and Dave Spilsbury but the one they had to be aware of was junior champ Cory McLeod.

Charleton booked his spot in the quarters with a good win against league president Ken Coker and Angela Spilsbury got there at the expense of Ray Milner.

Dave Hodgson also booked a spot and he faced Cory McLeod.

Hill, fresh after his exploits last weekend, would be matched with the difficult Olding and

David Spilsbury was to meet local man Mick Faulding.

Angela got the better of her match with Chaz Charleton never giving the Swan man much of a chance but McLeod gave Hodgson a lesson on how to bowl Starbeck going through 21-7.

Hill had a struggle against Olding, who could thrive at a higher level than the third division he plays in, the Bardsey man winning through 21-19.

Dave Spilsbury went from 8-6 down against Faulding to win 21-13 and make the semi where he will meet Hill.

In the first semi Angela soon built up a lead of 5-2 but local knowledge and youthful courage saw McLeod race to 14-5 as Spilsbury could find no match for the junior's lead

woods he eventually ran out 21-8.

The other semi was a much more close affair.

Spilsbury (D) stormed to a 7-0 lead but Hill pegged him back to 8-7.

Spilsbury took control again going 12-9 up before a sustained period with the jack saw Hill 16-12 in front.

Eventually Spilsbury found his length and pulled it back from 16-14 down to win 21-18 and look to take avenge on his good ladies defeat.

Would the young McLeod's nerves hold or would the experience of previous winner Spilsbury pull him through?

Spilsbury soon went 4-0 up but McLeod must have some fascination with the number five, as

when his opponent gets to five he seems to go into overdrive.

From 5-3 down he found his mark and platted the jack end after end forcing the usually placid Spilsbury to fire on three occasions.

McLeod went to 14-5 before a careless lead cost him the jack back into the match but McLeod wasn't going to let his chance of becoming the youngest winner of a major go and he ran out 21-11 to a standing ovation from the crowd.

Chris Light who had expertly officiated all day presented the trophies to a delighted McLeod whose proud parents looked on.

Starbeck's green was again superb testament to Andy Lumley the green-keeper and his staff but young McLeod can be

justly proud he was the best bowler on the day and at just 1 years old must have a tremen dous future ahead of him.

Federation National League On Sunday Starbeck host th federation match against UK Police.

North Yorkshire will be look ing for a good win to secure pro motion to the third division o the national league. The awa match is at Burton On Trent.

Wilf Shaw Pairs: Sunday Sep tember 24 sees the first showin of the Wilf Shaw pairs.

With £100 up for grabs it i sure to attract some goo entries, and there are a fe spaces left so those intereste should contact Carol Hawkin on 01423 881852. Entry is £8 pe pair and limited to 32 pairs

# 15

## (13 September 2006 – 12 September 2007)

### I can now pronounce you, not a bastard

My parents' wedding was 26 years after they started dating. At 15 years old I guess most kids don't get to experience their own parents' wedding, so in that sense I was lucky. I say I experienced it, but in truth, I don't remember much of it.

My parents weren't particularly the traditional type. My mum was brought up a Catholic but stopped going to church as she was terrified of one of the nuns who used to always shout at her. My dad was never pressured into going to church, so never did. My parents never felt like they needed to have a wedding to prove their love for one another, nor pay £20,000 to make it happen. What changed everything was Granny Cecilia's age. At the time she was 88 and flying to England for the last time. Her dream had always been to see her three children get married, so to put a smile on her face (and my mum's, hopefully) my dad proposed. He didn't get on one knee or anything, they were just sat on the sofa watching Traffic Cops on Channel 5.

They opted for a small ceremony in a registry office by The Stray in Harrogate, with Granny Cecilia and Nana Mavis both present, alongside me. This was the first time both mums had met each other! Granny and Nana held hands for the duration of the ceremony, watching Dad sign his bank account away.

Just kidding! It was a lovely day … until they kissed.

ON THE LIPS!

WAS THERE ANY NEED?

EWWWWWW.

With all their history of throwing parties, there was no way they weren't going to throw one on the biggest day of their lives. They hired a farmhouse, nestled down a long country lane, on the outskirts of Harrogate. They had decorations, lighting, beer kegs on every

hay bale, bands playing in the day and DJs at night. I invited five friends from school, who, like me, were too young to be exposed to that much alcohol. My childhood friend, Cal, was also there. He was a year older, which meant he was a year more experienced at drinking. This was the first time I was introduced to the drinking game 'Ring of Fire'. The last flashback I have is my dad running into the barn and dragging Sam away from the beer kegs. He was lying on his back with the tap free-flowing into his mouth.

The following morning, I was representing North Yorkshire in a highly regarded crown green tournament. This was the biggest game of my 'career' so far. I stumbled out of one of the barns at 8am covered in hay and stinking of cider, champagne, ale, piss and vomit. I looked like the scarecrow from the Wizard of Oz, if he'd spent the weekend at Oktoberfest.

I was drawn to play Dave Cowsill from Dewsbury. He was a well-respected player in the game, but I fancied my chances as Harrogate were hosting the tournament.

*If you don't want to read about bowls, please skip to page 347.

In hindsight, I should've told my captain to drop me for the first game (until I'd sobered up). I was all over the place. Crown green is about balance, accuracy and precision – none of which I had. My teammates were shaking their head, they'd never seen me play so bad. I scraped a 21-15 loss, but let my team down and was dropped for the next game. After the group stage, scores were totalled and we missed out on qualification by only a few points. Had I been sober/had my dad not proposed, maybe we would have qualified for the finals.

I wish I could say lessons were learnt, but there were plenty more matches to be played under the influence over the coming years. It's a hard life balancing a semi-professional career in crown green bowling and partying like a rock star.

# 16

## (13 September 2007 – 12 September 2008)

### Stinking attitude

Fresh from winning The Arthur Maude and Harrison Junior Classic, I was invited to the Yorkshire junior trials at Spen Victoria, Cleckheaton. Selfishly, I thought I was too good to be in the trials. My attitude stank. I wasn't up for it and lost my first two games. I kicked both of my bowls into the gutter, which echoed around the green. It's meant to be a game of etiquette. You can't behave like this representing Yorkshire. John Armitage, an experienced bowler, sat me down before my third game. He told me not to get worked up and if I won my final game it would be enough to make the squad.

I was up against Savo, who'd previously beaten me in The Pudsey Junior Classic. The game was tied at 19-19. I knew I had to impress the judges. I held my bowl above my head and said, 'This one is for the crowd.' I played the perfect bowl, nudging the jack towards my back bowl and scoring two to win the game.

### Bench warmer

I was eagerly awaiting the news as to whether I'd made the Yorkshire squad. The letter finally arrived in April. I'd been selected for the away squad but I was on the bench. I would only play if one of the 12 players dropped out. I was good enough to be in the starting team, but my behaviour had let me down.

I spent the entire season for Yorkshire on the bench. Every month I'd travel all over the country and have to watch the entire game without playing. I always supported my teammates who were on the green, but it felt like punishment. At the Yorkshire Junior Merit, it was my opportunity to prove the doubters wrong. Learning from past mistakes, I was focused and keen to show what I could do. I beat some of the county's best players before losing 21-20 in the final to Yorkshire's number-one junior at the time, Neil Ewart. I was so zoned in that I had no idea I'd qualified for the British Junior Finals.

The final of the British Junior Merit was held at Heswall Royal British Legion in Merseyside. It was a tricky green, large in size, with challenging hills. Wayne Ditchfield, who had won the last three British Junior Merits, was absent, so it became an open playing field. I'd lost 21-17 to Wayne in the Federation Junior Merit two years earlier. He was built like a 40-year-old man and was superb for his age.

In the first two games, I edged past Ben Percival of North Midlands 21-19 and Owen Jackson of North Lancs 21-19. I was satisfied with making the quarter-final, but I was playing well … really well. Wayne Ditchfield arrived to watch the final few rounds and shouted, 'Cory, you're on fire lad!'

I registered a 21-20 win against a South Yorkshire bowler which set me up with a semi-final tie against Josh Bradburn from Shropshire. I really was on fire, winning comfortably 21-12. On the other side of the draw Greg Smith from Warwick and Worcester was also making some noise. Whereas most of my games had been close affairs, he was demolishing his opponents to single figures. A big crowd remained for the final. Naively, I had no idea who Greg Smith was. Two Isle of Man competitors came over to me and said, 'Good luck' – I needed it.

Greg was on another level and beat me 21-10. Greg's now widely recognised as the best player in the game.

I played 13 games to reach that final. Four in the Harrogate qualifier, four in the Yorkshire qualifier and five in the British finals.

The following year, I played the 'anchor' position (Number 12) for the Yorkshire away team and we made it all the way to the British County Final, eventually losing to Greg Smith's Warwick and Worcester. I retired from junior bowls that day. Some would say I retired from bowls completely that day. Travelling, university, partying and even work became priority and my ability deteriorated.

## All these things I've done

After spending my early years at school messing about, I got my head down for the GCSE exams. This resulted in 8 Bs, 1 C and 1 D. Although I didn't get any As, my parents were still proud of me. Sam did great too, so as a reward our parents bought us Leeds Festival tickets.

It wasn't possible to break our festival virginity with a better line-up than the one we had. Metallica, Rage Against the Machine and The Killers headlined the Friday, Saturday and Sunday, respectively. At 16 years old, we had zero festival experience. This was evident upon arrival at the entrance, where we found thousands of people wheelbarrowing their supplies through the muddy terrain. We carried 96 cans of beer in plastic bags and didn't even have wellies. The Killers closed the festival with 'All These Things I've Done' and it's still one of the best things I've ever seen. Every single person in the crowd chanting 'I got soul, but I'm not a soldier' will stay with me forever.

Thankfully, that year we stayed in a tame part of the campsite, though we'd heard of the legend of 'Orange Hill'. It was the biggest hill on the festival site and by the final day it would become Yorkshire's very own Val d'Isere – but with mud, instead of snow. People used the slippery surface to ski, sledge and slide to the bottom. When we returned the following year, I made a name for myself. There was a collapsed wheelchair by the bins that my friends found. They fuelled me with beer and placed me in the wheelchair at the top of the hill. For some reason, I also ended up with a Fonejacker mask.

Passers-by gasped as my 'friends' released their grip and let gravity take its course. Everyone screamed – not because it was exciting, but because they thought I might die!

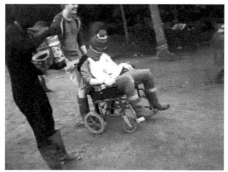 

I flew down the hill so fast the wheels started buckling and I veered off to the left, flying out the chair and crashing into a tent. Two people had to dive out of the way. There was a silence until my mates reached the bottom of the hill to check I was okay. Despite the cuts and bruises, I mustered the energy to fist pump the air and received a cheer from the crowd. I owed someone a new tent though.

Orange Hill was the place to be if you wanted an atmosphere, but on the final day of the festival a tradition started where people would go out of their way to destroy anything – and by destroy, I mean burn! Groups of festival-thugs would go around asking you to leave your tent so they could burn it. It was England's version of Woodstock '99. A deodorant can was thrown into a fire and blew up in our friend Phil's face.

In our third year, the tents next to us had a pig's head on a spike in the middle of their camp. The festival attracted some extremely disturbing and troubled people over the years. It rubbed off on us by year four. Someone in our group brought an extra tent to take a dump in because the 'long drop' toilets provided by the festival were so bad. One year, a girl dropped her handbag into the poo-pit and made a severe misjudgement in trying to retrieve it. She fell in and had to be rescued. She was forever known as 'Poo Girl' and her story even made the national newspapers. It was before the days of influencers so she probably would've got her own TV show if it had happened ten years later.

We played an evil trick on some people involving a Pringles can. As our tents were by the busy walkway, it was decided that each of us would piss into the empty Pringles can and we'd place it onto the walkway, hoping someone would kick it.

It couldn't have gone any better.

This 'lad' – who looked like a bit of a twat anyway – did a 'Jonny Wilkinson', cusping his hands and bending his knees, before taking a run-up and kicking the can as if it was the last minute of the 2003 Rugby World Cup Final. He kicked the base of the can so hard that the piss fired out the other end, all over his face. The best part was, he was with a group of girls and was trying to show off. We burst out laughing. Kids can be cruel.

#thingsyourenotproudof

# 17

## (13 September 2008 – 12 September 2009)

### Kindness makes the fat kid want to play football again

When I returned to school for my A-Levels, I found a friend in an unlikely source. It was my hilarious, new English teacher, Mr Pocock. Aside from his classes, he ran a football tournament on Friday lunchtimes called 'World Series,' contested by Years 11, 12 and 13. It was huge bragging rights in the school if you were the champions.

Although I was still a good, skilful player, I was going through a fat stage again in Year 12. The tournament attracted large crowds, including girls, so it was an opportunity to show off to them.

Unfortunately, during that period there were a small group of lads who started a chant, 'Go on fat boy!' I could hear it was aimed at me and had tears in my eyes whilst playing. Due to how competitive the games were, I was told by our captain that I wasn't selected one Friday lunchtime. This was unheard of as usually it was open to everyone and you could have unlimited substitutes. Mr Pocock noticed me leaving the changing room. 'Hey, where are you going?' I was sulking with my head down. 'They said I couldn't play.' He was furious. 'That's not on at all! Let me have a word!' I shrugged my shoulders and walked back into school.

The following week, Mr Pocock held an assembly and talked about the importance of inclusivity. He didn't mention any names, but used what happened to me as an example. It was an amazing act of kindness that has stayed with me to this day. That's what type of man he was and without the bond I had with him, I wouldn't have discovered my love for film and ended up studying it at university. The captain invited me back into the team and I ended up scoring the winning goal from the half-way line against the Year 13s in the final. Our entire year group came to watch and ran onto the pitch to celebrate with me. I went from zero to hero, thanks to Mr Pocock.

## Keep calm and pass!

I found the whole driving experience stressful when I was learning. I didn't enjoy the fact I wasn't good at something and I was jealous of my friends who were passing before me. I'm usually a calm person, but I would get road rage and become frustrated easily. After dozens of lessons with no improvements, my instructor suggested I take a break to clear my head. I returned after a few months and somehow passed first time. Dad was over the moon. 'Brilliant! I'm so proud of you!' This was the second time he'd said he was proud of me. Maybe I wasn't such a bad kid after all!

## Dan Rayiru, never forgotten

When you're young, you think you and everyone around you is invincible. In January 2009 I received news that still haunts me to this day: 'Your friends have been involved in a serious car accident.' One of my best friends from Rossett, Dan Rayiru, was in a critical condition in hospital and my other friends Josh and Daniel had serious injuries. Dan's older brother Craig and his best friend Joe died in the crash. They were just travelling to play in a football tournament and their lives were taken from them in an instant. Dan remained in hospital for 10 days. I remember hearing the news at school that he'd passed. I walked to the far side of the playground and sat with my head in my hands. We had so many good times together in school and on a weekend, playing for Killinghall Nomads and going to Sweden. Whilst I had issues with a lot of kids at Rossett, he was always good to me and I miss him dearly.

Dan, Craig and Joe. Never forgotten.

# 18
## (13 September 2009 – 12 September 2010)

### 18th birthday party

Adulthood! Not quite. I genuinely thought I was mature at the time. Looking back I was still a little kid. For my 18th birthday, I teamed up with my old school friend, Natalie. We hosted a black-and-white themed party at the Regency Pub in Harrogate and hired a DJ from Leeds. I was obsessed with Deadmau5 at the time, so when I gave the DJ the brief, I said he can play Deadmau5's latest album. He text back saying, 'HAHAHAHAHAHA.' I replied, 'Sorry, what?' He thought it was one of his mates winding him up. In the end, I let him control the music and it was an 18th birthday party to remember!

### What the fuck happened to you!

After years of using fake ID, I'd finally come of age. I was 18 and ready for my first clubbing experience. I'd been to Space in Leeds, but this was the first time I'd paid to see a DJ. Gatecrasher Leeds welcomed headliners Crookers and Laidback Luke. I was excited as this was a big step up from Viper Rooms and Moko in Harrogate.

All fuelled up on cheap cider, we headed inside. We were the youngest people in the club: innocent, naïve and donning our tacky, four-colour Topman T-shirts. The venue was pumping, with lasers spiralling around the smoky room to the beat of the music. We grabbed a couple of Blue WKDs and mingled our way into the crowd.

Laidback Luke took to the stage so we jumped up onto the platform in front of the DJ booth. The crowd screamed as he dropped his first track 'Show Me Love'. More and more people were forcing their way onto the platform. We were cramped in amongst a group of coked-up meatheads. I couldn't work out exactly where they were from but it sounded like Sunderland and their jaws looked like they were in Beijing. I bumped into one of them. He gave me a stern look and moved towards me. I couldn't hear what he was saying so leant in. He must've thought I was squaring up to him and began laying into me, swinging

left and right hooks. After the fourth or fifth swing he knocked me off the platform and onto the dancefloor. The crowd created a circle around us and he continued to pummel me. I was covered head-to-toe in blood so his mates jumped down to pull him off me. Even they were in shock.

Some people just can't handle their drugs ey …

As my blood was dripping all over the floor, I bumped into Dan Tullett (from Harrogate): 'What the fuck happened to you!?' Dan ushered me upstairs. 'We need to go to the toilets and get you cleaned up mate!' I barely recognised myself when I looked in the mirror and my ear had ripped open. I tried going back to enjoy the music but I was too worried I'd bump into him again. Soon after, we made the wise decision to leave and my first clubbing experience was ended prematurely.

# 19

## (13 September 2010 – 12 September 2011)

### Casino car crash

For my 19th birthday, we drove to Napoleons Casino in Leeds. I wish we hadn't. Firstly, I lost my birthday money and, secondly, I nearly died. After a few hours playing roulette and blackjack we set off in a four-car convoy back to Harrogate. We were at that age where you have cars that are too fast for you, so you can show off to the girls. Apart from me, I drove my mum's bright blue Citroen C3 granny bubble car.

For my birthday night, I was in my friend's souped-up Clio. After leaving the casino, one of our mates overtook us and sped away. This only egged my mate on and he put his foot down to chase him. Picking up speed, he began to overtake the car and then proceeded to overtake the van ahead. The van didn't see us and made a sharp right turn without indicating. I was sat front-left as we smashed into the van. We skidded right towards a metal fence. It felt like the end in those few split seconds.

My friend managed to turn the wheel in time and we missed the fence by a matter of inches. He was traumatised, aware he'd nearly killed his mates. We had two more friends in the back seat and miraculously no one was hurt. We were lucky, but we all learnt a big lesson that night. There's nothing cool about driving like a twat.

### Gap yah

After finishing school, me, Balley and Tom decided to have a 'gap yah' and backpack around South America for three months. Due to passing our GCSEs and A Levels, we were under the false pretence that we were now adults. It was more like Dum, Dumb and Dumber.

I believed we had every right to go to South America at 18/19 years of age, but looking back we were unprepared, immature little kids. Imagine my mate's mum not allowing him to play out in 'The Bronx of Harrogate' and here we were, venturing into one of the most dangerous and notoriously wild, chaotic parts of the world; swapping tea and scones for hookers and cocaine.

Joking about the hookers and the c …

We looked like the characters from The Inbetweeners as our parents waved us off at the bus stop; brand new backpacks and a Lonely Planet guide to South America in hand. I was upset as I was leaving my girlfriend at the time behind. I truly believed things would be okay if we stayed in touch every day.

## A warm welcome

Granny Cecilia had kindly arranged for a driver to collect us from Santiago airport and take us to Aunty Lis's home in Concón. The journey through the snow-capped Andes was providing flashbacks from my time there as a kid. I sat in the front testing my Spanish with the driver, whilst Tom and Balley snoozed in the back. I was excited for the three months ahead, but even more so to see my family again.

Granny was the first to greet us at the house. She gave us a big hug and kiss, and was instantly cracking jokes. We celebrated with dinner and a few glasses of Casillero del Diablo Reserva Cabernet Sauvignon – my parents' favourite.

We enjoyed two relaxing weeks with my family before loading our backpacks and embarking on our trip. One of the highlights from staying with my family was catching up with cousin Pablo. He's a cool guy who I've always looked up to. Pablo is now a world-renowned surfing photographer, but back then he was an amateur photographer, still

*Pablo's Instagram – @pablojimenez_photo*

studying and working full-time. He took time out of his busy schedule to teach us the basics of surfing. We were rubbish, but it was good fun. After a few hours' practice I could stand up for about half-a-second.

After surfing one day, Pablo invited us to a party. He was hosting pre-drinks at his apartment in Reñaca. With only one floor and three rooms, his house wasn't the biggest, but it was the dream for any surfer. All you had to do was roll out of bed, grab your shorts and board and be in the sea catching your first wave, all inside two minutes. The fridge was full of beers and the night out was set to be a big one. Someone should have warned us that going out drunk in a foreign country when you don't speak the native language was never going to turn out well.

Within five minutes of being in the club, one local guy ran up and booted me, tripping me up to the ground. I looked back and saw him and his mates laughing. They were either playing a prank because they saw a 'gringo' or it was an early warning sign that we weren't welcome. The rest of the night was fun and we started mingling with some other gringos in one corner of the club. It was 2am when me, Pablo and Balley were dancing with a group of American girls. However, it was only me, Pablo and Balley: 'Where the fuck is Tom?' We looked all over the club and there was no sign of him anywhere. Regrettably, we made the decision not to call Lis and worry her. We cabbed it back to Pablo's in the hope he was there. If he wasn't, that meant he'd gone back to Lis's house.

We woke up in Pablo's apartment six hours later to an irritating sound. The house phone (remember those?) was vibrating the table so much that empty beer bottles were falling off one by one, smashing into pieces on the ground. Pablo appeared from his bedroom rubbing sleep from his eye. 'Who is calling at this time?' Me and Balley were unresponsive, passed out amongst the broken beer bottles. Pablo wailed, 'Mama! Lo siento!' We could hear Lis shouting at him (in Spanish) down the phone. We fucked up. Apparently, Tom arrived home, but at 5am, chaperoned by two police officers who found him at the side of the highway being chased by a pack of wild dogs. His clothes were covered in dirt and blood from wrestling on the floor with the dogs. Thankfully, the police intervened and scared the dogs off. The police didn't speak any English but they mentioned 'casa,' which means house. Tom had no idea where we lived. We can laugh now, but apparently he was saying 'El tennis, el tennis!' This was enough for the cops to figure out he lived close to the tennis courts at the top of Lis's road.

## Out out

It was time for the first leg of our journey. We packed our belongings and said our goodbyes to Granny. I told her I was going to miss her homemade apricot jam every morning! The first destination on our itinerary was Buenos Aires. We opted for the budget option, taking a 24-hour coach from Viña all the way to the Argentine capital.

Lis drove us to the bus station in her old-school RAV4 Jeep; Ray-Bans on and windows down full, on a sweltering hot day. Towering sand dunes out of our left window and waves crashing against the Reñaca cliffs on our right. 'Do you know which bus you're taking?' Lis asked me. 'Yeah, there's a few different ones we can get so we'll check them out when we get there.' 'So you haven't even booked one yet? They get busy you know, especially at this time of year.'

Cut to three of us cramped at the back of a local bus, holding all our luggage on our knees.

The seats were barely wide enough for a five-year-old girl, never mind three 'well-built' lads. It wasn't long before Tom started complaining. 'Twenty-four hours on this!' I couldn't disagree with his frustration, it was uncomfortable and we knew it was going to be a long journey ahead. We looked out the right window to see the 'VIP' bus leaving the station. The passengers were reclining their seats and pulling down tables to rest their laptops and cold beverages.

Our bus was packed to the rafters with families and local workers, and to make matters worse, there was no air conditioning. Even the isle down the middle of the bus was full of people standing. More people attempted to squeeze on the bus. Tom, enraged, shouted down the bus: 'No more people!' The local passengers looked back to Tom in confusion as this was everyday life for them. Whilst Tom was distracted, admiring the reclining seats through the window, one of the local ladies tied her shopping bag to the luggage compartment above his head. As the bus started pulling away, the bag began to swing back and forth into Tom's face. Tom's blood started to boil and he went red in the face (from the bruising and because he was angry). Although the bus was uncomfortable, there were spectacular views of cactus-filled deserts, canyons and wineries, as the sun came up through the Andes.

We were exhausted but excited to explore the 'Paris of Latin America'. I pulled out my phone and searched 'Party hostel'. I'd heard the party scene in Buenos Aires was wild and I was keen to see if this vibrant city lived up to its reputation.

We arrived outside an abnormally Hagrid-sized wooden door. It required two of us to push the unnecessarily big door open. It revealed a huge, multi-storey hostel, with flags from every country in the world decorated all around the balconies. There was table football, a ping pong table, a pool table and even an indoor cinema. It was a young backpacker's paradise.

'Welcome to Milhouse Party Hostel!' Our jaws dropped as we were welcomed by a beautiful Columbian girl who approached us from the desk. 'My name is Tatiana and I am here to help you guys.' I looked to Balley, and Balley looked to Tom, and Tom looked to me. Tatiana continued whilst we composed ourselves, 'Please fill in these forms and we will get you booked in. Where have you travelled from?' Balley plucked up the courage to respond, 'Chile!' 'Oh this country is beautiful. How was your flight?' We looked at each other in embarrassment before Tom replied, 'We took a bus.' Tatiana was in shock. 'Oh my god. Are you okay? It is so far!'

Tatiana led us to the second floor and entered the code for the door, which opened up to a mixed 22-bed dormitory. There were people half-naked on their beds playing on their iPads, reading books and recovering from hangovers. The floor was scattered with dirty clothes, empty suitcases and four loud, humming fans rotating as they blew hot air across the room. Before she left, Tatiana shouted, 'Oh, and don't forget. Tonight is Beer Pong night. See you boys at the bar later for registration.' Balley turned to us, 'Did she just wink at me when she said that?' Tom settled it: 'I can categorically, hand on heart, even hand on the bible, say that she did not wink at you, no Balley.' He couldn't even pull girls in Weatherspoons, so I don't know why he thought he could pull a Spanish-speaking model from Bogotá.

I was taking a hot shower, minding my own business, when I could repeatedly hear 'Ooohhhh, Aaaahhhhh.' I assumed one of the lads had snuck a girl into the boys' showers. After I dried off and left the cubicle, I could hear it wasn't coming from the showers, but instead outside the building. I stuck my head out the window and saw a sign for 'Porn Cinema'. Our hostel was next door to an adult theatre and it seemed as if the film was coming to its climax.

We spent the first day walking down 9 de Julio Avenue, famous for being the widest avenue in the world. We had empanadas for lunch then worked our way towards the colourful La Boca neighbourhood, home to La Bombonera (Boca Juniors' stadium). There was so much happening as we made our way through the cobblestone streets. Couples danced, spinning each other around to the sound of local tango music. There was nearly as much love in the air as the porn cinema.

'Without the streets nor dusks of Buenos Aires, a tango cannot be written.' Local poet, Jorge Luis Borges.

We made our way back to the hostel, dancing down the street, showcasing our new tango moves. The sun was going down, signifying it was time to party. Crowds were beginning to form around the ping pong and pool tables, which had been converted into beer pong tables. If the human race was ever good for something it was inventing amazing drinking games.

It was there I met a guy called Rolo, also from Yorkshire. That first night in Buenos Aires, Rolo was what comedian Micky Flanagan calls, 'Out Out'. I followed his lead. After beer pong, he ushered me into a taxi and we headed to one of the big clubs. I knew cocaine was prevalent in South America, but I didn't think you could get it that easily. Rolo was in the front seat and turned around to me, 'You want some Charlie?' I was an innocent kid at that point. The only thing I'd seen in my life that was anything remotely similar to cocaine was when my mum used flour to bake cakes in the kitchen. 'From where?' I asked. 'From the taxi driver!' Lo and behold, the taxi driver (with his left hand on the wheel) pulled out a baggie with his right and racked up two lines on the arm rest. I thought to myself, If I'm ever going to have cocaine, I may as well do it in a taxi, with a random person I've just met in Buenos Aires, on my way to a super-club.

The club was Ibiza-esque; girls dancing on podiums, lasers, huge sound system and lots of bollocks-chatting. Around five in the morning, I found myself back on the world's widest avenue. After a night like that it also seemed like the world's longest avenue. I got my GPS (my brain) mixed up and walked the wrong way. It took me an hour to realise I'd

been walking in the opposite direction to the hostel. I was still wired when I arrived back to my bunk and had a huge smile on my face.

After that night, I understood why Eric Clapton released a song about it.

We spent a few more days in BA before heading to the largest waterfall in the world, Iguazú Falls. We only ended up there because we saw a photo of it in the hostel and it looked cool. The majority of the river flows through Brazil, but most of the waterfalls are in Argentina. We spent a day on each side of the river. On the Argentinian side, there's a wooden viewing platform that hangs over the lip of the main waterfall. With the sheer force of the gushing water, it didn't feel safe at all! On the Brazil side, we booked a boat ride that took us under the waterfalls. It was an extra cost but worth the money – especially as there was a rainbow that looped over the river.

After five coaches, four buses and a taxi, we arrived back at Lis's house in Concón. It was nice to have a proper meal on the table and spend some time with the family for a few days before heading north to Antofagasta.

## The curious case of the apple and the gun

We became complacent as we settled into our new backpacking life.

'Let's have one more night out before we go!' 24 beers later, we were pretty drunk. For whatever reason, almost as if he had a vision, Tom bailed at the last minute and went to bed. It was midnight when Balley and I left the house. We walked up the sandy track and made our way to the bus stop on the main road. As we arrived, three local lads (our age) started shouting in Spanish across the road. We thought they were joking so we laughed and shouted back. Seconds later, they pulled up three balaclavas, whipped out three guns and stormed across the road. We stood still in shock. They shouted, 'Dinero, dinero, teléfono, teléfono!' Stupidly, I had all my travel money in my back pocket and there was no way I was handing it over to them. It all happened so fast and I lost the ability to speak Spanish. I didn't even have a phone on me and wasn't sure how to explain that. They had zero patience and became more aggressive the more we weren't responding. Eventually, one of the guys hit me on the head with the gun, knocking me to the floor. As blood dripped from my scalp, he stood over me and pointed the gun in my face.

It was at that precise moment, our bus (and saviour) arrived. The bus was full of passengers and the driver beeped his horn repeatedly to startle the thugs. All three of them looked at each other, unsure what to do. Balley and I took the opportunity to jump up and run as fast as we could. We zigzagged through the streets of Concón until we finally reached the coast. After 20 minutes of running, I noticed Balley was still clutching onto his apple that he brought from the house. He had been holding it for the entire ordeal. I asked him how he managed to keep hold of it whilst having a gun to his head. 'I dunno, I was hungry.' He bit into the apple and with an eye over our shoulder, we began the journey back to Lis's house.

During the altercation, we lost our house key. When we arrived home, we had to climb over the gate and onto the roof (where our bedroom window was). Tom woke up to us knocking at the window. He was perplexed with his eyes half open. 'What on earth are you two doing?' 'We were held at gunpoint and lost our key, so had to come home.' He didn't believe us and was angry we'd woken him up. 'Oh, shut up! Close the window and go to bed!'

Antofagasta is situated in the northern part of Chile's Atacama Desert, and whilst it's famous for mining and copper production, I like to believe it's also famous for being the birthplace of my father, Ronald Ian McLeod. Albeit briefly, it was nice to see where he spent his first few years on Earth, before heading to San Pedro de Atacama.

## Driest place on Earth

I was blown away by the Atacama Desert. We chose front seats on the top deck of the bus. It was one long, straight road into the desert. I felt like we'd landed on Mars. There was no life anywhere, only red sand and rock.

Surrounded by hypnotic salt flats and fiery volcanic geysers, San Pedro de Atacama was one cool little town. The buildings were straight out of the Wild West, with saloon-style swinging doors and guys walking around with cowboy hats. The first day we were wandering around when a southern chap by the name of Will stopped us and asked, simply, 'Are you English?' We replied, 'Why indeed we are good sir!' (We didn't, we don't actually speak like that). Will had been travelling the world solo for nine months and was craving some company. He seemed friendly so we booked into the same hostel and signed up to the salt flats' tour.

Known as the driest place on Earth, I wasn't expecting to experience any water. This was until I was stood on the edge of a desert pool, being egged on to jump. I'd say it was 10m high – enough to give you the jitters. Adjacent to this was a salt-water lagoon, reminiscent

of the Dead Sea in Jordan. I was so content with life; the sun was beaming down and I had my feet up, floating in the water with my best mates.

The following day, we explored caves and sand-boarded down the biggest dune I'd ever seen in my life. It took an hour to climb and we were down to the bottom in ten seconds. Well, I bailed halfway down and landed on my arse. You could hear the screams from Antofagasta, and it still hurts ten years later.

After spending the entire night lying awake in agony, we were up early to visit El Tatio, the largest geyser field in the southern hemisphere. It was easily the coldest I'd ever been. I couldn't believe what a contrast it was to the heat of daytime. Call me uneducated, but I genuinely thought the desert never got cold! The geysers reach their peak of activity between 5am and 8am, which is why we had to get up so goddamn-early! Thankfully, there were thermal pools close by where we could recover and bathe in the scolding volcanic temperatures.

We went stargazing that evening after discovering we were in the least polluted sky in the world. My neck was cranked back and mouth wide open. I was in awe of how clear the sky was. I'd never seen so many stars in my life.

I've always been fascinated by space. People think I'm whacko, but I always remind others to 'look up.' People are so glued into their life, society, work, stress, relationships, that they forget what is up there. We're just a tiny speck, in amongst millions of galaxies, shooting through space. For me, people need to relax and enjoy life for what it is. It doesn't matter that you missed a deadline, it doesn't matter that you missed a payment, it doesn't matter that you forgot to wish your cousin a happy birthday (that much).

The following morning, my girlfriend broke the news to me that she wanted to break up. She was finding it difficult not seeing me and had exams when I was due back. This would disrupt her revision and results as I would want to see her all the time. I wish I could've said, 'I understand and sorry for putting you in that position going away for so long,' but instead, I took it badly and sulked.

## Oxygen is underrated

The next coach journey was to Cusco, Peru and took 20 hours. We'd been on so many buses and coaches by this point that we were used to it. I kind of enjoyed it. Locked away in a box

for a while, then you wake up somewhere completely brand new and exciting. Perspective. One of the stops along the way was at Lake Titicaca, believed to be the birthplace of the Incas. As we climbed towards Cusco, the shortness of breath started becoming noticeable.

We made the wise decision to spend a week acclimatising before attempting Machu Picchu. This proved necessary as I could barely walk around the town square without feeling like I had to sit down. The planned week of acclimatising was also a planned week of rest and recuperation as we'd had a lot of heavy nights out. Our plans were scuppered when we found out how good the nightlife was in Cusco. There were a couple of nightclubs and bars off the town square – one being the infamous Mama Africa. Kids would run up to you in the street and give you free drink tokens. You'd have a drink in their bar, come outside and a kid from another club would give you a free drink for their bar. Free drinks all night!

Mama Africa was the place to be at the end of the night. The club was famous for people dancing wildly on the bar. This was where we met Gary Miller from Inverness. He was having the time of his life, swinging his T-shirt around his head to electro house music. We loved his energy so agreed to meet him at the club again the following night … and the next six nights after that.

Once again, we had opted for a party hostel. Yes, they can be noisy at times, but it's a great way to meet people as they organise social events every night of the week. One night they hosted a table football tournament where we met Emil and Anders from Denmark. Then there was a salsa night where we found ourselves dancing next to four stacked Iranian soldiers … as you do. They explained how they were trained to kill and we became scared, backing away slowly (like that Homer-Simpson-backing-into-the-bush GIF).

It was safe to say, after that week, we were fully acclimatised.

## City above the clouds

The day finally arrived when we set foot on the sacred Inca Trail trek. Machu Picchu was the destination; an ancient Inca settlement hidden from the outside world until 1911. We were instructed to meet our team leader, Will, and the rest of the group outside the bus station in Cusco. Being one of the Seven Wonders of the World, I was excited. Even more so, that 33 years earlier my dad and Lis had been there. Our tour group consisted of 15 people from all corners of the globe, but it was the British and Aussies we spent most of our time with. There were three lads from Australia travelling together: Michael, Adam and Shane. Zara and Leonie were friends from England and Australia, then there was Nathan and Matt, also from the UK. Everyone had a great sense of humour so we were laughing from the very first minute of boarding the bus.

We began our journey at Qorihuayrachina; a picturesque train station close to Ollantaytambo. The towering mountains and snaking river made for a beautiful backdrop as we made our first steps through the valley. I was feeling great on the first day, cruising up ahead and enjoying the scenery. Each night, we would pitch our tents at the designated 'campsite' and the local porters would prepare hot meals. It was a good excuse for a bonding

session and a nice way to reflect on the day's experiences. Alarms were set for sunrise and before you finished lacing your boots, the porters would be there with a cup of hot tea.

For the next few days, we encountered llamas, ruins, weird bugs and even warning signs for bears! Everything was new and exciting, the only downside was the toilet situation. I was holding everything in as the excretion facilities weren't too pleasant. As we arrived at Puyupatamarca ('The City Above the Clouds'), it had all become too much. I couldn't hold it in anymore. I had two choices: either shit at the ruins or shit in the woods – where it said 'Beware of Bears'. I opted for the 10 per cent chance that I would get mauled by a bear, rather than wake up on the front page of National Geographic. I could already see the headline – 'The Shitty Above the Clouds'. On the third day, I struggled with the altitude, puffing my inhaler every few minutes.

I wondered how it was possible for the porters to carry so much weight on their backs, yet still be faster than us. Our guide explained how the locals chew coca leaves to counter the altitude sickness. It clearly works! I called my porter 'Pablo Es-gofar' (I didn't).

After four days of uphill hiking, humid temperatures and irritating bites and blisters, we reached the gateway to Machu Picchu. It was overcast with fog – not what we'd hoped for. We couldn't see anything! Eventually, the cloud fragmented, revealing the magnificent ruins of Machu Picchu. It felt biblical. Everyone in the group was exhausted but I persuaded Balley and Tom to join me on the trip up to Huayna Picchu, so I could sit on the same rock my dad once sat on.

It was carnage when we returned to Cusco. Nobody had touched a drop of beer the entire time so we were eager for a night out. I don't know who pulled out the coke in

the men's toilets, but someone did. Before you knew it, I was sniffing a line of Peru's finest off the toilet basin. I stumbled out of Mama Africa around five in the morning. Unfortunately, I was mugged for a second time.

One guy, who was a few inches taller, squared up to me and pulled out a knife. Again, he shouted, 'Dinero.' I learnt my lesson from last time. I gave him all the cash I had on me. I was taking too long so he grabbed my throat and strangled me until I withdrew 150 Peruvian soles from my back pocket. Funnily enough, Tom (best friend, Tom) walked past and was so oblivious to what was going on that he just shouted at me, 'Cory, come on! Let's go get a kebab!' He walked off and left me. I was being manhandled on the Adam's apple to the point where I couldn't even get any words out to display my frustration. Thankfully, the guy took the money and withdrew the knife.

Karma exists. Well, at least I think it does – I'll explain. The following night we were out again. On our way to the bars, I spotted the guy who mugged me. I told Nathan immediately. He grabbed me and asked, 'Are you sure? Are you positive?' I said, 'Yes, positive. That's him!' Nathan saw a police car parked up and ran over waving his arms. 'That man over there stole my friend's money!' The two policemen got out of the car and followed us over to the entrance to one of the clubs where the man was standing. Before they approached, they asked again if it was him. We said, 'Yes!' and pointed. I just wanted my money back to be honest, that's all I cared about.

After receiving confirmation it was him, the two 'law enforcers' pushed him up against the wall and beat him to a pulp with their batons. He fell into a heap on the floor, screaming and holding his legs in agony. They shouted at him and he got up, handed the money over, then hobbled away into the darkness of the dimly lit Cusco streets. I kinda felt bad on the guy. I had no idea what his situation was. He must have been struggling to have to mug tourists. We waited for the policemen to hand over the money. Instead, they returned to their car and drove away.

## Route 36

Next stop on our South American adventure was La Paz, Bolivia, the highest capital city in the world (3,625m). We arrived during the nationwide protests against the government and President Evo Morales. Teachers and healthcare workers were on strike, demanding a 15 per cent pay rise. Our coach couldn't reach the city due to roadblocks so we had to pay a local to take us into the city. For the duration of our stay, we had to stay clear of certain roads to avoid clashes with police. Of course, we still managed to have a good time. We reunited with Matt and Nathan, who were arriving into La Paz on the same day.

Our reunion involved entering the hottest curry in the world challenge in one of the restaurants and going to the world's first cocaine bar. Nathan, Tom and myself entered the curry challenge, whilst Balley and Matt opted for a korma. It was like having the Mordor volcano in your stomach. Nathan and Tom managed to finish theirs but at the halfway stage I was struggling. I was sweating profusely and my stomach was rumbling. I didn't know if I was going to shit myself or throw up first – there was a good chance it would be both at the same time! As Balley and Matt had finished their mildly pathetic curries, it allowed me to use their bowls to throw up in. First, I threw up into Balley's bowl, filling it perfectly to the brim and then I moved straight to Matt's and continued to fill up his – again, perfectly to the brim. It was impressive how I managed to not get any on the table. I wanted to complete the challenge so the restaurant staff agreed if I washed the bowls in the kitchen, I could come back and finish it. I powered through, finished it and they awarded me the T-shirt to prove I had completed it.

Some locals told us about 'Route 36', an illegal coke bar in La Paz. The location changes every few weeks and it isn't advertised. The only way to get there is to try your luck with the taxi drivers and ask them to take you to Route 36. Some of them won't know the location or want to take you there, but some of them do. On our third time of asking, we found a taxi that would take us. This particular bar was located on a dark street and the neighbourhood looked sketchy. When we left the taxi, there were two men in black leather jackets holding radios. They radioed up to the bar, which was on the floor above and gave us the nod to head upstairs. The creaky, wooden stairs were dimly lit, so when we arrived into the bar it was a bit of a shock to see how bright it was.

The bar and furniture were bright white, with only the tables made of glass. There were six booths and people were casually sniffing lines … and chatting – a lot! We shared a booth with another group. Balley and Tom weren't too keen on the whole thing so headed back to the hotel. When travelling, sometimes you have to embrace the experience that presents itself and just go for it. It was once in a lifetime so I thought I may as well tick it off the list. I was gobsmacked when the waiter arrived at the table with a menu of different types of cocaine. When in Rome … or La Paz. We spent the whole night having 'deep and meaningful' chats with absolute strangers – it was great! Nathan had a few lines too many, because when he returned home, he was convinced he was cold and took a boiling hot shower, scolding himself.

## Death road

We were coming to the end of our time in South America and also to the end of our funds. I had two things left on my bucket list for the trip: cycle 'Death Road' and visit Salar de Uyuni. It was the perfect time to visit Salar de Uyuni as it was the wet season, which gives it that spectacular mirror effect. Regrettably, it was proving to be a logistical nightmare and I'd already experienced the Atacama Desert salt flats, so I opted for the thrill of cycling down Death Road. With drops of up to 2,000ft and 2-300 deaths annually (in years gone by), the North Yungas Road wound up with its nickname, for a reason! After a new, alternative road was constructed in 2006, traffic was significantly reduced, opening the door for many tour companies to turn Death Road into a tourist attraction. This gave thrill-seekers like me the opportunity to cycle down the most dangerous sections of the road. Balley and Tom's parents wanted them home in one piece and they were low on cash, so they chose the comfort of staying at home. Thankfully, Nathan and Matt were up for it.

I couldn't believe how fast we were cycling down this death-defying road. On one particular corner, my back wheel skidded in the dirt and rocks trickled over the edge, disappearing into the depths of the valley. After a full day of cycling, I became cocky and

decided to film whilst cycling. Whilst at full speed, I was filming behind me and when I turned back I saw a truck coming the other way. The only way to get around him was to go on the cliff side. My heart beat a million miles an hour as I navigated through the small gap between the truck and the drop.

## Applying for University

Whilst we were in South America, Tom and I were applying for university. Balley wasn't interested and had his heart set on finding a tennis coaching job. Being so far from home wasn't ideal as it meant we couldn't look around the campuses. I had to make a choice between Liverpool John Moores University, Nottingham Trent University and Leeds Metropolitan University, to study Film and Television Production. Following a Skype call with the head lecturer at Leeds, I decided it was the best place for me. There was no way I was living at home with my parents though! I began applying for accommodation straight away.

Growing up, I was never sure what I wanted to do at university. It was thanks to three teachers that I developed a passion for film. My Media teachers, Caroline and Helen, were legends and I always looked forward to their classes (even when I'd be hungover on the Friday). Also, I've called them by their first names because I think they've changed surnames since. They were good fun and made the classes engaging. Mr Pocock was of course the other one – the best ever.

| Likes | Dislikes |
|---|---|
| Sweets | School          Running |
| Football | Bullies |
| Crown Green Bowling      Friends | Manchester United      Tomatoes |
| Steven Gerrard      Ten-Pin Bowling | Beer |
| Liverpool | |
| Girls      Art | Cats      Daily Photos |
| World Series      Vodka | Rejection      Losing |
| Radiohead | |

10 - 20 Years

# 20

## (13 September 2011 – 12 September 2012)

### Freshers

After all the travelling, I was eagerly awaiting starting university. Even if I didn't get a good grade, I wanted the experience of meeting new people and living away from home. I applied for what was known as the 'party flats' – Opal 1 accommodation, on Kirkstall Road. I shared a flat with Harriet, Emma and Lydia from Manchester, and Tom from London. We agreed to host the hall's first party. By 6pm, the flat was full and we partied

all through the night. Well, most people did … I passed out by 10pm. I introduced the Ring of Fire drinking game and was victim to one of the earlier rounds, drinking a shit mix of everyone's alcohol. I woke up at 5am wanting to vomit. I checked my phone and had messages from people I'd met at the party. One of them was Shehraz, who was still awake and invited me to his flat for a game of Fifa.

Shehraz lived with Chris and Will. They were likeminded people and we became close mates. Another person I met was Olly who lived in the flat opposite. My birthday was coming up so I invited them for a Nandos, along with my flatmates. Out of the 16 freshers' nights, our group went out for 14 of them. Back then I could wake up without a hangover and go again.

## Naked mile

Aside from partying, I signed up for trials with the university football teams. I made it through and was selected for the third team. This meant I was invited down to the initiation ceremony. Our ceremony involved sitting in a circle in underwear and being asked a series of personal questions – all in front of the other sports teams (including the girls' hockey team). If they didn't like your answer you had to do a forfeit and down excessively strong, disgusting drinks. They finished by pairing us up and tying our ankles and wrists together. We were forced to 'run' a naked mile. All the other teams made their way outside, whistling, cheering and laughing at our expense. My partner and I were having trouble coordinating any kind of rhythm and we kept falling over onto the concrete. We finished last. By the end of it, I was covered head-to-toe in cuts and bruises. I looked like I'd been attacked by piranhas.

When it came to the first line-up for the third team, my name wasn't on the list. I wasn't too bothered as I'd got to know a guy called Sam Ward through one of the university Facebook groups. He was joining a local football team run by two guys in the year above. This would keep my football needs satisfied, whilst not being so serious that I couldn't enjoy my social life. We ended up winning the league and coming runners-up in the cup that season. Sam went on to start his own team called Carnegie FC the following season and invited me to join.

## A picture of a pint of Peroni and a piece of pizza at the Leaning Tower of Pisa in Pisa

I'd always been loose and spontaneous, but I met my equal in Chris Wright at University. He was a similar character to me, always looking to have fun at any given opportunity. Napoleons casino was next door to our halls, so one night we decided to try our luck. We won £40 each and rather than spend it on a night out, we booked the cheapest flight we could find – £30 return to Pisa (Italy) leaving the following day. Our flatmates thought we were crazy but to us that was an appropriate way to spend the money.

We'd spent our student loans and bursaries during freshers' week so Chris filled a bag of his PlayStation games and DVDs and sold them at a local store – meaning we had £70 between us for two nights in Pisa. We hadn't done any research and couldn't speak a word of Italian. I knew the words Maldini and Pirlo, but that was about it. We booked a hostel for €12 euros each for the first night, took advantage of the complimentary breakfast then headed to the Leaning Tower of Pisa. It was blue skies with a temperature of 20 degrees celsius. Despite having little money, it was nice to relax by the funny-shaped-tower.

Our second allocation of money was spent on a Peroni and a pizza. We posted a photo of us online titled 'A Picture of a Pint of Peroni and a Piece of Pizza at the Leaning Tower of Pisa in Pisa' - this was a shock to our parents, who had no idea.

By the end of the day we had no money left and no means of paying for another night at the hostel. A group of American girls found our story hilarious and bought us drinks, then shamefully we snuck back into the hostel and slept under the pool tables.

A year later, one of the girls recognised me on TV and found me on Facebook.

## Film school

Studying on a film course is different to studying medicine or mathematics. It attracts a lot of interesting, quirky and artistic people. Bruce Cook, who starred in the film Thunderpants (with Rupert Grint and Stephen Fry), was even studying on the course! The first project was to write, direct and edit a short film. I volunteered to be the director. I had zero experience but thought I'd throw myself in the deep end. We filmed an interrogation scene and it went terribly. There was no structure, it didn't make sense and the acting was terrible. Despite this, it was a good bonding session and I made some new friends.

One of them was Josh, who is still one of my best mates to this day. He was in the same accommodation so we hung out regularly. We were passionate about film (obviously) and watched one every night, as well as playing FIFA until stupid o'clock. For our first night out together, we were invited by one of the girls from our course to a place called MiNT Club. It was a dingy, underground club with horrible music (or so we thought). Everyone in there was on drugs and barely any of the music had lyrics. Oh how naïve we were! We lasted an hour before leaving. We were quite drunk (as we were trying to reach the level of the people on drugs) so went for a kebab to soak up the booze. Josh ordered first and waited outside whilst I placed my order. The guy behind the counter looked at me funny. 'Is your mate okay?' I turned around and Josh stumbled, before face-planting into the shop window. He'd fainted and as he collapsed to the ground, his jeans fell down to his ankles. I ran outside to check if he was okay and helped him pull his trousers back up. In that moment, a guy in a Range Rover drove past. 'Oi, you two, get a room!' Great, thanks mate. Josh came back around and couldn't remember any of it. We collected our kebabs from the counter and walked home like nothing had happened.

Josh was the reason I first got into DJing. He sold me his Numark Mixtrack Pro for £50. I was hooked and spent hours in my bedroom practicing. Once I learnt the basics, I began DJing friends' house parties.

## Bwian Bwewewy

I was working at the Swan on the Stray pub, bored out of my mind when my friend Charles text me. 'Would you like to go to Amsterdam in two days?' Why, yes I would! I spent the remainder of the night being as nice as possible to the customers so they would tip me and fund my upcoming weed binge. Drew, another one of my favourite spontaneous people also said, 'YES!' – with capital letters. Armed with Drew's new video camera, we boarded the £36 ferry from Hull. One of our favourite music videos at the time was Tommy Trash feat. Mr Wilson – 'All My Friends'. The idea came to make a parody video of it, so for the next three days we filmed ourselves being as ill as humanly possible.

Our definition of 'ill' – ridiculous, stupid, silly, spontaneous, disgusting, unnecessary.

You can find the parody video on YouTube if you search 'Tommy Trash – All My Friends Parody'.

The ferry was loose and it didn't help that there was a casino. All our bets were coming in, we were buying random people shots … I felt like Alan in The Hangover when he beats the casino. Rather than enjoy our winnings, we went back to the roulette table and lost everything.

Good night though.

Our friends from Leeds, Dom and Richard, were also in Amsterdam, so we arranged to stay in the same hostel. The hostel was a dump. Five of us cramped in a tiny room on the top floor. The stairs were narrow and steep as the Leaning Tower of Pisa. Downstairs had a café. Café in Dutch means sells weed and coffee.

The café had four small tables, each equipped with a chess/checkers board. Drew and I sat down by one of the checkers boards. Little did we know, after one Lemon Haze joint each, this game of checkers would last three hours. Being 'Dam virgins, we picked the strongest weed in Amsterdam and toked like it was our last day on Earth. I developed a severe inability to focus and every move of the checkers piece seemed too difficult to comprehend. I'd finally move to another square, then we'd burst out laughing. Everything became so funny and Charles didn't help matters. He convinced himself that he had Buggs Bunny teeth growing out of his mouth and was panicking, trying to push them back in. This made Drew and I laugh even more. Eventually, it became too much for Charles and he ran upstairs.

We heard tales of a venue called 'Banana Bar' (Bananenbar) - lap dances involving bananas. Being young, naïve and irresponsible, this tickled our fancy. It also tickled our nose. We sat down on an L-shaped sofa and the ladies delivered drinks, touching our inner thighs inappropriately. One of them suggested a group lap dance. We looked at each other and nodded, not anticipating what was about to happen next. After 'warming' herself up, she pulled out a fresh-from-the-grocery banana, as yellow as Bart Simpson's face. She asked one of the lads to unpeel the banana then placed it inside a place where bananas don't usually belong.

Our host commenced the evening's proceedings by dancing all over Dom – he didn't know where to look, bless him! Things escalated quickly when she shouted "Eat it!" Dom's eyebrows left the Earth's atmosphere in disbelief. Richard gave him a nudge and he took a small bite from the banana, that was still... yeah – there! Next up for a nibble was Richard, shortly followed by Charles. The banana was now down to its final third. This whole experience brought a new meaning to the term Continental Breakfast. Poor Drew was last in line. I'd clocked this so I took a massive bite, leaving only a tiny bit of the banana left. "Oh God!" said Drew, as he anticipated a full-nose-dive. He couldn't bring himself to do it so she grabbed the back of his head and shoved him into that last inch of banana.

The following day we booked a tour of the Heineken Factory. We'd had enough fruit so Drew suggested a wake-and-bake joint for breakfast. Bad idea! We got so high, even more than the previous day. Drew could barely speak and was struggling to say the word 'brewery'. He kept saying, 'When are we going to the Heineken Bwewewy?' I couldn't stop laughing. I'd reply, 'The what?' Drew would shout 'Bwewewy!' This made me laugh even more, so I kept it going. 'Bwian's Bwewewy? Bwian's Bwewewy ... Bwian who lives on Bwewewy Wane? Owwwww, that Bwian!' This went on all day and we were in stitches.

Someone suggested buying a space cake each for the journey home. Mine hit me right as we boarded the coach to the ferry. As I took my seat, two imaginary arms grew out of my hip and started clapping repeatedly. The imaginary arms started clapping faster and faster. I wanted to burst into tears. I looked out the window and could still see the clapping hands in the corner of my eye. It lasted the entire journey to the ferry port. As we approached passport control, I asked the guys, 'Are you sure you haven't left any weed or space cakes in your luggage?' Charles checked his pocket, 'No, all good!' Drew patted his jean pocket, 'Oh my god!' Drew left a bag of weed in his pocket and had to run out of the terminal to dispose of it in a bin.

## Wasteland

Towards the end of our first university year we were given the opportunity to work on a heist feature film called Wasteland (or The Rise, as it's also known) as part of our work experience. Despite not being paid, I learnt more in that two-month period than I learnt on the entire course. Nothing against the course or lecturers, but I found the on-the-job experience more beneficial than sitting in a classroom. We also had the privilege of working every day with Matthew Lewis (Neville Longbottom in the Harry Potter films), Luke Treadaway (Clash of the Titans), Vanessa Kirby (Best Supporting Actress at the 2018 BAFTA Awards), Gerard Kearns (Shameless) and Iwan Rheon, who played one of my favourite characters – Ramsay Bolton in Game of Thrones.

With schedule and budget restraints, Josh and I were assigned as stunt doubles. We were handed Iwan and Luke's outfits and instructed to drive the car for some long-shot scenes while the main camera team shot close-ups with Iwan and Luke. The scenes we shot that day (driving across the Yorkshire countryside) ended up making the opening scene of the movie.

The film was available on Netflix and I saw it as an option on an Etihad flight soon after. At the wrap party, I made out with two of my on-set bosses. I was scared of them during filming, so it's funny how things work out. As I kissed one of them, Iwan gave me a nod and smiled. That was the last time I saw Iwan until he was on my television screen in Game of Thrones.

## Tomorrowland

I was obsessed with house music, so when I landed a ticket to Tomorrowland 2012 I was over the moon! I first heard about it after watching the 'aftermovie' from the 2011 festival, which went viral. Unfortunately, I wasn't the only person to have watched the aftermovie and it sold out in minutes. I was distraught, until I received a call from my friend from Newcastle, Adam Dawkins. His mate, Eddie Robb, had a travel company called As You Like It. Eddie had one package left, including one weekend ticket and travel via Amsterdam. Before he even finished the sentence, I said 'YES!' and transferred the money.

Dawkins was the only person I knew on the trip, but I was confident there would be like-minded people. From the minute I reached the ferry port, everyone was so friendly and keen to get the party started – as early as possible! I first met Tom Higham. He was a DJ in Newcastle and we hit it off instantly because of our identical music taste. Tom introduced me to his friend, Billy, and later Sean, David and Sarah from Scotland joined the conversation. The majority of the group were from Scotland and it wasn't long before they started the Scottish chant 'Here we, here we, here we fucking go!'

The ferry was even more chaotic than the time I went to Amsterdam to eat a banana. Tom DJ'd to a full dancefloor the entire night and two people from our group ended up in the on-board jail. We were given an hour to explore Amsterdam before continuing to Belgium. Of course, we took advantage of the situation. Billy and I had space cakes and laughed uncontrollably the entire way. Thankfully, I didn't grow an extra pair of clapping arms this time.

I was so accustomed to the rain, mud and debauchery of Leeds Festival. Here, everyone was so happy, the sun was out, there were people from almost every country in the world and everybody was respecting the land. I was gobsmacked people were actually using the waste bins for their litter. Although I'd watched the aftermovie a thousand times, the view of the main stage still shocked me. The end of the walkway from the campsite revealed the bowl-shaped main stage. Each year, the festival takes on a theme. This year, the theme was 'The Book of Wisdom'. The décor consisted of a giant LED screen and books lined up beside one another. It was the best festival stage I'd ever seen. We explored the rest of the site; it was like a Disneyland for adults. There were stages floating in the water, rave caves and ferris wheels.

At this point in my life, I'd never even considered ecstasy. I found music euphoric, even when sober. Eventually the jealousy kicked in. I was having an amazing time but the people I was with were on another level. As Avicii arrived on stage to play the headline set, they offered me some. I wasn't well-educated on drugs. The temperature had hit 32 degrees celsius when I took the happy-pill, but I hadn't been drinking any water, only beer and cider.

I was extremely dehydrated and collapsed in the crowd. My friends panicked and forced water down my throat. I recovered, then collapsed again. I was so confused, but once I hydrated properly I felt good and started coming up.

I'd been waiting years to see Eric Prydz, but due to flooding at the dance tent, they weren't allowing any more people in. I bumped into Ross from the Scottish gang who was equally disappointed. We knew we had to find a way in. I don't know what Ross was on but there was a river surrounding the dance tent and he suggested we trek through the forest and swim up river so we could avoid detection and jump over the fence. Covered in mud and drenched to the core, we successfully hopped over the fence and blended into the crowd. I tweeted this story and Eric Prydz reposted it.

# 21

## (13 September 2012 – 12 September 2013)

### RPT

After a year of living in student halls, it was time to find a house for our second year. Most students lived in the areas of Hyde Park and Headingly, with Headingly being the more affluent. We left it to the last minute and couldn't afford the more affluent area. There was just one available house left. It was on Royal Park Terrace, in Hyde Park, so we nicknamed it 'RPT'. We were proud of RPT, despite having rats living in the floorboards for the entire year.

### Viral

A few weeks after moving into the house, we released our daily photo project. It was time to convert Dad's 'flick book' idea into a time-lapse film, released on YouTube. Dad spent three months scanning the old photos and lining them up. The next job was the music, so I approached my good friend Tom. He was studying music technology and seemed like the perfect person to ask. He teamed up with his classmate George and began working in the studio straight away. I gave them a short brief: 'Something melodic and uplifting, but not cheesy.' They came back with a track one week later. We were so impressed and it was exactly what we were looking for!

We released '21 Years' on 26 September 2012. The link was shared many times that evening and received hundreds of views by the time we went to bed. By the morning, it had 2,000. A few days later, the Harrogate Advertiser got hold of the story and asked if they could interview us. The story made the front page and it wasn't long before the Yorkshire Post and the national newspapers published the story.

It was a crazy time. After a few weeks, the video reached 900,000 views. In anticipation of the video reaching one million views, me and my housemates went for a night out to celebrate. It was on 950,000 when we returned from the club. By the time we woke up, it

was on 2.5 million! The story had gone worldwide. The next week was a bombardment of interview requests from all over the world. We started with a 'live' interview on ITV. They filmed 30 minutes before airing so we rushed back to RPT to watch it.

We received loads of messages from people saying they'd seen us on TV. My housemates were excited so insisted we go out – like they needed an excuse! I was oblivious to the magnitude of it. Random people were coming up to me saying they saw me on TV. It was surreal.

We were interviewed on BBC Radio 4 by Sian Williams and Richard Coles, then CBS America paid for us to go down to London. We were chauffeured in a Mercedes and housed in a classy London hotel. The story aired on CBS This Morning a few weeks later and the video jumped by another three million views. I had tweets from celebrities, such as Alyssa Milano, who said, 'Wow! Is this you?' and Sebastian Ingrosso (Swedish House Mafia), who said it was 'Cool'. Over the next weeks and months we did podcasts in Canada, interviews for Brazilian, Japanese and Australian TV and a few other small bits. We knew it wouldn't last forever but enjoyed the ride. I received an obscene amount of friend requests and DMs, and even had to turn down a few marriage proposals!

Having to take a photo every day was a struggle at times. I didn't always understand or appreciate what was happening. In fact, I found it annoying during my teenage years. I could be at my friend's house for a sleepover and my dad would still drive over to take the photo before it turned midnight. If he forgot during the day and it was late at night, he would wake me up and take the photo. It was an old-fashioned camera back then, so the flash would sting my eyes. He never cheated and refused to take the photo if it was after midnight. For the few days he forgot (or for camera issues), he placed a rough sketch in the project of what I would have looked like on that day.

Whether it be my football matches or parties he went to, my dad always documented everything with his camera. I was recently at one of my parents' friend's houses. My dad filmed one of their old parties and gave them a copy as a gift. It had footage of his late

wife and you could see how much it meant to him to see that bit of film. People found it annoying that he always had a camera with him, but now they appreciate it as they can look back at the memories all these years later – me included!

Thanks to the interviews and advertisement revenue on YouTube, we made a bit of money from 21 Years – not a lot, but a nice little bonus. I was mistaken in thinking Dad was going to share it with me. Instead, he bought a new washing machine and a toilet that cleans your arse with a remote control.

## MiNT

Second year was a completely different experience to the first year. Parties changed, we changed. Instead of pre-drinking out of a fruit bowl and going on a bar crawl, we attended house parties. House parties were a big thing in Hyde Park and Headingly as many of the houses had soundproofed basements – perfect for raves. If you walked through Hyde Park in the middle of the night, you couldn't go five seconds without seeing a party. Although you might not have been able to hear it, you'd see crowds of people queuing to get in or taking a break from the music and lighting a fag. We went from leaving MiNT Club in first year, because the 'music was shite', to going there every single Thursday in second year. We ended up at a load of wicked afterparties – yeah, I said wicked. It felt like we were living in the *Human Traffic* film. 'All that exists now, is clubs, pubs and parties. I'm going to never-never land with ma chosen family, man.' Life was all about the music. We went to our Uni classes, but the talk was always about when and where the next party was.

MiNT Club was our church. We used to go to an underground party called Teknicolor and every week it would be the same crowd in there. It became a family, all brought together by the love of music … okay, yes and a little help from our friend ecstasy. I became close with a guy called Billy from Manchester. We had a platform on the right-hand side of the club that we would always meet at. It was a little higher than the rest of the crowd, so we could look down on everyone beneath us raving. Every night was incredible, but it would always go so quickly. Before you knew it, you were back in class, melting to the desk.

## One cold winter night

One of our other favourite venues in Leeds was Canal Mills. It was a legendary warehouse party held once a month. In January 2013, in the middle of winter, we booked to see Eats Everything, Ben Pearce, Mosca and Waze & Odyssey. In the week leading up to the party, it snowed every single day. News circulated online that it was going to be cancelled. Most of the roads around the city were deemed too unsafe to drive on. This is where the power of the 'Leeds spirit' came into play. Nothing can get in the way of a person from Leeds and their party – even 4ft-deep snow!

Our group heard nothing to say it was officially cancelled, but we were a bit sceptical as to whether it would still go ahead. The only way to get there was to walk, so we put our wellies on and trekked three miles through the snow. As we approached, we noticed other groups of young people making the treacherous journey across Leeds. It was a sign of hope, but our worry was that even if the party did go ahead, there wouldn't be enough people to make it memorable. Oh, how we were wrong! The warehouse was full and the atmosphere was electric! Despite ditching the usual rave attire for wellies, scarves and woolly hats, every single person had made it. Everyone we talked to was saying the same thing: 'We didn't expect anyone else to be here!'

I tweeted about it a few years later. Eats Everything and Waze & Odyssey replied, laughing about how legendary it was.

## Afterparty

One night at MiNT Club, myself and Anthony were pretty high and invited everyone to our friend's house for an afterparty. We found this out later – we couldn't remember doing it! Six of us went back to the house to have a few drinks and wind down. We heard a knock at the door. Two lads said they had arrived for the afterparty. We told them we were chilling but they were more than welcome to join. Every five minutes after that we received a knock at the door, with more and more people arriving for this unbeknown afterparty. Eventually, when my friend asked one of the newcomers how they ended up at the house, they said, 'Oh, two guys called Anthony and Cory were going around the club telling people this address.' Anthony and I shrugged our shoulders. Our friends who owned the house were annoyed we'd invited so many strangers, but found it too funny to be truly pissed off. Within an hour, the house was packed. Anthony turned to me and said, 'Well, we may as well have an afterparty now!'

## As you like it

After missing out on a Tomorrowland ticket for 2013, I was depressed. I would have done anything for a ticket – and that I did! In a genius move to provide marketing for the As You Like It company, Eddie decided to run a UK-wide competition to become a Festival Ambassador. The lucky winner would be invited to attend some of Europe's best festivals, documenting the journey along the way. After several online interviews, I made it into the final three. I was joined by Rachel from Liverpool and Kayleigh from Scotland. The next stage of the selection process was to travel to Manchester and spend a full day completing silly challenges and tasks. The activities included choreographing a dance routine with the general public, finding a celebrity and persuading passengers on a packed double-decker bus to sing a song with you.

Eddie and his team had a fun day laughing at our expense. Unfortunately, just as we thought it was over, there was one final surprise. Eddie pulled out a bottle of Jägermeister and suggested we take a few shots. The final task, was to … at peak-time … on a Saturday night … in the middle of Manchester … in a busy bar … do a stand-up comedy routine.

With only 30 minutes' notice, it's fair to say we all struggled. I read five one-liner jokes that I Googled and ended with my 'Blind I Spy Story'. It received the biggest (only) laugh of them all. Eddie congratulated us and said he'd be in touch.

## Leeds cup final

My dad used to film all my football matches as a kid, but would always miss my best goals. His excuses would range from going to the toilet, turning to speak to one of the other parents or his video camera running out of battery. When Carnegie FC made the Leeds Cup Final, I asked my dad to come over to Leeds to film it. There was a decent crowd at the stadium so it was a big occasion for a lot of us. I was playing attacking midfield, supporting our striker Jimmy. It was a tense affair on a windy night in West Yorkshire. After 45 minutes, the game was tied at 0-0.

Our gaffer, Sam, and captain, Billy, rallied the troops and got us pumped up for the second half. After several close attempts, we won a promising free-kick in the 70th minute. As we did with all our set pieces, Josh aimed for Jimmy's head, as he was the tallest player

on the pitch. Josh struck the ball perfectly. Jimmy flicked the header to me and I took it on the half-volley, smashing it into the net! Our travelling supporters went wild and I was smothered to the ground. Our opposition scored two late goals and spoiled the end-of-season party (although we still went out). I asked Dad if he recorded my goal. 'Oh, was it you that scored? I thought it was someone else! I think so.'

## LHP

I was invited to DJ a whole host of different house parties across Leeds in my first two years at university, but none were as good LHP. 'Leeds House Party' looked like any normal terraced house, but the door in the kitchen led downstairs into one of the best club venues I'd ever been to. It was a like a mini-Berghain. The creaky wooden floorboard descended into complete darkness.

As you arrived into the basement, there was a red-lit chillout area to the left and the main dancefloor to the right. The acoustics were surprisingly good; you could have a conversation in the left room despite the music thumping in the right. The club room had

a stack of speakers on either side of the decks, a smoke machine and lasers. I remember opening my set with wAFF – 'Jo Johnson,' Patrick Topping – 'What Do You Mean' and Luigi Madonna – 'Summer Sensation'. It's still, to this day, the best set I've ever played. The crowd were bashing the wooden beams supporting the ceiling, meaning dust was dropping down all over the decks and on top of people's heads – but no one cared! I dropped 'Starlight' by The Supermen Lovers in the middle of two techno tracks and the ceiling almost collapsed!

## Festival ambassador

As You Like It announced me as the winner of the festival ambassador job. I was going to all of Europe's best festivals – for free! A few weeks before I was set to embark on the summer of a lifetime, I received a call from the boss, Eddie. He explained how the company were having a few issues and it wouldn't be possible to send me to all the festivals. Eddie was a good friend of mine and he would have loved to send me to all the festivals if he could. As an apology, he gave me his VIP ticket to Ultra Europe in Croatia, all paid for and staying in the same hotels as the DJs. He also threw in a free ticket for Tomorrowland Festival, which was two weeks later. All in all, it wasn't what I was expecting, but it was still set to be an awesome summer!

## The ten Americans

A few days before Ultra Europe, the cameraman I was meant to be travelling with pulled out. Eddie asked if I had any mates who were good with cameras I could take with me. My best mate Sam was always up for anything, so I told Eddie he could do the job. I called

Sam and told him he was coming to Croatia. He said, 'Fuck yes!' then, 'Oh shit, it's my graduation that weekend!' I was like, 'Mate, it's Ultra Europe, for free!' Sam paused for a while. 'Okay, let me speak to the 'rents.' He called an hour later: 'They're letting me miss the graduation but they're not happy!' Me: 'Great! By the way, have you got a camera? You're going as an official photographer.' Sam: 'What?'

I can be known to influence my friends from time to time. One of my mates said he went to a festival in Croatia because he thought 'What would Cory do?' He couldn't afford to go and didn't have any holiday left, but he booked it anyway and went. He ended up getting fired for missing work, but at least he had a good time!

We arrived in Split with Sam's ancient little, beaten-up, digital Canon camera and two backpacks full of rave clothes. We messed up the directions to the Radisson Blu Hotel and ended up walking two hours in the sweltering heat. We were exhausted and had two options: either crash in bed or start drinking. We opted for the fun version and cracked open a beer on the balcony. When we looked down, we saw none other than Carl Cox entering the building. We were ecstatic as he was one of our favourite DJs.

By 4pm, Sam and I were smashed. We went to the second floor to use the computers to let our friends and family know we were having a good time and to tag @AsYouLikeIt on some posts. For you kids out there … we used to use Internet Cafés to access Facebook. One flustered American by the name of Erfan sat on the computer opposite. He was sweating and clicking aggressively on the mouse. We asked him what was up: 'Bro, me and my friends accidentally booked the Radisson Blu in Dubrovnik instead of Split and there's no availability in any other hotel!' I replied, 'Shit mate, that sucks!' Sam and I were a few drinks deep and had a little chat between ourselves. A few minutes later, we turned to Erfan. 'Mate, you can crash in our place if you want.' 'Are you serious? There's ten of us!' 'Yeah! Fuck it.'

Ten American lads, with suitcases, rucksacks and duty-free bags full of booze, arrived into our suite. Three slept on the balcony, four in the corridor, one joined us in the bed and two slept in the bathroom. They could've been anyone but they turned out to be legends and were so grateful. So grateful, they offered some of their ecstasy. This ecstasy turned out to be the best ecstasy I'd ever had. Karma.

This festival was also where I truly got into techno music. On the way to the toilet we passed the techno stage. Swedish DJ Adam Beyer was playing Alan Fitzpatrick's track 'In The Beginning', which was going off. We forgot about needing a piss and raved for the entire set. The following night, after friends Jonny and Josh had arrived, we headed into the festival for Day Two. We hadn't taken the ecstasy the night before so we were looking forward to it. We danced our way through the crowds, talking to everyone we passed. Some of the people I met that night I still talk to, including my Croatian friend Anamaria.

We were having fun in the crowd but realised we hadn't made use of the fact Sam was an 'official' festival photographer and that I was an 'official' festival ambassador. We decided to try our luck getting into VIP. We said to Jonny and Josh, 'We'll be back within

30 minutes, we're going to check out VIP. Stay right here.' We were confronted by two security guards at the entrance: 'VIP passes please.' 'Sorry, we don't have a VIP pass, but we are official Ultra Europe photographers and ambassadors.' We pulled out the documents from our bag which Eddie had sent us. They looked puzzled. 'Where is your camera?' Sam puffed his cheeks, looked at me for answers (of which I had none) and shamefully reached down into the bottom of his bag, pulling out the ancient Canon camera. Both security guards looked perplexed: 'Go on, on you go.' I thought that meant fuck off, but they waved us into VIP!

We were like two little children who had just been let into Santa's Grotto on Christmas Eve and went straight to the bar for shots to celebrate. The guy next to us was a captain on one of the yachts and had access to the top VIP floor: 'Boys, come with me!' The security on each floor stopped us, but the camera and the documents passed and we were let up! By this point, the ecstasy was flowing through every part of my body and it truly felt like I was flying above the crowd. We were so high that we completely forgot to go back and find Jonny and Josh. On our way out we saw them sat up against a wall covered in rave paint. They looked like they'd also had a good night. We watched the sunrise by the marina, which was the perfect end, to what is still the best night of my life!

Sam and I managed two hours' sleep before boarding a ferry to Hvar Island, where the festival was hosting an exclusive pool party. We were suffering, but the fresh air soon brought us back around. We hit the jackpot. Eddie's suite was overlooking the pool party and the likes of NERVO, Steve Aoki and Dada Life were all staying in the rooms next door. It felt like a spring break party: thousands of young people raving in the pool to some of the world's biggest DJs.

# 22

## (13 September 2013 – 12 September 2014)

### Dubai

My Chilean cousin, Danny, had been pestering me to come work with him in Dubai. He was the general manager of a catering company and had been enjoying life in the 'sandpit' for the past five years. I was approaching the end of my course and was on track for a 2:1 or 2:2. For the final project, we had to write, direct and edit a short film, which would be shown in a local cinema. All students were split into four groups and roles were distributed. I was given the role of editor, along with my friend Brandon. I was excited for the project as it was a fun story. It was a mockumentary zombie film, and I volunteered to be one of the main zombies. We hired a television actor for the lead role and booked a professional make-up team.

Despite being editor, I spent every day on set, helping the crew and acting. The filming went well, resulting in some great footage! When it came to the edit, Brandon and I were slow to get going. Not because we were lazy but because we were working out which angle to go with. Either to follow a linear narrative or think outside the box. One of our classmates, who wasn't part of the editing team, kept entering the room to pitch ideas and change things – it was frustrating! With time running out, we worked through the night for three consecutive evenings and moved the ending of the film to the start. It wasn't the safe option but we believed it was funnier by changing the order of the scenes.

Our classmate complained to the head of department. It's like telling Tarantino he can't use cartoons or excessive blood splatters - sort of. Without a second chance, they removed us from the film. We were upset and disappointed. The head of department said our only option was to write, direct and edit our own film, in a week. ONE WEEK!

We tried our best to make it happen, but there wasn't enough time. The only way we could pass the year was if we came back for three months in September to redo the project. That meant paying extra money for the course, accommodation and changing all our future plans. Although I didn't want to disappoint my parents by not completing the course, I had Dubai in the back of my mind. I took a step back and looked at the bigger picture. If I don't move to Dubai now, I may never move. I took the leap of faith. Three months later, I was on a plane to Dubai.

Some of my friends from the film course went on to work in television and film. Most notably, Matt Robinson who appeared in the BBC's Bodyguard and the film 1917 – my favourite war film!

## The high life

Sam also finished Uni (although, he actually got grades n' that) and agreed to join me in the Middle East. His mum asked me on the morning of departure what I thought about the move: 'I feel upset not knowing when I'll see my parents again.' Sam laughed and called me pathetic. Although I'd see my parents again, this was the day I truly left home.

Along with two other interns, we were housed in an unfurnished flat in the outer-outskirts of Dubai. The Burj Khalifa and Burj Al Arab were the size of ants on the skyline. After complaining, the company's warehouse team delivered some of their event furniture. We didn't have Wi-Fi or a TV so spent a lot of time in the Arabic restaurant below. For my first shift at work, the supervisor was training me how to become more 'Dubai'. To me, canapés were sausage rolls and cheese triangle sandwiches. I had to get used to the fancy canapé names and learn to speak more eloquently.

As much as offering canapés to people more fortunate killed me, it was the door that would open many great opportunities and experiences. I met Emily, who introduced me to DJ Mark Knight and his tour manager Adam, who invited us to party with them. Another night, we met a prince who invited us to his suite in the Burj Al Arab. He had a stack of cash and tipped every person he passed 500 dirhams. The suite, decorated in red velvet and gold, had three butlers on hand, offering lobsters, steak and champagne.

Each year, the company caters on the yachts at the Abu Dhabi Formula One. There are 50-60 yachts and DJs play all day and night. Rich party goers and celebrities jump boat-to-boat, partying for the entire weekend. It's even fun as a waiter! On the final night of my first Formula One weekend, we finished our shift and gatecrashed some parties. It was a crazy night. I woke up and couldn't remember a thing. When I checked my phone for evidence, I found a photo of David Haye taking a selfie of me, him and my friend Adam. I couldn't stop laughing and tweeted the photo. News outlets picked it up and it became a headline – something along the lines of 'David Haye parties in Dubai, despite having passport seized'. We catered for Lindsey Lohan, Kendrick Lamar, David Hasselhoff and Craig David, among others. I also served Dwight Yorke, Andy Cole and Jermaine Jenas. As a football fan, this was cool for me, even if they did play for teams I hate!

## DJing the biggest NYE private party in Dubai

After three months of waitering, we hit the jackpot! One of our clients was hosting a NYE party in his luxurious apartment on the Palm Jumeirah. The soirée was also located

where they were breaking the record for the world's largest firework display. It was a big party to say the least, and we couldn't fuck it up! Our roommate Lily became good friends with him and persuaded him to let me and Sam DJ. We called ourselves 'The Mixer'. 700 people were on the guestlist and we'd only DJ'd a few house parties. The client's right-hand man was a guy he called 'The Brain'. He claimed to be a genius and was knowledgeable on everything, including music. He even told stories of when he used to party with Paul Oakenfold. We had a meeting to discuss the vision for the music. The Brain wanted 'cool music'. He mentioned playing Orbital and I said I was already picturing playing 'Halcyon' as the sun came up. He was impressed.

That was lesson number one for our illustrious DJ career in Dubai – don't listen to the client! We barely had any commercial music for the party and, unfortunately, most parties in Dubai require commercial music. As guests became more drunk, they wanted to dance and we were running out of ideas – we even played the same song three times! The upper class in Dubai expect the best and we certainly weren't the best DJs in Dubai – at that time, anyway. One woman came up to the booth shouting and swearing in our face saying

we were shit. We weren't bad DJs, we just didn't have enough music. It was embarrassing, but I still finished with 'Halycon' by Orbital as the sun came up.

## The beach

After our internship, we wanted to treat ourselves. We'd saved up enough money in tips alone, never mind the party we DJ'd. One of our dreams had always been to go to Thailand. Aside from Wedding Crashers, The Beach was our favourite hangover film. There was something about Richard rocking up in a new country and immersing himself into a new culture that appealed to us. The warm weather, beautiful beaches and cheap beer was a bonus!

Sam's girlfriend surprised him by booking a flight to Dubai on the same dates we had planned to go, so I ended up travelling alone and he joined the following week. Luckily, my other mates from Harrogate (Luke, Tom and Greg), were also travelling in south-east Asia at the time. I opted for Bangkok as my starting point. Swapping luxury penthouse parties for Khao San Road was a bit of an adjustment, but one I was willing to embrace.

As ever, I landed in a foreign country with zero planning. All I knew, was I needed to reach Khao San Road and there would be hostels in abundance. Khao San Road is where all the backpackers stay and is known for its many bars, street food markets and the infamous 'Ping Pong' shows. I was trying to find a taxi outside the airport when a guy on a scooter shouted 'Khao San Road my friend?' It's like he read my mind … or I looked like a stereotypical backpacker. To settle into my new environment, I ignored the voice (my mum's) in my head and, with a degree of negligence, jumped on the back of the scooter. There was no helmet, so I hugged my new friend as tightly as I could. We darted through the streets, dodging oncoming traffic and pedestrians. Despite the risk, I had a huge grin on my face. I'd been working my ass off in Dubai and finally felt free again!

It was only mid-afternoon, but it already looked like they were preparing for the chaos that would ensue at night. There were hostel signs wherever you looked, but one in particular stood out - 'Hostel with rooftop bar'. Sold! This was slightly more upmarket, but it was the first day of the holiday. By the time I had faffed around checking in, I was so exhausted that I collapsed fully clothed onto the bed. Luke was arriving later so I messaged instructions of how to find me. Four hours flew by and I was rudely awakened by Luke's large fist banging at the door.

Rather than join me in bed (not like that), he was full of energy and ready to hit the town. Bangkok can be intimidating at night so I was grateful to have someone to share the debauchery with. We joined a party on the rooftop and ordered our first cocktails of the night. We smiled and nodded at each other. It felt like the beginning of The Hangover Part II movie (apart from we were hoping not to end up with a monk in a wheelchair, or lose a finger).

Things escalated quickly. It was carnage; Bingtang-vest-wearing-tourists (mainly Brits) stumbling all over the place, tuk-tuks beeping their horns and a sea of multicoloured buckets and scorpion remains. Usually this would be an awful thing to witness but I guess this is how this particular area makes all their money. Yet again, foreign countries taking advantage of inebriated Brits … how dare they!

It was 11pm and the night was in full swing. We'd spent most of the night sharing a table with a cockney guy who had spent the last five years living in Thailand with his local girlfriend. They suggested going to a Ping Pong show. Intrigued to experience this global phenomenon, we accepted the offer without a moment's hesitation. We jumped on the back of a tuk-tuk and made our way through the bustling streets. By this point, we'd had three buckets each so riding in the back of the tuk-tuk was making me dizzy. Everything was moving fast and my vision was distorted.

I've never seen so much talent in one tent! It was like the Cirque du Soleil, but with a twist. I was in awe of what these women could do! They were like the Harlem Globe Trotters of Thailand, doing trick shots into cups, catching the ping pong balls with the skill and precision of Zinedine Zidane and throwing darts at balloons using their pelvis muscles with the accuracy of Phil 'The Power' Taylor.

On to a nightclub, where Luke claimed he got with 'an absolute worldie'. He wouldn't stop talking about her on the way home.

I had to break it to him that it was actually a boy with braces.

I couldn't muster the strength for one more night in Bangkok, so I was happy we'd agreed to take an overnight coach south towards Koh Phangan. This is where we would meet Tom, who was joining us for The Full Moon Party. The event attracts thousands of tourists each month, with parties continuing until sunrise the following day. A line of beach bars pump music all night, ranging from house music, techno, drum and bass, reggae and psychedelic trance. The footage I'd seen online looked amazing!

Usually I prefer the budget option of an overnight coach, but when you're with someone like Luke who has the loudest snore imaginable it can be somewhat painful. I didn't sleep for the entire 14-hour journey. Of course, he slept the whole way there and looked fresh as a daisy as we arrived at the ferry port. There was a real buzz about the place. Three coachloads of young backpackers boarded the ferry to Koh Phagnan and it wasn't long before the party started.

The Full Moon Party was the following night so after reuniting with Tom we got some well-deserved rest before 'the world's most famous party'.

The girls in the adjacent cabin had neon, glow-in-the-dark UV paint. The result: a snake on my face and 'Harrogate' down my arm in capital letters – so cool. By 7pm, the beach was overflowing with neon-painted ravers. We jumped through a ring of fire then danced our way across the beach, stopping at different parties. One minute we were grooving to reggae, the next we were stomping and fist-pumping to trance. At the end of the beach, sat way up on the hillside, was Mushy Mountain, a place you can buy mushroom shakes (a lot of them). I didn't leave Mushy Mountain until the sun came up. I lost my old friends and made new ones. It was amazing, euphoric and one of the best nights of my life.

## Everything in its right place

A great song by Radiohead, but also a great way to describe our time in south-east Asia. Our friend Greg was travelling to Gili Islands with ten friends and invited us to join him. Whilst Sam was flying from Dubai, Luke and I made our way south on another overnight coach to catch a cheap flight from Kuala Lumpur. I couldn't endure another night on a bus with Luke's snoring so double-dropped some Xanax. Taking one dose helps you relax if you're struggling to sleep. Taking two… well, you're fucked.

I had 24 hours in Kuala Lumpur and spent 23 of them trying to find somewhere to sleep. I was sleeping on park benches, in disabled parking spaces, at the bowling alley, in the middle of roads … anywhere that had a surface. To revitalise me, Luke took me to Starbucks and I even fell asleep there, face down on the table. I was looking forward to seeing the Petronas Towers as well …

## Hell of a trip!

I'd never slept so much in my life! On to Bali, and I was recharged and ready to party. Luke, Sam and I spent one night on the mainland before taking a severely battered and

bruised 'public boat' to the Gili Islands. It looked like it had been peppered by a machine gun. The crew spent the entire journey trying to keep us afloat, using buckets to remove the water. The Gili Islands consist of three islands: Gili Trawangan, the party island, Gili Meno, the romantic island, and Gili Air, the chill-out island. We opted for Trawangan where Greg greeted us with an ice-cold beer.

It was heaven on earth ... the water surrounding the island was crystal clear and perfect for snorkelling and diving. The only modes of transport on the island were bicycles and

horse and cart. In the day we sunbathed and at night we partied. On the first night, we noticed a sign above one of the bars: 'Buy Mushroom Shakes Here'. I rubbed my hands together, 'Brilliant! I'll take two!'

We headed back to the hostel to get ready for a beach rave. The hostel was run by two locals who were laughing outside. They waved us over. 'You want good time?' 'No mate, I'm fine thanks.' 'No, no. You like mushroom tea?' I was two shakes down but keen to try anything. I took a big swig – it tasted like Coca-Cola. It was delicious!

They delivered two litres of the concoction to our room, and instead of the beach rave five of us sat in our hostel room for the entire night. It was one hell of a trip. We took it in turns to stand at the end of the bed and do stand-up comedy sketches. I'd give everything I own to have that whole experience on tape. Everything we said was funny. We gave names to each other and the objects in the room. Luke became 'The Big Red Giant' because he's big and he was sunburnt. Erika was 'The Yellow Mermaid' because she had long blonde hair and a sparkly dress. We even gave a name to the sheet of cloth that was blowing in the doorway due to the fan being on – that was 'Gusty Gail' (she was my favourite). By 7am, my jaw was aching. I was clamping my mouth shut with both hands as I couldn't stop laughing.

After a few hours' sleep (with Gusty Gail flapping beside me), we packed the snorkels and made the 100m walk down the dirt track to the beach. There was no sign of a comedown as I sunk my toes into the soft sand. We swam with exotic fish and had cocktails delivered from a nearby bar. There were parties every night of the week, but this one particular evening was the biggest of the month. You didn't have to ask us twice.

We returned to the hostel and placed an order: 'Five litres of the Coca-Cola-Mushroom-Rocket-Fuel-Shake, please!' There was a lot of hype about the party.

Everyone we met was talking about it and the shops were full of backpackers raiding fridges for spirits and beers. Everyone was sharing a bottle of the mushy shake between two or three, but I ended up with a full litre to myself. What could possibly go wrong? I downed most of it before the party. The DJ was playing fast-paced psy-trance music and hundreds of loved-up ravers were dancing amongst lasers, under the clear night sky.

I was able to enjoy ten minutes of the rave before experiencing the most intense mushroom come up. I felt like I had rockets attached to my feet and I was launching into another dimension. My entire body was erupting with an irrepressible tingling sensation; mouth wide open and eyes rolling to the back of my head. Jenny (Greg's friend) noticed I was struggling to contain the euphoria. She sat me down against a wall away from the party. The universe was spinning around me. You know when you're on the Waltzers at the fairground and you're going so fast everything becomes blurry and you feel sick? Imagine adding a Ferrari engine to it. I was seeing glimpses of objects and the rave in the distance, but my brain couldn't physically take in all the information. Jenny made the wise decision to walk me back to the hostel, which was 500m down the beach.

I'm sure there's more to psychedelics. I could read the sign for the hostel perfectly. I stood in the same spot the following day (sober) and couldn't read any of it!

After weathering the storm, I noticed the mushrooms had enhanced my senses. Jenny tried putting me to bed but I insisted I wanted to be outside. I sat in a plastic chair

under a big tree, captivated by the wildlife. I could hear the formation of an ant colony on a branch, a spider spinning its web, it was incredible! I felt so immersed in nature for the first time in my life. I developed a deep realisation and appreciation that we are all one. From that day forward I have looked at life through a different lens and felt more love towards insects and smaller creatures.

The rest of the group consumed the perfect number of mushrooms, giving them a nice balance of hallucinations and ecstasy. After the rave, they watched the sun come up and said the sky was a blend of colours they'd never seen before. I was jealous but glad they had a good night. Anyway, I'd made friends with an ant colony. I even named them: Tiny, Mini, Munchkin, Shortstop, Itzy Bitzy, Stumpy, Elfie, Midgie, Lil Wayne, Pixie, Nugget, Sweet-Pea, Kiddo and Little Red Riding Hood.

Yeah, I officially lost my mind that night.

## Exploring Lombok's empty beaches

We had an unbelievable week, but it was time for a new adventure on the adjacent island of Lombok, a larger island with winding jungle roads and untouched beaches. We convoyed through the mountains on scooters, stopping at every beach along the way. It didn't seem real. Every beach we stopped at looked unique and had nobody on it (apart from the guys selling coconuts).

The more confident we became on the scooters, the faster we drove them, and without anybody saying a word a race was established. It was stupid and reckless but the adrenalin rush from overtaking someone or dodging oncoming traffic was undeniable. I felt like a poor man's Lewis Hamilton. Myself, Joe and Sam were in the podium positions for the majority of the race. An hour in, I overtook two lorries to gain an advantage. As I came out of the bend and accelerated away, everyone gasped. My back tyre aquaplaned on the wet tarmac and it looked (and felt) certain I would fall to my death. Somehow, I managed to level out and regain control. Joe, Sam and the rest of the group knew that was a wake-up

call to slow down and conceded the race. I knew I was tempting fate with that manoeuvre so promised I'd stop riding like a twat.

After all that dangerous driving, Sam crashed his scooter arriving into a restaurant car park. He lost balance and flipped over his handlebars, landing heavily onto his knee, ripping his skin open. Unfortunately, we were in the middle of the jungle with no nearby hospital. The locals called a nurse who stitched him up with bamboo. It was nasty and they didn't give him any anaesthetic. Thankfully, he was still pumped on adrenalin from finishing in second place in the Formula Nine Grand Prix.

Before returning to Thailand, there was time for a few relaxing days in Ubud and one (more) night out, in Kuta. In Ubud, we upgraded to a hotel with a heated outdoor pool. I don't know why they bother having a sanctuary for the monkeys, they climb over the walls anyway! The Balinese long-tail monkeys were causing havoc; climbing lampposts, hanging from telephone lines and even taking a bath in our pool!

Kuta was similar to Bangkok; many backpacker bars and street food stalls. Kuta also boasted the oldest club on the island, Skygarden, where Jenny, Luke, Sam and I would spend our final night in Indonesia. The nightclub (which had seven different rooms), consisted of cheap drink deals, sticky floors and banging commercial music … and who could forget the prostitutes hanging around the dancefloor hoping to make a quick buck. It was fun, but Sam and I were up early to fulfil our dream of visiting Maya Bay, better known in popular culture as The Beach.

## Paradise

My 'The Beach Playlist' was good to go. I'd downloaded all the tracks from the soundtrack and was ready to become Richard – a young 20-something, looking to travel into the unknown and escape reality. Of course, it wasn't quite like that. Due to the film's success, tourism in Koh Phi Phi and Maya Bay exploded and the tropical jungles and exquisite beaches were now full of tourists. We spent the last of our cash on five nights at a cheap hostel located at the back of a laundrette in Koh Phi Phi. We spent the first day in Western Union trying to get money sent over from the UK. It was a stressful experience. We couldn't even afford a Pad Thai. Thankfully, there was a local woman (also in the queue), who provided us with some much needed morale. We asked her name and she said, 'Winnie The Pooh.' We laughed and asked her to prove it. She responded by lifting her arms in the air revealing the name tattooed on her biceps.

It wasn't time to call for Mummy's help just yet. Through Sam's perseverance, we managed to get hold of some baht. It wasn't a lot of baht, but it was enough to get us through the next five days. We arrived back at the hostel exhausted from the ordeal, but two Swedish girls, Emma and Louise had just arrived, full of energy and ready to party! 'We must go out!' demanded Emma. It was hard to say no. Sam had three buckets too many and thought he was in a fit state to dive through a flaming hoop at the beach party. The skin from his whole left leg burnt off as he misjudged one of the jumps. Any progress that had been made since

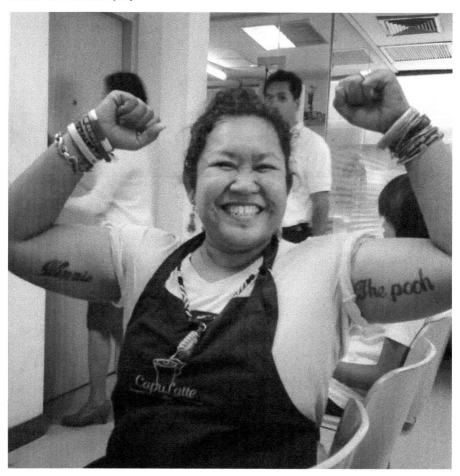

the scooter accident had been undone. A normal person would go to hospital. He thought it would be a better idea to run into the sea to cool off and buy another bucket to numb the pain. We carried on partying through the night and Sam continued to dive through the flaming hoop. Finally, I was able to say to someone else, 'You idiot!'

I was hoping to go to Maya Bay the following morning, but we spent most the day in hospital. Instead, I hiked through the jungle for a sunset view of Koh Phi Phi.

On the way up, there were memorial plaques from the devastating tsunami of December 2004. 4,000 people lost their lives and almost all the island's infrastructure was destroyed.

After days of messing about treating Sam's leg, we were finally able to make the short boat trip to Maya Bay. I'd been dreaming about it for years, seeing that iconic outline of the island, hidden in amongst the clouds, walking out from the jungle and seeing The Beach for the first time (whilst Moby's 'Porcelain' is playing). As the boat entered the bay, there were at least 50 other boats already parked up. The Beach was full of tourists drinking beer, taking selfies and even littering. This was not how I'd imagined it! How was this allowed to happen? Was I part of the problem?

Maya Bay finally closed in 2019 due to intense pressures on the marine ecosystem. Up to 5,000 tourists a day were turning up during the busy season.

It was still cool seeing the same spots where Richard, Françoise and Étienne had been in the film and we managed to check out the other side of the island where there was a turquoise lagoon with tropical coloured fish. Hopefully they can manage it better in the future and restrict how many tourists visit per day.

'I just feel like everyone tries to do something different, but you always wind up doing the same damn thing.' – Leonardo Di Caprio (as Richard) in The Beach (2000).

After Thailand, we returned to the UK to catch up with family and friends.

It wasn't long before we were off gallivanting again though ...

## The White Isle

From seeing footage of Sven Vath and Carl Cox in the 90s, Ibiza had always been a dream destination. I was with Luke, Edge and George at The World's End pub in Knaresborough. Keen as ever for a spontaneous trip, I hunted down cheap flights and pitched the idea to go... in three days. They weren't too sure. I ordered four more pints – 30-minutes later we had return flights to Ibiza booked.

We were all buzzing and I couldn't have been sharing my first time in Ibiza with any better people. Like me, all three of them were into their music and wanted to see the same DJs and experience the same clubs. Will, Chris, Daisy, Olly and Johnny, friends from Harrogate,

were also in Ibiza so we met at their apartment for pre-drinks before heading to Sankeys for the Tribal Sessions opening party. Patrick Topping was playing. It was cool to see him doing so well after meeting him at a party in Newcastle a year earlier. I remember hearing his tracks 'What Do You Mean' and 'Walk On' and thinking this guy is going to be famous!

Whilst doing my business in a toilet cubicle, I noticed some graffiti on the wall. It read "Don't take life so seriously. It's not like your going to survive." It seemed fitting and I liked that they used your instead of you're. My misconstrued interpretation was that the grammar mistake was a lesson for people who stress too easily, reminding them to relax and enjoy life.

Those four nights in Ibiza couldn't have gone any better. We witnessed the flying planes over DC10, the sun coming up inside Amnesia and the sun setting at Café Del Mar. Another dream ticked off.

## Peace in the dark

As many of my schoolfriends attended university in Sheffield, I'd take the coach down frequently. Every summer there is a family-friendly festival called Peace in the Park. After the festival concludes, (on an entirely independent basis) local youths (those bloody youths!!) organise Peace in the Dark, a raver-friendly festival. The location changes every year and is revealed through an automated voice message. This particular year, it was held in a farmer's field, down a long country lane. We had the address but it was pitch black so we didn't have a clue where we were going. We travelled as far as we could before the taxi driver gave up and told us to get out. As we stepped out, we heard a repetitive thud. We followed the sound of the beat and arrived at a gate. Two policeman flashed us with a torch. I was so close to my first illegal rave. I'd heard so many good stories from my dad's partying days in the late 80s – I wanted a taste of it!

'On you go lads, have a good night! Stay safe!' They waved us on and offered directions, the complete opposite of what we were expecting! The police ended up playing more of a stewarding role and were on standby if anything went wrong. As we made our way down to the farm we saw a line of cars. Each car was kitted out with speakers and decks, and each 'stage' had a different genre of music. There were 4/500 people present; beers in the air, loving life, raving in this secluded farm. We partied to 160bpm reggae music as the sun came up. It wasn't my usual preference but that's why it was unique and memorable.

Dancing with your mates, enjoying each other's company, the music, the vibe, that's life right there.

## Hideout

My dad told me about 1989 being 'The Summer of Rave', but this started to feel like my version of that. My friend Sam Hodgson couldn't make Hideout Festival in Croatia, so offered his two VIP tickets. I didn't need a professional photographer this time, but there was still only one person to ask – Sam Hodson (yes, the Sam Hodson without a 'g').

We only knew a handful of people going. There was Ben Parkes, who used to play for our junior football rivals Harrogate Railway, Donna from university and Ross and his mates, who

were a few years below at school. Ross had two beds left in his villa so invited us to stay with him. We never got on with boys in the years' below. We didn't like them and they didn't like us. There was no reason for it, it was just petty school behaviour. Once you leave school, you discover age doesn't matter – what matters is what you have in common. In this case, it was music. We partied for seven days with only a few hours' sleep a night. Those ten lads from school who we supposedly didn't like became good friends of ours and we still hang out to this day.

After an eventful summer, it was time to head back to Dubai for another season.

# 23

## (13 September 2014 – 12 September 2015)

### Living the dream

During my first year in Dubai, I was standing on Barasti beach and turned to Sam: 'It would be so cool to live in one of those high-rise towers!' Who would have known, one year later, we would be! Stuart, a friend of cousin Danny, was moving in with his partner so needed someone to take his master room in a shared apartment. We couldn't believe how lucky we were! We'd gone from a flat with no furniture, in the middle of nowhere, to a luxury apartment overlooking the beach.

We had six flatmates. Five of them were quiet, working professional people. The other, Salvador, was also a working professional, but loved to party. We hit it off instantly and it wasn't long before we decided to throw our first flat party. Our flatmates weren't happy, but there wasn't much they could do when a sea of people started arriving through the door. Salva's mates, Jordi and Raul, knew a lot of air hostesses so invited them all – and I mean all! There were six guys and 40 cabin crew girls raving in our living room. As we had installed lasers and speakers, the flatmates called the landlord and even threatened to call the police. The landlord turned up to shut the party down but it was so good he ended up staying and getting drunk. It was his first drink in two years.

## Meeting British royalty

I'd met a lot of celebrities during my first season. It was cool, but I'd never been starstruck, until I met British royalty. Our company was booked as caterers and Prince Harry was the

special guest. For some reason (maybe because I was from Harrogate and vaguely posh), I was chosen as Prince Harry's private server. I'd never been so nervous. For the first hour, I followed him around with a tray of fresh juices, bending the knee as I served. I looked like a moron. I asked him four times if he'd like one and he said no every time. 'JUST TAKE THE JUICE HARRY SO I CAN TELL MY GRANDKIDS!'

Once he'd sat down for dinner, I was given the task of placing the napkin on his lap. Right as I was about to place the napkin, my friend snatched it off me and did it herself. Her desperation to get close to his crotch was too funny to hold any grudges. Sat beside Harry was Geri Halliwell and her husband Christian Horner.

I was given a real inside, first-hand look at Harry as a person. He seemed down to earth with a good sense of humour. It was a real shame to see what later unfolded. After the dinner concluded, people from other tables started requesting to have photos with him. He politely declined but they kept disturbing him and interrupting his conversations. Eventually, he stood up and firmly announced, 'If I take a photo with one of you, then everyone will want a photo.' He looked stressed and the final straw was when a woman grabbed him. 'Please! Just a quick selfie?' He had to run away, accompanied by two security guards.

## The party never stops

I'd been away from the party scene for some time. Dubai had some awesome clubs but I was missing those 'proper' parties. I was at home watching YouTube clips of Ibiza and it was one particular video of a Sven Vath afterparty that made me want to try a season. Sam was equally keen, and in May 2015 we booked a one-way flight from Dubai to Spain. Darius Syrossian (famous tech-house DJ) was looking for another housemate for his villa in Ibiza. I began talking to him through a mutual friend and agreed to move in. Unfortunately, at the last minute, the EDM duo, NERVO, came in with a more lucrative offer for the villa and it fell through. It would have been a hell of a season living with Darius and his mates!

As well as Ibiza, we had Tomorrowland in July and the Rickshaw Run in August. Naïvely, we thought we could just hop on a flight to each of them and come back to Ibiza straight after. We threw a leaving party (as we always do) then boarded a flight to Barcelona. Our connecting flight to Ibiza wasn't until 6:30am the following morning so it was the perfect opportunity to explore the city. What started as an innocent sangria on Las Ramblas, turned into a bar crawl/tour around the city. Bottles of beer were only one euro, so we kept buying them!

It was 7pm when we arrived back at the hostel. Most of the backpackers were heading to one of the big clubs in the city. 'It would be rude not to!' declared Sam. I'd seen that look in his eyes before. I replied cautiously, 'We need to set an alarm for 3am so we have enough time to get to the airport.' I knew what we were like so I enforced some ground rules.

I woke up at 5am, the flight was at 6:30am, and Sam wasn't anywhere to be seen. I rang him, messaged him, even emailed him! By 7am, I accepted we'd have to miss the flight …

seeing as it had already taken off. I fell back to sleep and woke up at midday. There was still no sign of him. I posted on Facebook:

@Sam Hodson - If you don't come back to the hostel in the next 34 minutes I'm booking a one way flight to Geneva for 12 euros.

Thirty-four minutes later, he rocked up to the hostel. He looked like he'd come from a paintballing party, covered in sweat, dirt, bruises and neon ink. 'Don't ask.' I never did ask and we boarded a flight to Ibiza the following day.

Landing in the party capital of the world felt as special as the first time. With it being his first time in Ibiza, Sam spent the entire taxi ride with his head out of the window. The roads were littered with palm trees and billboard advertisements of the islands biggest DJs and parties. You feel the buzz and excitement running through your veins, way before you even get to the clubs! The plan was to secure a job selling tickets, which would pay for our nights out and accommodation.

Life was good. Every evening, we would drink cider and watch the sunset at Café del Mar. People would arrive early to sit on the rocks outside, waiting patiently to witness one of the most famous sunsets in the world. The moment the sun disappeared beyond the horizon, you'd hear roars and clapping, signifying the start of the night. After befriending one of the bar owners, we were handed free tickets to the Es Paradís opening party.

It really was Paradís. The glamorous club has been around since the mid-70s and had that old-school-Ibiza feel. Stardust's 'Music Sounds Better With You' was echoing around the club as we walked in. Dancers in corsets were swinging on giant hoops above the stage and flashing bright lights would reveal all kinds of weird and wonderful people. We saw a couple in their 60s doing the tango through the crowds of young people. It was a night full of classic Ibiza anthems, but they eventually dimmed the lights and took us through a few hours of dark techno. I hugged Sam, a lot. By 7am, the sun was coming up. My eyes were closed and hands in the air for the entirety of the final song: 'Jaguar' by DJ Rolando. What a start to our season in Ibiza!

We were good at networking during our time in Ibiza, meeting pretty much every worker on the island. The whole idea of networking was to find work. Instead, it was night out … after night out … after night out. That's what we were there for though, right? We spent most of our time in Viva! bar in San Antonio. They had discounted drinks and we became friends with Max who worked there. They had a boat party coming up, but it seemed out of budget for us. We told Max we DJ'd in Dubai, so he proposed an offer: 'If you DJ our pre-party, I'll give you free tickets to the party.' 'Deal!' We played for an hour and, although it wasn't a 'super club', we'd officially DJ'D IN IBIZA!

As the boat headed for the abyss of the Mediterranean Sea, we were hit by a monumental thunderstorm. The boat was rocking so much that all of us were sliding to the left, crashing into the sides, then flying back to the right. Despite the harsh, horizontal rain and the flooded dancefloor, the music never stopped. I guess that's the definition of Ibiza – the party never stops! It was such a wild and memorable boat party that I still talk to the people I met that day.

Will and Jonny (Harrogate) had also arrived for the season – just in time for the Amnesia opening party. Amnesia was my favourite dancefloor on the island and the club hosted my favourite party, Cocoon. We arrived at 2am and partied until midday. I was hugging and kissing strangers, and dancing like I'd never danced before. The last track I remember was Apollonia playing Alex Braxe & Fred Falke, 'Intro'. Pure bliss.

I'm not sure if it was this night or a few weeks later in Amnesia, but I bumped into the English comedian Jack Whitehall on the stairs. I said, 'Alright mate!' He replied, 'Hey!' in his soft, posh but endearing voice. I looked at myself in the mirror to check I wasn't tripping.

Through partying at Cocoon, we met an Aussie called Donovan. He owned one of the greatest ginger beards I'd ever seen and had a heart of gold. I'm not sure if he liked it or not, but we nicknamed him 'the Techno Viking'. It wasn't just because he had a giant

ginger beard, it was also because he used to stomp so hard on the ground it shook everyone around him. Donovan was a talented writer and wrote many articles on the clubbing scene in Ibiza.

Along with Lewis (who we met on the boat), the four of us went to every bar, club and party you can think of on the island. After a month of solid raving, Sam announced he'd had enough and I didn't blame him. I don't understand how people can party like that for six months straight. Sam flew back to the UK at the end of June and left me in Ibiza, running on a rather unsustainable budget. Thankfully, Will and his friends from Leeds took me in for a week. They knew I was low on cash, so I used to cook for my rent. Once July came, it was almost as if a friend from back home was landing in Ibiza every day of the week. My friends were always on holiday mode and my minerals were deteriorating. It reached the point I couldn't keep up anymore and I flew back home.

Unfortunately, during my stay in Ibiza, I had my phone stolen at one of the parties. I was gutted as I lost some daily photos from the project that I didn't have backed up. I was upset and still feel guilty that I didn't take more care.

I had two weeks back home (including Cocoon in the Park festival in Leeds), then I was on the ferry to Tomorrowland for the fourth time. By this point, I was getting indications I was partying too much. Anxiety was becoming more frequent and the days after were becoming much harder to deal with.

It was one busy Sunday morning working at the pub that changed everything. The bar was heaving and I had my first proper anxiety attack. I ran out of the bar and into the street, but the street was full of people, so I ran back inside and locked myself in the toilet cubicle. I was so scared. One of my colleagues came to check up on me. I was close to tears and eventually sent home.

When I arrived home, I closed the curtains and locked my bedroom door. This would be the first of many days I would lie in darkness, hiding from my troubles.

## 3500km across India in a tuk-tuk

Thanks to the YouTube channel JacksGap, I'd heard of this 'thing' in India called The Rickshaw Run. This unique race, created by The Adventurists, invites 80 teams to travel 3,500km across India, from Shillong to Kochi, in beaten-up tuk-tuks. Surprisingly, after pitching the idea to Danny and Sam, they were keen to join. Partying in Ibiza for two months, followed by a weekend at Tomorrowland wasn't the ideal preparation. There was a lot of logistics involved just to make it to the start line in north-east India. Danny's flight from Dubai landed three hours earlier. He had to wait around, but at least it gave him time to cool off. We left it to the last minute to apply for a visa and almost didn't make the flight.

We loaded our backpacks onto a tuk-tuk taxi and headed towards the hotel. It was glorious sunshine, but as we climbed into the mountains the heavens opened. The roads

flooded and we could barely navigate through the puddles without the tyres and engine clogging up. What should have been an hour journey took three and it was pitch black by the time we arrived. Shillong is a damp town close to the Himalayas and the capital of Meghalaya, meaning 'The Abode of Clouds.' Mawsynram, close to Shillong, is known as the wettest place on Earth. A football match had been arranged for 6am the following morning – the Rickshaw Runners versus the local press. I'm assuming it was early so they could play before starting work.

The boys were fast asleep when I left. The size of the stadium was impressive considering the location, almost like a mini Bernabéu. Many locals came to watch us foreign idiots play against their local heroes. After Ibiza and Tomorrowland, I felt as fit as a 45-year-old Brazilian Ronaldo coming on in a charity match. It was 3-1 to the home team so they subbed me and another English guy, Phil, on. Phil scored a 30-yard screamer and I managed to poke home a late equaliser. Rather than break any hearts with a penalty shootout, we called it a draw.

That night, they organised a party for all the teams to drink together. It was fun meeting everyone but resulted in some sore heads the following morning. For check-in day, we had to register, paint and pimp-up our rickshaws. Our design included the Chile and UK flags, a shark's mouth on the front and our faces on the side.

Other teams converted their rickshaws into Batmobiles and ours looked like Dot Cotton's shopping trolley. We purchased shower curtains to stop rain entering through the sides, three pillows so we could sleep and three bottles of juice – not Nitrous Oxide, but orange juice to cure our hangover. Everyone else had neon lights, generators and even extension cables fitted so they could charge their phones. We ran out of space when painting our team name. One girl approached, confused: 'I don't understand your rickshaw. The name makes no sense.'

I came up with the team name on the journey over. I remember my former English teacher Mr Pocock telling me about a football headline where they replaced supercalifragilisticexpialidocious with 'Super Caley Go Ballistic, Celtic Are Atrocious' after the underdogs, Inverness Caledonian Thistle, beat Celtic in the Scottish Cup.

Our team name – 'Super Danny Goes Ballistic, Tuk-Tuk's Are Atrocious.'

Despite the rain and 7am start, there was a real buzz in the air on race day. Everyone was excited to see what the next three weeks had in store. All teams shook hands and wished each other luck. We all needed it ... especially us!

The starting gun shot into the sky and we embarked on the journey of our lives (the journey that might end our lives). Within 30 seconds, two tuk-tuks broke down – a sign of things to come. We raced ahead. Sam seemed the most capable during the practice runs so was our designated driver, with Danny and I cramped in the back. We only tested the shower curtains capabilities when stationary. In our intoxicated state, we didn't take wind into consideration, nor the physics of motion. The curtains were flapping in the storm, drenching us and our pillows. The first hour was winding, downhill roads, leading out of the mountains before a welcome break in the clouds.

As we approached the next village, we noticed the first casualty. One of the rickshaws veered off the road and crashed into a ditch. Thankfully, they were all okay and we helped them back on the road. As we waved goodbye, our front wheel buckled and rolled down the hill. Danny and Sam jumped out to stop the tin can toppling over whilst I chased the runaway wheel.

Hour one.

After returning our wheel to its rightful place, we began making progress. After four hours of beautiful countryside we reached our first city. Thousands of people, cars and cattle crossing the roads in any-which-way they pleased. When the traffic lights turned red, cows would casually approach our rickshaw. However, it wasn't them I was worried about! Out of nowhere, a cross-dresser reached through the shower curtains and grabbed Danny's balls. He screamed in agony and shoved the intruder back onto the road. Me and Sam found it funny. Danny felt violated.

That wasn't the last cross-dresser we saw that day. Some Aussie Rickshaw Runners were being interviewed by local TV. John and Kyle were dressed in red overalls (which they vowed to wear for the entire journey), and Jon and Sam were dressed as Alice in Wonderland and The Mad Hatter. Jon and Sam's rickshaw was painted as a giant Cheshire Cat so they attracted a lot of attention on the roads. After being side-tracked by the media frenzy, it was time to find a hotel. Our data barely worked and the Wi-Fi was about as

useful as an emu in a china shop. Finding a place to stay each night was heavily reliant on finding a sign in English or asking strangers in the street. Many villages had never even seen a tourist so finding a hotel proved difficult.

Apart from losing a wheel in the first hour, the first two days weren't too bad in terms of breakdowns. We were hopeful we'd landed one of the more efficient rickshaws and that we might even have a chance of winning the race. However, tensions were building inside the tuk-tuk and the claustrophobic environment was driving us insane. The arguments were ridiculous – Who was the worst driver? Who had the worst music taste? Who was the worst at directions? Danny (General Manager Danny) took charge and said, 'Fuck you two, I'm driving from now on.' I volunteered to be co-pilot and help with directions. Danny turned, expecting to see me on Google Maps, but instead I was on Instagram. He went ape shit for burning all his 4G data. In fairness, it was taking me ages to find a filter that would desaturate the blood-boiling veins on his face.

After a few hours of silence, Danny pulled off the highway and into a restaurant. 'Order food, I'm off to get directions. And you're fucking paying.' He'd run out of data on his phone so couldn't use Google Maps anymore. The resulting conversation with the restaurant owner was that we could either take the main highway to the next major city, which would take three days.

Or.

'You can take the ISIS road, which will take a day or two.'

In north-east India, there are large areas occupied by Islamic State. We had a decision to make. We're in a race but how much are we prepared to risk our lives to reach the finish line? We pondered on the predicament over a Kadai Paneer curry. The man advised against going down the ISIS road; he could see the naivety in our faces. Danny was still fuming and not thinking logically: 'We're taking the short cut!'

As we rode into the distance (with a giant UK flag on the back of our rickshaw), the restaurant owner shouted, 'Good luck!'

It was like the beginning of a horror film. The sky turned grey, everyone we passed stopped smiling and black and white flags became more frequent on the side of the road. If we were lost in any other ISIS territory we would've been captured instantly. As we were driving through rural India in a pimped-up tuk-tuk, with a shark, three cartoon faces and a shit team name (plus some offensive flags), it threw them off a little.

Reluctantly, after four hours driving, we pulled into a gas station. Locals stared as we filled up the tank. A group whispered to each other and approached whilst Danny was inside paying. We waved him to hurry. He did that disjointed walk, a bit like when you're late for a bus. As we sped away, we noticed two snipers in watchtowers. The area was being overseen by local military. At sunset, we approached a village where kids were playing in the street. We decided this would be a safe place to stay the night. They were the first smiles we'd seen in ten hours. As we travelled down the high street, a group of locals congregated outside one of the hotels. The locals spotted us and ran towards us. After being tense all day, we assumed the worst. Instead, it was kids with cameras wanting to take selfies. As the crowds separated, we noticed the Aussies' tuk-tuks. John waved us over: 'Don't worry, we're the first tourists to ever pass through their village.'

All worries were forgotten but it was back on the ISIS road the following morning. The Aussies were drunk and driving all over (a bit like the locals). From this day, it felt like we were breaking down every 30 minutes. Most the journey was through barren countryside so when we broke down, there was no one around. All we could do was wait for a local to drive past and ask if they knew a mechanic. The weather became brutally hot as we travelled south so we realised the importance of stocking up on water.

We found ourselves stuck in a traffic jam. You know when a kid has toy cars and smashes them together, leaving them facing different directions – it looked like that! Some Rickshaw Runners were up ahead so we squeezed through gaps in the traffic to say hello. One team consisted of Kevin from Canada and brothers Conrad and Phil from South Africa. The other, an all-girl group who were living in Beijing. Tamera, Linda and Nina were sharing two rickshaws as their friends had dropped out.

Meeting them was a blessing in disguise. All three teams agreed to convoy for the rest of the trip, meaning swapping tuk-tuks and spending time with different people – a stress relief for three lads full of testosterone. Kevin and Phil were semi-qualified mechanics, so every time we broke down they would be under the rickshaws saving the day. Danny, Sam and I were in charge of team morale. This meant organising curry, beer and games at the end of each arduous day.

We were mistaken thinking we'd seen the last of black and white flags and frowning faces. The following afternoon, two rickshaws surrendered once more. Where we broke down looked like ISIS headquarters, and within seconds 300 locals surrounded us. It wasn't the friendly attention we'd received previously. For the first time, Kevin and Phil were unable to fix the rickshaws.

As we escorted the rickshaws to a mechanic, two kids tried grabbing Linda's bag. A trustworthy-looking man in a semi-ironed business shirt whispered in our ears, 'You need to leave before dark, otherwise you're in trouble.' The sun was disappearing behind the trees and tensions were starting to mount. The girls were being harassed so we decided Sam and I would drive them in the working tuk-tuks to the nearest hotel. Kevin, Phil, Conrad and Danny stayed at the mechanics and attempted to calm the situation. It wasn't an easy decision leaving my cousin but the girls' safety was the priority.

Both mine and Sam's headlights blew moments after setting off. The roads were dangerous in India. Trucks the size of Amazon warehouses drove 120kmph down the highways. The drivers work incredibly long hours which is hazardous when you're behind the wheel of a 20-tonne truck. Tamera had the genius idea of using iPhone torch lights to guide us. It saved our lives as endless trucks whizzed past, millimetres from us. After two traumatic hours we reached a hotel.

We checked in and waited for news from the guys. I received one text from Danny – 'A gang threatened to stab us.' We tried calling back but their phones were dead. After an hour of waiting, I'd had enough. I couldn't leave my cousin in the middle of India with his life in danger. I threw my rucksack in the rickshaw and started the engine. At that moment, the guys flew past. I shouted 'DANNNNNN!' and he saw me just in time. I've never hugged my cousin so tightly. We celebrated in the only way we knew how: curry and beers!

The story even made the front page in our local paper.

The majority of India is beautiful, especially the rural areas. Lush green fields and stunning lakes running all the way to the Himalayas. Unfortunately, we witnessed another side of it. We saw kids who had their legs removed wheeling around on planks of wood begging for money. We'd been so immersed into the adventure that we forgot about the extent of poverty in India.

A local volunteer invited us to a nearby orphanage. We were sceptical at first, unsure whether we'd be welcome. Thankfully, the kids loved us, and we loved them! We played a game of cricket and Nina and Linda (make-up artists) painted their faces as different jungle animals.

Despite the breakdowns and stomach upsets, we were having an unbelievable time and the recent events brought us closer as a group. After days of travelling through countryside, we made it to the coastal town of Puri. We'd acquired some weed and organised a group wake and bake. Alarms were set for 6am to catch sunrise at the beach. We sat on the sand and not one of us said a word. The moment felt special and we were enjoying the silence. This was until we heard a fart, which was followed by several more. We looked to our left, and to our horror a local man had pulled his pants down and was squatting in the sand taking a dump. Half of Mumbai fell out his ass. The moment was over but it was nice while it lasted.

The coastal road led us to Chilika Lake, home to the world's largest breeding colony of flamingos. To cross the lake, we had to board an old wooden ferry. Me and the guys were top deck, telling stories and joking around. We looked down and noticed Linda and Nina being comforted by Tamera. There was clearly something up as they were in floods of tears. They'd been the soul of the party up to this point, always smiling and having fun.

What they told us didn't seem real. News had broken in Beijing that a woman had been randomly attacked with a samurai sword outside a shopping centre, and later died. This woman was one of their best friends. We didn't know what to say, we didn't know what words would be of comfort. I can't even imagine what they were going through. There was lots of hugging and crying. This was the day we all became a family and I discovered that Linda and Nina were (and are) two of the bravest people I have ever met in my life. They carried on with the journey and put the news to one side so as not to ruin the trip.

The rickshaws were falling apart and breaking down constantly. Our unrealistic dreams of finishing the race in time were deteriorating. We were spending more time in mechanics than driving. Sam came up with the idea to buy a cricket bat and ball. Each time we stopped, we had a game of cricket with the locals. Despite not speaking the same language, it was amazing to have a connection with these strangers, simply by introducing a bat and ball.

We were in India for one reason – adventure. Adventure was getting the better of us. As we were breaking down constantly, a divide in the group was beginning to form. Some were discussing options in a constructive manner, whereas others were shouting. We were behind schedule and the only chance of making it to the finish line on time was to drive through the night for three consecutive nights. The other option was to pay a truck to take the rickshaws.

Reasons for not continuing: one, it would be dangerous driving at night with trucks driving at full speed. Two, we were exhausted and would risk falling asleep at the wheel. Three, there was no chance our rickshaws would make it to the end anyway.

Reasons for continuing: One, it would be cheating riding a truck to the finish line. Two, we've come so far, we may as well try finish it. Three, adventure.

We called a team meeting at 11pm, taking it in turns to voice our opinion. Each person had a different viewpoint. Conrad wanted to continue regardless. Whilst he was blunt in his argument, he made good points and I agreed we'd come so far and had to overcome our obstacles. Tamera showed her wisdom by voting we take the truck. I felt we'd become such a tight family that there was no way we could split up. My view was, either we all continue together or all take the truck. The discussions resulted in us pressing forward in the rickshaws. Tamera was disappointed but happy we were sticking together.

We drove through the night, swapping drivers every few hours. Sam had driven most of the day so slept first. Whilst driving, I kept nodding off and had to repeatedly slap myself in the face. Feeling responsible for Sam's safety, I signalled the others and requested we pull over. 'Let's reach the next town, then we can stop' they replied.

Moments later, there was a bang, followed by several thuds … and screams I'll never forget. Kevin and Tamera's rickshaw had been clipped by a truck that veered off the highway. 'It's on my leg, it's on my leg!' yelled Tamera. The rickshaw rolled off the side of the road and landed on Tamera's leg. We ran as fast as we could to help lift it off. Tamera's leg was gushing with blood so we wrapped it with our shirts and called an ambulance. Tamera was suffering but remained calm. We held her hand and tried to take her mind off it. Tamera was asleep when they were hit and woke up to bashing her head on the roof and tumbling out the side door.

Bizarrely, the local press arrived before the ambulance. They were journalists looking to have a story written before the papers were printed. Eventually, the medics arrived and put Tamera onto a stretcher. We didn't want to leave her alone so Linda and Nina accompanied her in the ambulance. The damage to her leg was so bad they had to take her to Chennai hospital, four hours away.

As ever, we were surrounded by half the town moments later. The local press were asking questions and taking photos. Conrad was going berserk and losing his patience. The sun was coming up and we needed a plan. All our rickshaws were fucked so we had to find a truck willing to take us to Kochi at an affordable price. One man approached and offered to help. He returned one hour later and proposed an obscene price. We'd refuse the offer then he'd go away for another hour to find another truck. Each time the price would be way over budget. This went on all day in the scorching sun.

It was 4pm and we still hadn't found a truck. We were drained, burnt and fed up. Most of our group weren't smokers, but we all had a cigarette that day. 'Why don't we fix them?' Kevin muttered. 'What?' we replied collectively. That option was never even considered. We physically couldn't finish in time with the incompetent rickshaws we had. At the rate they were breaking down we'd miss our flight, never mind the finishers' party. Kevin stood up and took a more commanding approach: 'Seriously, let's find a mechanic and see what happens. Let's give it one last go!' It was as if Jesus Christ had been resurrected and was guiding us to our destiny. The band was back together. We kickstarted the four tuk-tuk's that were rattling like my mum's pots and pans in the kitchen and headed to the nearest mechanic. The nearest mechanic was 500m away and the rickshaws still managed to break down. We explained we'd had no luck with mechanics and begged: 'Please do the best job you can!'

We waited patiently in the restaurant next door. 45 minutes passed when there was a knock at the window. 'Boss, it's ready.' From our experience, if it took 45 minutes to fix, it would take 45 minutes to break down. Kevin took the first rickshaw for a whirl. 'What the fuck!?' The fact we could hear his expletives above the noise of the engine was a good sign. We hopped in the remaining tuk-tuks. Four happy, healthy tuk-tuks circled freely, like four overjoyed whales being released from SeaWorld.

This was the best our rickshaws had ever sounded. 'How much money do you want? We'll pay anything!' The mechanic replied, 'A photo please.' He refused to take any money. We couldn't believe it. He was the best mechanic of the entire trip and didn't want anything, only a photo to remember the unlikely crossing of paths.

We revved up the squeaky-clean engines and flew down the highway at full speed towards Chennai, where the girls were staying. Arriving into Chennai was reminiscent of a real-life Mario Kart game; dodging obstacles and overtaking on winding downhill roads. Adrenalin was high and belief we could finish the race was restored. It was early evening when we arrived at the ITC Grand Chola five-star hotel. We were covered in muck but that didn't stop us pulling up next to a Bentley and tossing our keys to the valet. The staff and guests were appalled, but thanks to Tamera we had a reservation. We did need a shower though.

And sauna, massage, manicure, pedicure and haircut.

Our night in luxury was bliss and well deserved. Tamera returned from hospital and was dressed in a robe, drinking a glass of wine. She insisted on finishing the race so hired a driver to take her to the end, whilst we drove the now-trusted rickshaws. For the rest of the journey we didn't break down once. The only negative from the final few days was a trip to McDonalds. We'd eaten curry for breakfast, lunch and dinner for three weeks, so when we saw the 'golden arches' we had tears of joy. Our insides must've been so used to the local street food that the Big Macs came flooding out quicker than a lie from Boris Johnson's mouth. We all had a serious case of the shits so the only thing stopping us crossing the finish line on time were the volcanic eruptions coming out of our backsides.

The final day was frantic. Most competitors had already arrived at the finish line, some even three days earlier. We'd been through so much, it would've been disastrous not to receive a finisher's medal. We had to board a ferry to reach the final stretch. When we arrived at the port, there was a mile-long queue. In desperation, we went down the line begging people to let us overtake. We explained our situation but people weren't so

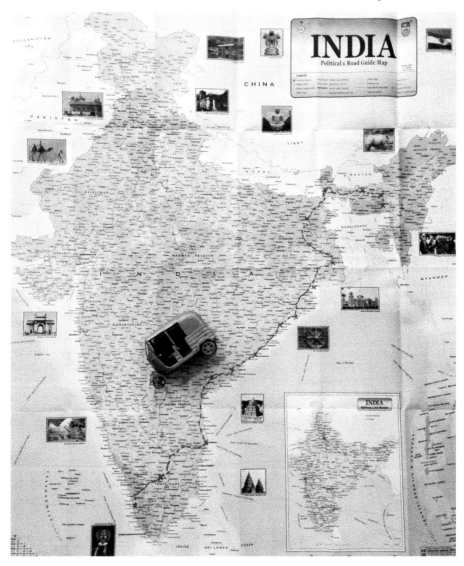

understanding. We managed to get far enough to secure a spot on the second scheduled ferry, meaning we'd arrive 30 minutes after cut-off time. It was a bittersweet ending. The staff and fellow competitors were still there but the chequered flag had been removed. The fact we even made it was an achievement in itself.

We finished the trip with an awards ceremony. I won the 'The Swiss Award' for being the most calm in difficult situations.

After the conclusion of the race, Red Bull published an article on their website about the Rickshaw Run and included my photo of our model rickshaw travelling across the map of India.

# 24

## (13 September 2015 – 12 September 2016)

### Not living the dream

I was back in the UK, broke and needed work. My friends were working at a market research company. The work sounded easy so I went for an interview. I was overqualified by being on time, wearing a buttoned-up shirt and having shiny shoes. They asked if I could start straight away – as in, right at that moment. I'd never felt so wanted. I'd be with my mates every day, having a laugh and saving cash until I figured out what to do next. Sounds fun right? No. It was cold calling big, angry, 40-year-old, burly builders and asking them to do a 30-minute survey. 'Oh hello, is this Kevin Platt from Stoke-on-Trent?' 'Who the fuck is this and where did you get my number? And the name's Kev. Don't call me Kevin.' 'Sorry sir, I'm calling from a market research company in Harrogate and I'd like to ask a few questions.' 'Listen kid, I don't have time for your stupid surveys, go waste someone else's time!'

As I was new in the job, I worked hard to convert my surveys. I was impressing the supervisor with ten or more completed surveys per day but couldn't work out why everyone else could only manage four or five. A week into the job I realised how glued in I was to the screen and my headset that I didn't notice the chaos around me. People were gaming, watching videos on YouTube and reading which celebrity's cat got stuck up a tree.

The CEO's five-year-old daughter used to crawl around the room, throwing toys at us whilst we 'tried' to work. She refused to pay for a babysitter during holidays so let her child cause havoc, high on Freddos and Fruit Pastilles. Sometimes, she'd ask one of the girls in the office to drive her daughter home and babysit her there. The babysitting role was painful, but I'd rather be sat on the sofa of a big country house watching Nickleodeon than bothering Kevin. Sorry, *Kev. It didn't take long for me to settle in. As long as I hit four or five surveys a day, I wouldn't get fired, so that was the plan until I worked out what to do next.

## Help

My anxiety became increasingly worse. What started as something that happened occasionally turned into a daily nightmare. I'd developed derealisation disorder, a spin-off from anxiety. I felt detached from reality and couldn't look my parents in the face without questioning their existence. It was scary. I thought normality would never return and I was stuck in a nightmare I couldn't get out of.

I used to come home every day and go straight to my room and turn the light off. The darkness helped. The less information or reasons my brain had to panic the better. I'd watch light-hearted movies every night to help alleviate the shortness of breath, erratic blinking and negative thoughts. Mum kept asking if I was alright; she could sense something was up. I'd claim I was fine. 'I'm just tired from work.' It's not nice lying to your mum but I knew if she was upset that would make me more upset. I accepted I'd have to battle this alone.

It's always better to speak to someone. They're your family and friends for a reason and they'd rather help you than see you suffer. There's no shame in asking for help.

It became so bad I had to leave work on multiple occasions and fake an injury at football so I could leave the pitch. I caught myself staring at the sky, questioning why we were all running around a bit of grass, kicking a ball made of air and synthetic leather.

Actually, I'm not the first person to question that.

## Shutting down

Warehouse Project in Manchester was coming up and there was a stellar line-up, including: Tale of Us, Scuba and Joy Orbison. I knew a group from Harrogate who were going so hitched a ride and stayed at their friend's student accommodation. These lads were a few years younger and I mistakenly thought I had the minerals to keep up with them. The ecstasy that night was strong and making me hallucinate. Betting odds were popping up all over the dancefloor above people's heads. The DJ had odds of 3-1. I took cash from my wallet and tried placing a bet. I'd officially lost my marbles.

We continued drinking back at the house and someone passed me a joint. After two drags my body didn't know if it was up or down. I hyperventilated and collapsed on the floor. This wasn't just a panic attack, I felt like I was going to have a heart attack. I was barely conscious and my vision turned grey. I was shutting down. I asked the lads to call an ambulance but they were too scared. Everyone in the house was either too high, stoned or twisted to deal with the situation. It took nine hours to start feeling normal again.

## Good fortune

We'd formed a 'gang' at the office. Not a throw-eggs-at-your-window-kind-of-gang but a group of friends, who, on occasion, would be mischievous. As well as the occasional survey, we would play games, send memes and make jokes to pass the time. The lads were betting on how many corners Azerbaijan under-17s would get in the first half of a football match. I became hooked and started making decent money betting on the number of goals in a game. In two days, I turned £20 into £1,300.

This was the time of the Conor McGregor craze. Tom invited us over to watch the upcoming fight against Nate Diaz in UFC 196. I had other ideas after winning big. I looked up flights to Las Vegas where the fight was taking place. I called the embassy, fast-tracked a visa and booked a flight leaving the following day via Dublin and Philadelphia. The next job was to break the news to my boss. I told them I won a competition and it was too good an opportunity to miss.

My parents have always been supportive of my spontaneity. They were excited for me, but if they knew I'd made the money from a bet, not so much. Before I knew it, I was boarding a flight to Dublin. I sampled seven pints of Guinness before a layover in Philadelphia. After chilling out, maxing and relaxing all cool, it was time for Vegas. I had crippling anxiety for the duration of the flight and was cramped between two John Candy look-alikes. They were wearing Hawaiian shirts and carrying briefcases, ready to gamble their week's wages on slot machines.

The iconic lights glistened as we descended into Sin City. 'Welcome to Fabulous Las Vegas Nevada.' After spending my winnings on the airfare and fight ticket, the only accommodation I could afford was a manky hostel on the outskirts of the city. Hookers and dealers congregated around street corners, whilst pimps patrolled the streets in American lowriders. I went from a quiet Yorkshire town to Grand Theft Auto in less than 24 hours. Sam Hodgson heard I'd landed in Vegas and put me in touch with his Harrogate friends Ally, Josh and Adam who were also there. They invited me to join them at the weigh-in the following day.

I woke up in a dormitory adjacent to a Japanese guy who couldn't speak English. The Harrogate lads weren't free until the afternoon so I invited him for breakfast (using hand gestures). I discovered everything in America truly was in XXL. When I ordered beer, the waitress delivered a two-pint glass. My new friend raised two fingers. I thought it was the peace sign but he wanted a beer for himself. I was surprised considering it was 9am and he seemed like the most innocent guy in the world.

He was giggling and stumbling whilst we toured The Hangover movie locations. It felt surreal rocking up to the wedding chapel drunk and I was hoping I wouldn't wake up on the Caesars Palace roof. Later, I joined the Harrogate lads who were staying at the MGM Grand (where the fight was taking place). After a few drinks they told me to check out of my hostel and move into their luxurious top floor suite. I couldn't believe my luck. 'Ohhhh Conor McGregor, Ohhhh Conor McGregor' echoed through the streets of Vegas as we queued for the weigh-in. It felt like a football match as Joe Rogan called the names of both fighters. Irish fans in their green, white and orange scarves chanted, 'Ole, Ole, Ole!'

Conor was the big favourite, and Nate, UFC's 'bad boy' was booed at any opportunity. The weigh-in spilled into the streets and Irish fans started chanting, 'Shoes off, for the boys in green!' 2,000 Irish fans (and us) were dancing with one shoe in the air. This was soon replaced with 'Clothes off, for the boys in green!' Adam, being Adam, removed his clothes and joined the Irish fans. Without going into details, it was a wild night. You know the drill … What happens in Vegas, stays in Vegas.

We got suited and booted on fight day and ordered a bottle of champagne to the room. I felt grateful. Thanks to the lads, my night was a million times better than it would've been. Despite ordering separate tickets we managed to sneak our way into the same section and find four empty seats.

It was set to be a night of upsets as Holly Holm lost to Miesha Tate in the previous fight. In the main event, Conor started well, showboating with spinning leg kicks. After landing some good shots, he began to tire and Nate took advantage, finishing him by submission. The Irish fans were stunned but it didn't stop them (and us) partying until the early hours. We even bumped into Bruce Buffer!

Some hours later, I woke up parched, face down on the floor of the suite. I went to the mini-mart to grab a juice. Outside the shop, I noticed Nate Diaz's entourage. He was happily taking photos with fans so I pulled out my phone. As I opened the camera, my phone died. I was gutted but it was cool to see him post-fight and I had a new-found respect for him. He seemed like a nice guy.

Good things come from shit situations.

If I didn't work in a market research job begging builders to do surveys, I never would've ended up in Vegas.

My luck continued as I arrived into Los Angeles for two days before flying home. School friend Chris Child was road tripping the US with his friend Kieron and happened to be arriving in California the day I arrived. We toured the Hollywood Sign, Griffith Park Observatory, Hollywood Walk of Fame and Sunset Boulevard, before sleeping in the back of their camper van on Venice Beach.

The following day, I met up with Harrogate friends Liam Palmer and James MacLaverty at Hermosa Beach.

Wherever you go in the world, you bump into someone you know! Rachel, who I battled for the As You Like It job, lost her friends at the 2014 World Cup in Brazil. Amongst thousands of people, she got talking to a guy who was from her area in Liverpool. They shared a drink and added each other on Facebook, finding one mutual friend – me. The guy was Mike Armstrong, my old Carnegie FC teammate.

After several hours of sunbathing, I headed to a nearby café. One of the first posts I saw online was my Spanish friend Laura Rose checking in at Los Angeles airport. She was cabin crew for Emirates. We met for dinner before I flew out the following morning. As icing on the cake, classmate Henry Blunt was visiting Dublin whilst I was on my return layover. I had one final Guinness before confronting angry builders again.

## Time warp

I faced a predicament. I was in my mid-20s and loved raving. Music was a big part of my life, but my anxiety was becoming unbearable. There were tickets left for Time Warp Festival in Germany and I'd always wanted to go. I thought, if I don't go now, I'll never go. Uni friend Billy was going with a few friends, so I purchased a ticket and booked a flight. After watching Mainz beat Augsburg 4-2, we boarded the train to Mannheim. I was feeling anxious, but once the beers settled I relaxed and could look forward to the night ahead.

The festival is held inside a giant airport hangar and clubbers party through the night and into the next day. By sunrise, my phone had died and I lost everyone. I only knew it was daytime because I used one of the portaloos outside. I remembered an old video I saw online of Laurent Guarnier playing Andi Müller's remix of 'Everything In Its Right Place' by Radiohead as the sun was coming up. I overheard someone say he was playing so rushed over and as I arrived to the room, the intro of 'Everything In Its Right Place' came on. I was speechless. I closed my eyes, raised my arms and smiled for the duration of the song.

As the song ended, I had an anxiety attack. The pure ecstasy of the song and what I had taken, reached such a high that it all came crashing down. I was freaking out. My phone was dead, I couldn't speak German and I felt like my heart was about to explode. I paced the festival searching for Billy, but couldn't see him anywhere. It was similar to my experience in Manchester, apart from being stuck in the middle of an airport hangar in Germany. I was taking breathers in portaloos to limit distractions and focus on my breathing. Portaloos that were smeared in shit and used condoms. Two hours passed before I saw my group entering one of the rooms. They could see I was in a bad way. My breathing was irregular, I was blinking a lot and stumbling. They tried persuading me to dance it off and bought me an orange juice, but it wasn't happening.

I felt bad. They were having the best night of their life but had to look after me. Although I didn't know Billy that well, he persuaded his mates to leave the festival early and take me home. I accepted my death in the taxi and have flashbacks of collapsing on the pavement as I tried to leave. Billy offered me his bed and my body twitched to the point of exhaustion until I fell asleep. In truth, I didn't know if I had fallen asleep or passed away.

I woke up ashamed and apologised. However, they dismissed it and said they've all had bad nights. Maybe everything was in its right place. Maybe I did need the ecstasy of the Radiohead song and the anxiety attack as a wake-up call that I needed to sort myself out.

## Self-help

It reached the point where I had to seek professional help. I was experiencing intense head pressures which were unbearable. When I spoke to the doctor, he didn't even know what derealisation was. It made me question whether there is enough research or services available for people struggling with mental health. I was asked to complete a very basic multi-choice survey on the computer. It was almost laughable how bad it was, and they still prescribed me anti-depressants. After researching online and self-diagnosing a brain tumour, I asked to be referred to the hospital where I had an MRI scan. It was a daunting experience lying inside a machine whilst electrical pulses scanned my brain. They made an incredibly loud, literally shocking sound.

The results came back negative – they didn't find anything. Although desperate, I refused to take the anti-depressants. I was worried about relying on them to feel good and becoming addicted. I left the hospital that morning knowing it was down to me to fix it. I made a plan: gym every day, clean diet, no alcohol, no partying and I would get back into football. My friend Alex Myers had trials for Knaresborough Town Reserves, so I set myself the goal of making their starting 11 for the first match of the new season. It was a strong reserve team. For perspective, their first team had Seb Carol who was in the squad for AS Monaco in the Champions League Final in 2004. Funnily enough, the manager of the first team was my old PE teacher, Paul Stansfield.

I also noticed trials advertised for York City futsal team. I was a skilful player and futsal always intrigued me, so I signed up. In the days leading up to the trials, I lifted weights every morning, ate clean in the day and ran in the evenings. Considering I was still far from match fitness, I did well at both trials and was invited back. Taking part in the Futsal training drills made me realise how meticulous and tactical the game is – it's not just about skill. I was frustrated by the lack of freedom on the ball and always had to think three plays ahead. I'd been watching too many futsal highlight videos.

Three of the players were members of the England national futsal team. A 'nutmeg' is the most embarrassing thing you can do to an opponent in sport. I try and do it all the time in games (maybe too much). I never get nutmegged because I see it coming. It's a different story when you're defending against the England captain. I got too tight and my arrogance led me to being nutmegged twice within five seconds. Still to this day, I have no idea what he did. I was mortified but it was the reality check I needed. Despite being twisted inside out, I was selected for the upcoming tournament in Gateshead, where we would face three teams from the UK and the Australian youth team.

The fat was dropping off and I was starting to tone up. Our first pre-season game for Knaresborough was away in Huddersfield. Starting on the bench, I knew I had to make an impact when coming on. Whilst warming-up, I muttered to myself, 'Make some big tackles, win your headers and keep it simple.' The first thing I did was a crunching tackle on their forward. Even though a foul was given, I received a pat on the back and respect from my teammates. I didn't do anything on the ball that stood out but played good passes and never lost possession.

A week later, I made the 90-minute journey north to Gateshead for the futsal tournament. Only three trialists made the matchday squad, including Dave Hall and myself. We were nervous but looking forward to the challenge. Junior (coach) pulled out his whiteboard and talked through the tactics. As trialists, we were only expecting to come on for a few minutes of each game, so I was shocked when he announced me in the starting line-up alongside England internationals. I played safe for the majority of the game, letting the more experienced players lead the attacks. I was replaced in the second half but received high-fives from my teammates.

The next game was against the Australia youth team. Three weeks into my futsal career and I was already playing against Australia! They were younger than us and faster than us, so we sat deep. I defended well but received a bollocking from Junior, 'We need more goals from you!' In the third game, I came alive. Usually, you'd play short passes to get up the pitch, but space opened up ahead for me to run into. My teammate played a long, looping volley up the pitch and I jumped high (in what felt like slow motion) and controlled the ball majestically before squaring the ball for my other teammate to tap in. This match was being recorded and the commentator shouted, 'Wow! Great piece of skill by York City!'

At Knaresborough, the first day of the season was fast approaching and I was growing in confidence. Even when we trained with the first team, I didn't feel out of place. I was so focused on football that I didn't even realise how much my anxiety was improving. Alex and myself made the squad for the first match, away at Oxenhope. It was a great sense of achievement knowing I'd come from that incredibly dark place a few months earlier. However, the goal was to be in the starting 11.

Thirty minutes into the journey, we received a text saying we were in the starting line-up. Alex cranked the music and we celebrated wildly. Thirty-one minutes into the

journey, we heard a loud bang and Alex's car grounded to a halt. We called the manager expecting him to tell us to get the car fixed and go home. Instead: 'We need you! I'll get someone to pick you up.' We arrived one minute before kick-off, leaving no time for warm-ups or stretching. We were horrendous and subbed off early in the second half. The game finished 1-1 but it was a game we should've been winning. We sulked all the way home and Alex still had to find a way to retrieve his car from the side of a country road. It wasn't the dream start but at least I achieved my goal of making the first 11. I was proud of myself.

# 25

## (13 September 2016 – 12 September 2017)

### Confidence

I continued starting games, and, with some of the reserve players being promoted to the first team, I became one of the more experienced players. The gaffer, Mike Bligh, moved me to centre-back to provide solidity, with the younger kids playing further upfield. I'd never played defence before, but thanks to all the fitness training my whole game improved. I felt strong in the tackle, quick covering attackers runs in behind and was leaping much higher to win headers. My confidence playing football hadn't been this high for about 20

Photo credit – Craig Dinsdale

years! We were having a great season and made the final of a local cup. Unfortunately, away from football, I was having a torrid time. My market research job was cementing me into a deep depression. My anxiety had improved dramatically, but I was so fed up with calling builders and being told to fuck off.

## England in the sun

Charles and Josh were still in Australia and badgering me to come over. Sam had also been the previous year but I always thought of it as just England in the sun. It was November and bloody freezing. England in the sun sounded great! I was enjoying football so it was a difficult decision to leave, especially as I'd worked hard to secure a regular place in the side. I called Mike and he understood: 'Life gets in the way, I know it all too well. Go enjoy it while you can!' I applied for my visa that night and booked my flights (not direct of course). I decided to fly via Dubai to work at the Abu Dhabi Formula One, then spend three days in the Maldives, followed by five days in Sri Lanka. Balley had never been to Dubai so I persuaded him to come with me for a week. My DJ friend, Tom Higham, had also expressed interest. I knew Tom would love Dubai as there was a great, emerging party scene. I pitched to him that we could have a DJ company in Dubai together one day. He jumped at the chance and booked a flight over, staying with me and Balley at my cousin Danny's house.

They both had a cracking week. Tom even promised he would come back to Dubai to live. I wasn't sure if I believed him though! On my final day in Dubai, I wanted to thank Danny and his new girlfriend Heather for putting up with me and my mates for the week. I walked across the road to the local shop and bought them a hamper full of stuff they needed for the house. All my intentions were good that day. Before heading to the airport, I realised I'd forgotten to drain the batteries for my drone (which you're meant to do before boarding a plane). Running out of time, I pulled the drone out of the bag, placed it on the table and turned it on. I was expecting the lights to flash and slowly burn the battery. Instead, the propellers rotated and the drone started humming … LIFT OFF! The craft hovered at a 45-degree angle and nosedived into Danny's wall, chipping away at the new paint work.

Danny and Heather were relaxing in front of the TV when the drone took another turn and headed towards them. Heather screamed and leaped onto the sofa as it crash landed, spinning uncontrollably on the floor. I ran over and whacked it with a book, damaging the propellers. Danny looked at me like I'd just ruined Christmas. There was a dent in the wall and I heard Danny had to make it up to Heather by buying an expensive painting – a large one – to hide all the damage.

## Blue

Erika (who I met in Indonesia) was heading to the Maldives on the same day with her friend, Amy. Due to the extravagant prices, we went full-budget-mode. We shared a double

bed in a cheap hotel on the mainland and took a boat to the Cinnamon Dhonveli resort. It was only $80 for a full day, all inclusive. Most people believe you can only go to the Maldives if you're rich or on a honeymoon. It's not true. We sunbathed, drank cocktails, swam with exotic fish and I flew my drone (with its brand-new-spanking propellers).

And in case you weren't sure, the colour of the water in the Maldives really is that blue.

Erika flew back to Dubai because of work commitments, but Amy and I headed to Sri Lanka to meet her sister. We travelled all over the country in five days. Sri Lanka was beautiful and felt similar to the rural parts of India I had experienced on The Rickshaw Run.

The trains in Sri Lanka are incredible. Kandy to Ella is one of the most scenic and epic train journeys in the world. The carriage doors remain open allowing you to dangle your

legs as you pass through remote villages and tea plantations. I became far too comfortable and fell asleep. We approached a station with a high platform that would've taken both my legs off. Thankfully, Amy spotted the danger and shook me frantically. I only just lifted them in time, scraping both legs in the process.

We explored the Sigiriya rock before travelling to the foot of Adam's Peak, a 2,243m-high mountain. There are many beliefs and legends surrounding the holy mountain above the clouds. The boulder at the peak resembles a footprint which many believe is the footprint of the Buddha.

The sacred pilgrimage attracts thousands every year and people climb through the night to arrive for sunrise. The trail is illuminated by a band of dazzling lights which can be seen for miles. The trek was more difficult than I anticipated. Some steps were two-foot high and we found ourselves lunging upwards. Amy and I were breathless, sweating profusely, as a frail 70-year-old woman overtook us with a big smile on her face. We stopped complaining after that.

Thankfully, it was worth it! I've seen some good sunrises in my time but there was something special about this one. A gong echoed through the crowds as the sun appeared

from behind neighbouring mountains. The sky looked like it was on fire and cast a shadow of Adam's Peak on the surrounding plains. I was speechless, Amy was speechless and many of the pilgrims were crying, overjoyed with emotion.

After the knee-jerking descent down the mountain, we moved to Ella, where there was a hostel called Tomorrowland. I loved Tomorrowland in Belgium so was hoping for a similar vibe. We witnessed sunset and sunrise from the warmth of our sleeping bags in a treehouse. It was magical.

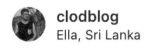

**clodblog**
Ella, Sri Lanka

•••

I was sad to be leaving. Amy's sister Casey had arrived and I had a nine-hour bus journey back to Colombo airport. I was first to board so placed my suitcase on the rear left seat and sat beside it. I was ready to relax with my music and enjoy the views, not anticipating what was about to happen for the next nine hours. At every stop, more and more school kids and workers got on the bus. Locals were standing on my toes and falling on me. I felt guilty about blocking a seat with my suitcase so stood up and gave away my seat. I was stood up for eight of the nine hours on that bus. A bus that had no air-con and three times the capacity it was meant to.

Maybe you just have to get lost to find yourself.

I definitely didn't find myself, that experience was fucking miserable.

## Good day mate

I eventually made it to Colombo, stinking of oil, dirt, and curry-flavoured crisps. Time was ticking but I was desperate for a wash so snuck into the hostel I'd previously stayed in and used their shower. At the airport check-in, I placed my suitcase on the belt: 27 kilograms. 'Sir, you've not paid for any baggage allowance.' My heart sank. 'I'm flying to

Australia! How can there be no baggage allowance!?' I'd never been on a long-haul flight without baggage allowance. It was ludicrous but I accepted I'd have to pay extra fees.

I nearly fainted when they asked for $300. I didn't even have $300. I'd been through so much chaperoning that suitcase to the airport as well. A 'lovely' man approached me and offered to help reduce the weight. He was dressed like airport staff and wheeled my suitcase to a nearby bench. Together, we unpacked my suitcase and he asked what items I didn't need. I needed it all! I was starting a new life in a foreign country with no money!

After an hour of going back and forth checking the weight, I'd filled several trash bins. To save items, I wore three T-shirts, three jumpers, two shorts, two pairs of trousers and three pairs of boxers. The only thing left in my suitcase was some smart clothes for a job interview. After paying a $50 fee, I wheeled my significantly lighter luggage to the security gates. The not-so-lovely man ran after me and grabbed me in an aggressive manner. 'Pay me one hundred dollars!' 'That's more than I paid for the luggage!' I lost patience and gave $25, ending the trip on a sour note.

Charles and Josh welcomed me in Sydney with a bottle of Australia's finest, Victoria Bitter. I was so exhausted that I could only manage one. Christmas Eve was the following day so we had enough to look forward to. I toured the Sydney Opera House, Harbour Bridge and Bondi Beach. I was in love. England in the sun was good! The 7-Eleven $1 Slurpee's were also a highlight. I had four that day.

For Christmas Day, we attended a beach party in Coogee. Beach parties happen every Christmas in Sydney, usually organised by Europeans on working holiday visas. For

obvious reasons, locals hate it and it can be incredibly dangerous as thousands of young people party in the sea off their heads. The waves were huge that day. I lost Charles for ten minutes and was worried for his safety. Thankfully, he appeared 100m down the beach where the current had taken him. We bought a plastic Christmas tree and decorated it with cheap tinsel, and erm, well… partied till the break of dawn, bitches!

Another reminder why you should always stay in touch with the people you meet.

Manda York was one of the Australians I camped with at Tomorrowland 2014. She noticed my Snapchat announcing I was moving to Australia and sent me a message offering her sofa until I found my feet. I landed in Australia with less than $200 so she was the angel I needed. Along with her housemates, Lauren and Kate, they welcomed me into their home for three weeks. Their place was in Surry Hills, a cool, hip (not cool whip – Family Guy joke, sorry!) area with lots of trendy bars, cafés and the world's best ice cream shop (Gelato Messina). Manda and I used to go on 'date nights' (as friends) after work. We'd order three scoops each … actually, no, I'd order three scoops and she'd have one, then we'd eat them on the park swings and catch up.

I spent the first few days sending my CV to as many restaurants and bars as I could. Emily (from market research days) put me in touch with her uni friend, Melissa. Mel was working as a hostess at Watson's Bay Boutique Hotel. The beach club/hotel was a

20-minute drive from Bondi Beach and the centrepiece of a rather affluent area. Through the week, elderly locals would walk down for tea, coffee and fish and chips. Weekends were totally different as the brunch would attract busloads of young people from the city. It was a beautiful harbourside spot with an incredible sunset view of the Sydney skyline.

Mel arranged an interview for me with venue manager Kylie. I got a haircut, dressed smart and arrived feeling confident. Kylie seemed cool and explained she was looking for

a personality. Someone who would work hard, have fun and get on with the rest of the team. The interview lasted five minutes and I was asked to start the following morning. My first shift was working 'the floor' with five Mexican guys, a young lad from Sydney and our supervisor, who was the most Aussie man you're ever likely to meet. He had a strong accent and wore a green hat with corks hanging below the brim. The floor was clearing empty glasses, plates and cutlery, ensuring the venue was always tidy. It was beneficial to learn that side of the job but I was moving to the bar the following day.

Surry Hills was 80 minutes from work and I didn't want to overstay my welcome so moved into a hostel in Bondi. Known for its luxurious beach, I didn't expect to be staying in a shit-hole when I moved there. The hostel was ten minutes up the road and the view of golden sand and blue sea was obstructed by drunks fighting outside a booze shop. An elderly Russian lady greeted me at reception. She barely spoke English and spent half the time shouting at her son (in Russian). It felt like a haunted house. The staircase had panels missing, the walls were peeling and it stank of dead cats.

I shared a room with a (constantly) drunk Irishman and a 45-year-old bogan Aussie who had been living there, in bunk beds, for three months! When I arrived home after work, he was passed out with a plate of spaghetti on his belly and six empty beer cans beside him. Oh, and his undies (which he'd washed in the sink) were drying on the steps to my top bunk.

I lasted two nights before registering myself as homeless (unofficially). Work hadn't paid me yet so I couldn't afford an upgrade. My Israeli colleague, Joanie, noticed me in the locker room with my suitcase and kindly offered for me to stay with her. My shift finished at 11pm but she said she'd stay awake to let me in. I was ready to collapse in some fresh bed sheets when Joanie answered the door. Something was wrong. She sneaked out in bare feet, quietly shutting the door behind her. The couple she was living with had fallen out and refused to let me stay. It was approaching midnight and I had a suitcase and five bags on me. Joanie instructed me to wait outside until they fell asleep. Joanie stayed up (bless her) and eventually let me in at 4am. I had to vacate before they woke up so only managed three hours sleep. Before I knew it, I was sat on my suitcase, on Bondi Beach, at seven in the morning. There were more seagulls than people. The beach was empty, bar a few surfers and health freaks doing yoga.

I arrived at work with a suitcase for the second day running.

## Funny how life works out

I count my lucky stars I met Gabriela from São Paulo that day. I was allocated a shift in the upstairs bar with her and she turned out to be one of the most special people I've ever met. Full of energy, always smiling, laughing and making everyone around her feel good. We hit it off and she invited me to a night out that evening. When I said yes, I didn't realise it was a Brazilian samba bar with 150 Brazilians. I had to pretend I could dance to samba all night. It was embarrassing but at least the 150 Brazilians had a good time laughing at me.

Along with her friends Bruna and Jack, we went back to Gabi's house in Double Bay for drinks. When we arrived, her flatmates were all partying.

There were five bedrooms, each with three or four people per room. The house was run by a French guy called Vincent. We shared a cigarette and he told me one of the guys was moving out in a weeks' time. I was in, but needed to figure something out until the space became available. Gabi shouted, 'Stay in our bed migo!' Gabi was sharing a double bed with three other Brazilian girls, and soon to be me.

'Migo' ended up sticking. My South American friends still call me Migo to this day.

It was a fun week with Gabi, Carol, Bhea and other Gabi. We worked in the day at Watsons then partied at night. The week flew by and I was ready to move into my new room, sharing with a French guy called Victor and a German guy called Fabian. It sounded like the start of a bad joke.

An Englishman, a Frenchman and a German walk into a house. They share a room, have a drink together, party together and against all odds, become best friends. We had a similar sense of humour and taste in music. Due to my previous anxiety issues, I hadn't partied for a long time. However, as my mental state had improved since arriving Down Under, it didn't take long for my housemates to persuade me to come out. It's crazy what a bit of vitamin D can do.

Our house, 'Manning Road', became infamous for parties. It was like a zoo at times with hundreds of people walking through the doors every weekend. Our favourite club night was S.A.S.H. and half the dancefloor used to come back for our afterparties. Sydney was

quickly becoming my favourite place in the world – at least to live, anyway. I was looking up things to do and discovered the St George Open Air Cinema in Sydney Harbour. It was a giant screen that raised from the water in front of the Opera House, showing both new and old films. Somehow, there were tickets left for the Trainspotting 2 premiere so I invited Carol to join me. She was still learning English so I had no idea how she was going to decipher Spud, Sick Boy and Begbie's Scottish accents.

I was a huge fan of the first film and Danny Boyle was my favourite director so I dragged Carol down early. We dressed to the nines, ate vol-au-vents and sipped champagne 'til the sun went down. As the venue started to fill, there was an announcement: 'Ladies and Gentleman, please put your hands together for our special guest, Mr Danny Boyle!' I nearly dropped my champagne glass. I had no idea he was attending! Danny introduced the film and explained how the idea for the sequel came to be. He received a round of applause and took his seat on the front row.

Carol was a good sport, laughing all the way through. In fairness, she was probably the first Brazilian to watch Trainspotting 2. I doubt she understood all the Scottish slang, such as, 'Aye, ya wee prick, yee,' but it was a fun night.

Josh and Charles both left Sydney so it was nice to have Jack Carter around (also from Harrogate). We got to know each other through our ex-girlfriends who were best mates. Jack was working as an Uber driver in Sydney, earning a good wage. On his breaks, he'd pick me up and take me for coffee. It was cute. It was beginning to feel like home. I had someone to spend time with from Harrogate, Manda, Lauren and Kate (who felt like family), and also my workmates and housemates. My original plan was to move to Melbourne after a few months, but life was good, so I stayed.

Due to my catering experience in Dubai, I was promoted to 'Food Pass Supervisor'. I was the first male to ever work on the food pass, let alone supervise. The male bartenders were jealous I was spending every day with 15 girls so started requesting shifts there. I was really enjoying my job. Not only because of the girls, it was just a fun place to work! My

two managers, Kylie and 'Frosty', became good friends of mine. Unfortunately, one of the other managers had something against me. He used to spend all day at the food pass to spend time with the girls, but Kylie said he didn't need to be there now I was supervising. He used to send me home for no reason and made me pay for ice cream which he used to give to the girls for free.

Nicknames are a serious thing in Australia; respected and stuck with, like a badge on a sleeve. It took me three months to find out Frosty's first name was Alexandra.

## The stars aligned

One of the best guys I met at work was Dan Folkes. He was a sweet Aussie guy with a wicked sense of humour. We used to close the bar together every Sunday. Each week, we'd agree to go for beers but by the end of the shift we'd be knackered and say, 'Ah fuck it, we'll go next week.' This went on for months. Eventually, the stars aligned and we agreed to go out. It was madness. We went to the Golden Sheaf in Double Bay. As we walked through the bar, we heard a call from a table in the smoking area. It was Izzy from work. She was sat with two older guys. As I approached the table, I recognised one of them. It was Suggsy! aka Graham McPherson, lead singer of British ska band, Madness. I was perplexed, wondering why Suggsy was in a tiny bar in Double Bay. I didn't play it cool, but I was in shock. 'I've seen you at Leeds Festival!' He was touring with Dean Mumford from The Rifles. They were both welcoming and shouted the bartender to bring more drinks.

We listened to their stories for hours. Suggsy told us when they were in the Top 10 touring Australia there was a queue of girls outside his hotel room wanting to meet him. The queue went down the corridor, down the stairs and around the block. Dean and I exchanged numbers and arranged to meet again the following night. When we met, they gifted three tickets to their show – Suggs: My Life Story. The show was a mixture of hilarious stories and music, with Dean playing the piano. Izzy couldn't make it so I invited Mel. Mel and her dad were huge fans of Madness so she was even more excited than me and Dan.

## Madness!

I sat in the Enmore Theatre thinking how ridiculous yet perfect it all was. Out of all the times we debated going out, the one we did resulted in us becoming mates with Suggsy and Deano (for a week).

'Alcohol, because no great story starts with someone drinking water.' - Some drunk guy, 2000 B.C.

The show was superb, and I'm not just saying that because I was mates with Suggsy and Deano (for a week). Suggsy's timing was like a professional comedian. His hilarious stories would segue into one of his classic songs. Deano was down to earth and seemed like one of the lads at the pub; you'd never imagine him being such a gifted piano player. After the show we were invited to the afterparty at a bar down the road.

I stayed in touch with Deano; he is a good soul. He told me he was playing in Leeds with The Rifles later that summer. Unfortunately, I wasn't in the UK, but my dad was. Dean didn't even know the bloke (my dad) but said he'd sort two free guestlist tickets. We were pissed-up in Sydney so I didn't think anything of it. A few months later, he sent two tickets out of the blue. I was astounded by his generosity. Dad was 61 at the time and cut the entire queue of young rockers, proudly saying, 'Excuse me, I'm on the guestlist!'

I faced a huge spanner in the works. My cousin, Katie was getting married in the UK. I miss every family event but apparently I'd promised to be at this one. My mum also threatened me with 'You HAVE to be there!' I considered flying via Hawaii and Alaska but they were so overpriced. Another option was flying via Nepal as I'd been toying with the idea of doing Everest Base Camp.

## Spontaneous decisions bring great results

It was a crazy last week leading up to my spontaneous decision. I lost my visa card at 'Transvestite Bingo', involving a bottle of Fireball and a 40-year-old Columbian. A day later, I almost died at the staff party. The owner of Watsons took me and the managers on his speedboat, to the island where the party was being held. We travelled a-million-miles-an-hour through Sydney harbour – so fast, one of the guys flew off and cracked his ribs. We were too busy holding on for dear life to notice he was missing. We arrived at the party in style (after we'd picked him up).

OH YES, OH YES! Next up was a Manning Road family outing to see DJ Carl Cox. 40 of us, all from different corners of the globe, came together, in the name of music. I spent the majority of the night with Fabian. We were so high that when the show finished at 4am, we booked a flight to Melbourne to see him again. We were crashing hard in the airport, questioning our life choices, whilst our housemates were in hysterics. I scratched my head for people we knew in Melbourne. Ross, who I stayed with at Hideout Festival, was online. I explained the situation. He said we were crazy, but, 'Of course you can crash at ours, we're going to see Carl Cox too!' Ross was hosting a pre-drinks starting at 10am, an hour after we were due to land.

We arrived feeling a little worse for wear but it wasn't long before they handed us a recovery beer. Ross was living with Michael (Hideout) and Matt, another friend from Harrogate. A steady stream of people arrived as the day went on. It was confusing leaving a nightclub to arrive at a pre-drinks with a load of new people, for the same night we were

just at, but in a completely different city. In our intoxicated state, we assumed we could buy tickets on the door. Unfortunately, in Melbourne, it was sold out! We searched online, Ross messaged his mates and we even tweeted Carl Cox. We'd travelled all that way and couldn't even go! You had to laugh. Whilst Ross and his mates went to the club, me and Fabian went to a few bars. We timed it so we arrived back at the same time. By that point, I was finished and went to bed. Fabian stayed up with them drinking, meaning he attended two pre-drinks, two nights out and two afterparties – all in one night, kind of.

Me and Fab did a quick tour of Melbourne before flying back to Sydney. I was bedbound for two days with exhaustion. In a bid to find some inspiration for my upcoming journey to the wedding, I watched the film Everest. I'd always dreamed of seeing Mount Everest. There was something special about it that intrigued me. The film finished and I booked a flight leaving 48-hours later.

*During the first COVID-19 lockdown, I converted my Everest Base Camp blog into a book and launched it on Amazon. I recommend reading the full story there. The shortened version is below. The book is titled 'How NOT to Trek to Mount Everest'.

## How not to trek to Mount Everest

It was the day before the flight and all I owned was flip-flops, shorts and vests. My options: buy hiking gear (expensive), buy hiking gear in Kathmandu (slightly cheaper) or ask around. Sydney wasn't the best place to be asking for winter clothes, but I got lucky. Richard, the floor guy from work, had been to Antarctica. I'd only known him a few months but he lent me his waterproof boots and extreme weather clothing. Legend.

It was hectic landing in Kathmandu. First, my drone was confiscated, then I had to navigate through peak-time traffic in search of a tour company. My travel-blogging friend Tom (@traveltomtom) had assured me there was no need to book treks in advance. After several near-death experiences in the taxi, I arrived at a small shop where I was greeted by Madan. Madan helped plan my trip and even got me on a flight to Lukla, leaving the following morning. By chance, Phil (who I met on the Rickshaw Run) was in Kathmandu so we met up for a beer.

Approaching the most dangerous airport in the world was as traumatic as it sounds. Fellow passengers screamed as the plane battled the high winds. As we approached the incredibly short runway, the pilot slammed on the breaks and made a sharp turn into what looked more like a supermarket car park than airport terminal. Ngima, my guide, clearly Facebook stalked me as he spotted me straight away.

The Lukla shops were overflowing with merchandise and hiking equipment. You could sense the excitement in the town. I'm not sure if this was in anticipation of the trek or relief at surviving the world's most dangerous airport.

Ngima seemed to know every local person we passed, acknowledging them with a handshake. It was a comfortable 8km to our first stop, Phakding. Although it can be warm in the daytime, it's a different story at night. I had to borrow extra blankets to survive the first night. The next stop was Namche Bazaar, where I'd planned to buy a sleeping bag. On the way up to Namche we arrived at two questionable bridges (visible in the 2015 Everest movie) – high up, dangling over glacial rapids. I didn't take notice of the higher one as I

assumed we wouldn't be crossing it. It turned out we were. It was like something out of an Indiana Jones movie.

From there on, it was an almost vertical climb and I began feeling the effect of the altitude. The temperature was also dropping significantly, meaning it was time to buy a sleeping bag. Unfortunately, none of the ATM's accepted MasterCard and I'd lost my Visa card in Sydney. I had a small amount of cash, but not enough to keep me alive for the rest of the trip. Again, I borrowed extra blankets, but this time I had to wear my clothes … and shoes to keep warm.

I woke up to snow-capped mountains on my doorstep and shared coffee with Takashi, a 57-year-old Japanese guy who was travelling alone. I befriended him as he'd been staying in the same lodges as me. We were advised to spend an extra night in Namche to acclimatise so embarked on a small hike to the first Everest viewpoint. I never imagined it to be as dramatic as it was. I had some kind of vertigo-infused anxiety attack where I was unable to look at it. I had to turn around for a while to compose myself. After that, I was in a state of euphoria.

The following day was a ruthless hike up to Tengboche. Despite the steep incline, a group of sherpa women carried the size of my dad's hoarding collection up the cliff face. My mum struggles with her Tesco bags, bless her … and the supermarket is only around the corner! It was getting late, a storm was brewing and there was still no sign of my mate from Tokyo. I was starting to get worried. He was having trouble with his knees and eventually arrived seven hours after me!

Thankfully, in Tengboche, I was able to get cashback at the hotel. It was too late to buy a sleeping bag but at least I had money to eat. At breakfast, I witnessed one of Earth's most unique sunrises. Due to the sheer size of Everest, the reflection created a second sun.

It was a pleasant walk up to the next village. I made friends with a local family who owned a restaurant. They had a lovable, playful kid so I spent an hour having lunch with him at his dinner table. I gave him a balloon and, amazingly, he broke into song, singing the full happy birthday chorus.

Emma, my colleague in Sydney, said she gave balloons to the local kids when she was there and they loved it, so I bought some to hand out.

When I arrived in Dingboche, I discovered Takashi was forced to cut his trip short. His knees couldn't take it anymore. I enjoyed his company and hoped to see him again. Carelessly, I washed my clothes and hung them out to dry. Minutes later, a hailstorm arrived out of nowhere and transformed my boxers into icicles. With the weather getting worse, it was becoming likely flights would be delayed out of Lukla – and I needed to make

the wedding! To save time, I skipped the recommended acclimatisation day in Dingboche. Stupid boy. An hour into the hike, I almost collapsed with altitude sickness and had to return to the lodge. On my way back, a blizzard swept through the valley.

I was freezing and concerned for my health so took an altitude sickness pill. After three hours in front of the fire I didn't get any warmer. Morale was low until Indian couple Priyanka and Kunal burst through the doors. They were hilarious and invited me to join their card game. The laughing warmed me up and I forgot about how bad I felt. Three snow-covered lads from Adelaide arrived from their acclimatisation hike and joined the game.

The lads invited me to join them for the hike up to Lobuche. They kept a slow, steady pace at all times. It made me realise how fast I'd been walking. From that moment, I had no troubles.

Thanks to my aching muscles, I slept like a baby in Lobuche. Feeling fresh, we set off walking to Everest Base Camp through a rocky valley, and the views were breath-taking,

quite literally! We walked adjacent to the Khumbu glacier and could hear the crackle of small avalanches. It startled a few people, but for me it added to the excitement. After a succession of teasing corners, the valley opened out, revealing the stunning Everest Base Camp. It was a special feeling.

The sunshine and clear blue skies soon turned to blizzard. It's crazy how quickly the weather turns up there. I tried to savour the moment for as long as possible. It was such an amazing feeling and sense of achievement, but I had to start making my way down as the storm was becoming treacherous.

News broke confirming flights were being delayed. Missing my flight meant missing the wedding. Missing the wedding, meant an angry mother. Ngima and I discussed the situation and convinced ourselves it was possible to cut the four days to Lukla, down to two and book onto an earlier flight. Fuelled by adrenalin and the increase in oxygen, we ran, with heavy backpacks, across the Himalayas back to Namche Bazaar, all in one day.

My knees were shaking, I'd never run that fast in my life. I felt like Usain Bolt, without the bolt. The locals wouldn't believe me when I said I had travelled from Goraksep. I treated myself to a pint in the 'World's Highest Irish Pub' and had an early night.

My whole body was in bits but the final leg of the journey was nothing in comparison to what we'd accomplished the previous day. It was all downhill to Lukla and not nearly as far. We ran the majority, meaning it only took a day and a half to reach Lukla Airport. There was no guarantee I could secure a seat on an earlier flight, but Ngima pulled a few strings. It was an emotional goodbye and we promised to meet again.

Arriving in Kathmandu meant I could have my first hot shower in almost two weeks. I must've stood in there for about 20 minutes. I was proud of what I'd achieved and there was a sense of satisfaction knowing I'd pulled it off without any planning or prior experience. Oh, and somehow, I made it to the wedding!

## The greatest place on Earth!

There really is no place like it. Hand on heart, I can safely say Glastonbury is my favourite place on planet Earth. I'd been watching the festival on TV for years but was never organised enough to apply for tickets. In 2016, the set that changed everything and gave me a kick up the arse was Underworld's headline set on the West Holt's Stage. Me and my dad pushed the sofas back in the living room, turned off the lights and raved. Following the show, I messaged Charles and insisted we buy tickets for 2017.

My parents attended Glastonbury from 1981 to 1986 and had many fond memories there. The 'hippie' Glastonbury spirit and love for people and life still exists today but it's organised better, with tighter security. In those days, people used to hop over the fence

(including my parents one year). Mum burst into tears struggling to scale the 7ft fence and Dad had to push her over. Another year, Mum and her friend hid in the footwell of the car whilst Dad drove into the festival. These days, the only way to get past security would be to hire a plane and parachute in.

Dad used to wear a radio cassette player around his neck and stand by the stages recording. You can find his recordings on his 'cloddyclips' YouTube channel. He said, 'Toilets were holes in the ground so you didn't want to pitch your tents nearby as shit would filter down the hills a couple of days into the weekend.'

## Dad's Glastonbury memories

1981    Photos :- B o W Pyramid, vans & tents. Colour, stage & tor.
            + crowd & tee pee

I'd only ever been to Knebworth in '76 and Deeply Vale in '79 so when a bunch of mates decided to hire a van and head to Glastonbury, I joined them. There were 8 or 9 of us in the van. Two would pay and drive in while the rest would climb over or under the fence and somehow meet up inside. I know I saw Rab Noakes, Decline and Fall, Hank Wangford, Supercharge, Aswad, Mother Gong and Hawkwind as I have photos. I have a couple more photos of bands I can't recognise.

1982   Photos :— Tumbling Die, Jackson Browne, Pink light + Tor. 'Aftermath

Same thing :— hire a van, two drive in and the rest nick in. A few of us had tickets for Frank Zappa + Hammersmith Odeon for Saturday night. We thought we would be able to just pop over to London, see F.Z. then drive back to Glastonbury and carry on where we left off. What could go wrong? **Mad!** I still have the unused ticket. I saw Van the Man, Jackson Browne but can't remember who else. I bumped into a friend who was selling cider, ~~from~~ with a mate, from the back of a van. He dropped a tab, 'Mickey Morse' I seem to remember and I have a photo of him giggling away while people queued up for cider. I can't remember who was on stage when a large inflatable die tumbled over the crowd. On its way back it was covered in mud or cow muck. I think it was this year when one of us pitched their tent under the pylon cables. It charged ~~up~~ the tent poles, with electricity and you would get a shock if you touched them.

1983   Photos :— Beer tent, changing signs, E.P. Thompson

I had bought a radio cassette player, some batteries and a couple of cassettes in order to record some performances. I managed to record some Moving Hearts, Tom Paxton, Incantation, Alexei Sayle, A Certain Ratio, Black Roots and Melanie. I managed to get some photos of Curtis Mayfield and I seem to remember he did around a twenty minute version of 'Move On Up'. I also got photos of Tom Paxton, Incantation, King Sunny Adé and UB40.

<u>1984</u>   Photo :- Marquee surfing, wrist band.

I was now at art college in Cambridge so I hired a car and travelled over to Worthy Farm with some fellow students. We drove in with one person in the boot and another in the rear foot well covered in our belongings. We bumped into our friends from Harrogate at our usual meeting place, just in front of the mixing desk when the bands were on. I managed to record some Weather Report, Fela Kuti, General Public, The Smiths, Fairport Convention, Christy Moore, Brass Construction, Paul Brady and John Martyn. Great weather this year.

<u>1985</u>

Not great weather this year! We made our way from Cambridge on public transport. My girlfriend and I were staying with a couple of friends in their tent. That was okay until they'd had enough of the mud by Sunday. They packed up and left, leaving us homeless. We managed to track down some friends from up north and sheltered in the back of their van. Another friend from up north, now living in London, had the great idea of buying a load of Wellington boots on the way to the festival. They sold in a flash. He managed to leave the site, load up with more wellies and flogged those too. He ended up giving us a lift back to London. I didn't take any photos this year as my camera lense fogged up with the damp. I made no sound recordings either. One image that stands out in my mind is of a dead umbrella poking out of the smooth mud in front of a deserted pyramid stage. The high point for me, was seeing Hugh Masekela on stage when a weak sun broke through the grey sky and lit him up.

1986 Photos :- ~~John Martyn~~ Green Fair, crowd thoroughfare
    I felt I had to go once again to shake off the muddy memories of '85. I seem to remember seeing The Pogues, Ruby Turner and The Housemartins. I definitely saw John Martyn, London Wainwright III, Robert Cray and Christy Moore as I recorded them. So this was the last time I went but I have some great memories.

## Peace and love

It was time to head to the promised land. We crammed as much as we could into our Morrison's trolleys and headed south. Our trolleys consisted of beer, cider, vodka, rum, water, some more beer and cider, and some bread and cheese slices. Essentials. Another 'essential', or what we thought was an essential purchase, was our very own, trusted, four-wheel, heavy-duty beer trolley that we ordered online. Rather than carry six bags each, we thought we'd use this to push all our supplies into the festival. It seemed genius at the time. We parked up, unpacked the boot (which was full to the brim) and loaded our very own, trusted, four-wheel, heavy-duty beer trolley. The queue only stretched 100m past some hedges at the end. 'Brilliant! We were smart setting off at 5am. We'll have camp set up and the first beers cracked in no time!'

Despite the constant yawns, spirits in the queue were high. Some groups were drinking before the sun had even come up, dancing around portable speakers. After a few hours, there were signs of movement which brought a cheer to the line. So far so good as we advanced forward at a steady pace. This was until the first corner - a 90-degree angle through bumpy mud-land. The trolley, holding the weight of the weekend on its shoulders, struggled to manoeuvre around the bend. The wheels buckled and more cans than you'd find in a Heinz beans factory came toppling off the trolley, crashing to the ground. Beer sprayed everywhere and we were stuck in the middle of the queue, embarrassed – with our very own, trusted, now three-wheel, heavy-duty beer trolley. Not one person stopped to help us. It became every man for themselves. People even started overtaking us. Twats! What ever happened to Peace and Love!?

The only positive was that there wasn't long left in the queue so we distributed the weight and advanced forward once more. Charles and Tatters dragged the wounded trolley whilst Josh and I carried as many bags as we could. It was a nightmare. The sun starting coming up and there were rumours it could be the hottest Glastonbury on record. Naturally, Josh and I split from Charles and Tatters as they kept having to stop to fix the trolley and realign it. Every time we glanced back, they were veering off the path. It looked like they were dragging their pissed-up mate out of a club.

The trolley capsized every time it made a turn, it was unbearable to watch. My three-litre bottle of cider kept falling off and rolling down the hill. Charles shouted, 'If that rolls off one more time, I'm booting it into the next farmer's field!' To cure us of our misery, Josh and I made the conscious decision to stop looking back. It was like that scene in The Beach where Sal leaves the Swedes out in the cold, so as not to ruin the vibe of the camp. We just wanted them out of site. As heavy as they were, I was glad to be carrying the bags. I still remember how vibrant the smiles on our faces were as we reached the end of the line by the hedges. Amidst all the excitement, pain and embarrassment, we'd been totally naïve and officially cemented ourselves into Glastonbury virgin folklore.

This wasn't the end of the queue. This was the queue to join the queue. The actual queue. The queue that would take another five hours. In the hottest Glastonbury on record.

The adjacent field had five separate queues filtering in to join the main queue. We weren't the only ones but that didn't make us feel any better. By 11am, the sun was beaming down and there wasn't a cloud in the sky. To make matters worse, Charles and Tatters had all the water. The main queue was enclosed by metal fencing, making it impossible to reunite. The only thing we had to keep hydrated were cans of cider. It wasn't the smartest idea but at least we could drown our sorrows.

The entrance looked like a mirage in the distance. I was dehydrated, drunk and everything was blurry. A girl in the queue sprayed me with her mini water fan and I honestly felt like marrying her on the spot. The torture endured until 3pm. We bumped into Dave Hall who was setting up camp by a large oak tree. Heatstroke was hitting us hard and the shade looked inviting so we pitched nearby. In our delirious state, we erected the tent close to the long drops. Tatters returned from a food vendor furious and insisted we move. Thank God he did as the smell in that spot five days later was unfathomable.

Long Drops – The legendary open-top cubicles that can be found all over the festival site.

In fairness to Glastonbury, the campsite toilets have improved and they're trying to be more environmentally friendly. When you take a dump, you collect a cup of sawdust and throw it on top after you've done the business, helping mask the smell, and the waste is turned into compost for crops.

Bit of a shitty invention if you ask me.

Flags at Glastonbury have become iconic. Watching the TV coverage, you'll see thousands of flags with funny photos, memes and political statements. The flags that go unnoticed (the real heroes) are the ones that line up alongside each path. Much of the site was exposed so people were taking cover in the shadow of each flag. Whilst amusing, there were no available flag shadows for me. I noticed an ice cream van up ahead. Despite the large queue, I nestled myself on the ground at the front and tried to sleep.

Temperatures dropped so we walked up to the G-L-A-S-T-O-N-B-U-R-Y sign for a sunset view of the festival site.

Wednesday was fairly innocent so we were feeling fresh and raring to go for Thursday. The festival had come to life. It was packed, everywhere! It was so busy that we couldn't even get inside the tent for Eats Everything's daytime set. Thankfully, Josh spotted speakers

outside the tent with space to dance. My parents had warned me it was important to set meeting points if you lose each other. By 3pm, Thursday, we learnt that lesson. Charles and Tatters disappeared and we didn't see them again until Friday morning.

## Happy days!

That Thursday was one of the best days I've ever had and the actual festival hadn't even started yet. Morale was so high all day. We covered every inch of the grounds, dropping in at different parties and joining random campsite's drinking games.

Highlight from Eats Everything set was when he played Basement Jaxx's 'Rendez-Vu'. Thousands of people outside the tent were going wild, flailing their arms and embracing each other.

I presumed it was Friday morning and opened one eye to gather information on my surroundings. I was in my tent, but in the porch, on the hard floor. Charles was spread across my compartment with his ass out, snoring loudly and occasionally farting. I joined Josh for some fresh air outside. He'd converted the butchered trolley into a seat by flipping it upside down. I was craving fresh lemonade and wanted to see Haçienda Classiçal open the Pyramid Stage so persuaded Josh to join. Business was booming for juice bars, smoothie bars … and even oxygen bars, which all had huge queues. Josh questioned, 'Could last night have been that heavy you need oxygen pumped into your mouth and nostrils through a pipe?' I shrugged my shoulders, but in the back of my mind I was thinking – Yes, that's exactly what I need.

Haçienda Classiçal played less-banging versions of famous dance songs. It was the perfect start to the Friday and the beginning of our road to recovery. Following them was Paul Carrack, whose keyboard player, James Locke, was in my class at school. It was cool seeing an old friend tearing it up on the world's most iconic stage. For the rest of the day, I let the lads decide what stages we went to. All I was bothered about was being at the front for Radiohead at 9:30pm. Anything that came before was fine by me. Josh recommended Royal Blood, who were the highlight of the day. I've never enjoyed a band so much without knowing any songs.

The sun was setting, meaning it was time for Radiohead. I'd seen them at Leeds Festival in 2009 for their In Rainbows tour, but it wasn't the same. The crowd was shit and there were too many kids who didn't appreciate them. One even shouted, 'Play something we know!' At Glasto', on the grandest stage of all, the crowd were 90 per cent 'Radiohead heads'. My parents brought me up on The Bends and OK Computer and they soon became my favourite band. There was something unique about them. From Thom Yorke's voice, to the experimental music and inventive videos, even to the way they released albums, such as the 'pay what you wish' download of In Rainbows.

I'd dreamed of being at the front, with a beer in hand, tears in my eyes and singing my heart out. A few songs into the show, a girl approached me. Usually, I would be inclined to partake in a kiss during a concert … but it was Radiohead, my favourite band. I'd arrived two hours early to secure a spot at the front and didn't want to be distracted. Josh shook his head in disbelief as me and this girl started making out (for pretty much the whole set). Every time I tried singing a lyric I'd be dragged back in. The set wasn't as rocky as the headline slot they played in 2003, but it was still a masterpiece and I was unequivocally fulfilled. They finished with Karma Police and the crowd chanted, 'For a minute there, I lost myself, I lost myself, I lost myselllllllffffffff' all the way back to the campsites.

The great thing about Glastonbury is that you can see your favourite bands in the day and your favourite DJs at night. From midnight, thousands gather at 'the Naughty Corner' on the far side of the festival. Other late-night options include: Arcadia, a giant Spider that blasts flames and techno, and The Rabbit Hole where we saw the highly energetic Confidence Man – one of the sets of the weekend! When it comes to clothes, anything goes at Glastonbury. By 5am, at The Temple Stage, I was dressed as Santa Claus and Charles had a Kim Jong-un jumper on. We didn't look out of place though. It was a sea of misfits all dancing on different levels of this colosseum-like arena. Sunrise seemed like the perfect time to head to the legendary stone circle.

The monument, comprising of 20 stones, is a common place for people to wind down after the night's antics. The previous day, the festival had organised an unofficial world record attempt for the largest ever human peace sign. 15,000 people turned up to show solidarity for the recent terrorist attacks in Manchester and London. The world record was broken and it sent a powerful message that I was proud to be a part of. Fast forward to Saturday morning and we were lying down with a ciggie and a tinnie, listening to music and watching the sun come up. Two shirtless lads in ripped jeans were lying next to us staring into the sky and giggling. They were in another dimension but no harm to anyone.

Nestled somewhere within our deep chats about space, UFO's and the afterlife, someone mentioned 'The Piano Bar' – a secret place in the festival grounds that changes location every year. It's always difficult to find and you have to pick up clues over the weekend. We noticed a small, consistent flow of people walking to the top corner of stone circle. Out of sight from the rest of the festival, there was a queue of 15 people and an Irish man dressed as a Leprechaun. He had the strongest accent I've ever heard and kept repeating a riddle. If you could decipher the riddle (which was already difficult due to his accent) you whispered in his ear and he'd grant you access into the woodland. In 45 minutes, not one person solved the riddle. We were about to leave when we overheard someone say the correct answer. So it wasn't obvious we'd cheated, we hung around for a few minutes before whispering the answer in the Leprechaun's ear.

The woodland led into a tunnel that required us to crawl on all fours. After 20 metres, it turned to complete darkness. I imagine you're thinking this is all one massive trip. As we shuffled further into the abyss we could hear faint noises. I turned back to look at the lads but couldn't see a thing. Eventually, it opened up, revealing a small cave with 30 people crammed together facing a stage. We were giddy and talking loudly as we clambered out of the tunnel. When we jumped down, every single person turned to us and put their finger to their lips and shushed us. I muttered 'What the fuck?' which echoed around the cave.

I felt like I'd joined a cult. We discovered that in order to remain in the cave, you weren't allowed to speak. If anyone spoke you had to shush them. Initially, I was offended at being told to shush, but the longer we were there the more fun it became shushing the new arrivals. The act on stage was a weird Irish folk band. I don't think they'd mind me saying that, you have to be weird to play a gig at 8am, hidden behind a Leprechaun, at the end of a pitch-black tunnel, with no talking or singing allowed. I'm a big fan of Damien Dempsey and Christy Moore (Irish folk legends) so it's nothing against that genre of music. They'd talk gibberish for ten minutes, then play a two-minute song, then talk gibberish again. Nothing they said made sense, it was like they were muddling the order of words in a sentence. Either it was part of the act or I was imagining it and it was time for bed.

The highlight of Saturday was Liam Gallagher's daytime set at the Other Stage. He came out to 'Fuckin' in the Bushes' and the place erupted. Beer cans sprayed everywhere like freshly popped bottles of Vueve. It felt like a Slipknot concert, there were mosh pits everywhere! By the end of the set, I'd lost Tatters. Thankfully, we had a new rule: if you lose each other, meet back at the tents. 'The greatest frontman of all time' closed his set with an emotional take of 'Don't Look Back In Anger', which he dedicated to the victims of the Manchester and London terror attacks, and Grenfell Tower tragedy.

'I've never done that before. That's kind of like everyone's song for the moment because of all the shit that's going down in the world, so I thought, if our kid's (meaning brother,

Noel) not going to do it for them then I'll do it for them. And I thought I did alright actually. It's nice to be back, man, playing some tunes to the beautiful people.' – Liam Gallagher speaking with Jo Whiley after the show.

We rounded off Saturday by seeing Goldie's '92–'94 rave set at Arcadia, followed by Foo Fighters at the Pyramid Stage and Fatboy Slim at the Sonic tent. I say rounded off … we still had eight hours to go at the Naughty Corner. At Fatboy Slim, there was a four-year-old girl with glow sticks raving on her dad's shoulders. That alone sums up Glastonbury.

Back in the 90s, if my parents left me alone in the living room, I would run to my dad's CD collection, grab Fatboy Slim's album, You've Come a Long Way, Baby and skip to track three – 'F**king in Heaven'. I'd open all the windows, turn the volume up and let 'Fatboy Slim is fucking in heaven, Fatboy Slim is fucking in heaven, Fatboy Slim is fucking in heaven, fucking 'n fucking 'n fucking in heaven' run, until my parents came sprinting back in the room to shut the stereo off and call me a little twat. This was a game I enjoyed playing regularly.

By Sunday, we wanted the Pyramid Stage to fall on top of us. The only way to survive our stinking hangovers was to drink through it. After several beer bongs we'd run out of alcohol.

Sometimes the Lord looks down on you, and in this situation he did. Thank you, Lord.

Charles went on one of his daily walks. It's usually when he's drunk and needs to clear his head. In his dazed and confused state, he stumbled across two young lads sat beside a tent with an unopened 24-crate of Carling lager. One of them looked up at Charles: 'Oi mate. Do you want this crate for a quid?' Charles was gobsmacked. 'A quid? Sure!' The thought crossed his mind that all the cans could be full of piss, but it was a risk he was willing to take, for a quid. All of a sudden, the other lad tapped his mate on the shoulder and whispered (but loud enough for Charles to hear), 'We can't give it for only a quid, that's ridiculous!' Charles had £10 he was willing to part with, but after a discussion, they came back with a revised offer. 'Oi mate! We'll give you it for two quid. How about that?' In disbelief, Charles rushed to his pocket, chucked them a £2 coin and hurried back. Carling isn't usually my beer of choice but when you're desperate and offered the deal of the century, you have to take it!

Charles left our tent a very drunk man who wasn't much use to anyone and came back a hero. We gave him a round of applause and cracked open the first warm can.

Festival tip – Good things only happen when you're drunk. If you're ever in a desperate situation, send your drunk mate on a walk and he'll stumble into something great.

The sun was shining and Chic were about to play 'The Legends Slot' on the Pyramid Stage. As we were getting ready, we noticed something glistening in the sunlight under the tent. Charles asked, 'What is that?' I stuck my hand under the tent and pulled out a three-litre bottle of God's very own, Strongbow cider. 'Yesssssss! I knew this would come in useful!' Charles and Tatters didn't look too impressed after the misery it caused them in the queue – but every cloudy cider has a silver lining right?

Despite consistently losing each other all weekend and ending up with random groups of people, all four of us were back together for the final day. No one else, just us and our bottle of cider. Tears of joy ran down our cheeks as Chic walked on stage. It was the perfect pick-me-up music for a Sunday afternoon. 'Wee aree familyyyy! Heyy, heyy, heyy, heyy, yeaahhhh!' The set finished with thousands of people clapping and chanting 'These are the good times!' They really were good times and morale was restored.

Following Chic, we saw London Grammar and Goldfrapp, who I knew from listening to my dad's Q magazine CDs as a kid. Ed Sheeran was headlining the Pyramid Stage. As talented as he is, it wasn't my cup of tea so I went solo to see Justice at the West Holts Stage. Sam persuaded me to see Bullet for My Valentine instead of Justice at Leeds Festival 2008, so I was excited to finally see them. They put on an amazing light show and fired out glow sticks for everyone in the crowd. With their French bomber jackets and long curled hair, they finished the set by standing on top of the DJ booth and lighting cigarettes – they looked cool as fuck.

By midnight I was done, and so was Tatters, who I met back at the campsite. He was driving us home the following morning so I was glad he was being sensible. It was a different story for Charles and Josh, who stayed out till 6am. Idiots.

The drive home is the worst part of going to any festival. After six hours of heart palpations and toilet stops, we made it back to Harrogate and the comfort of our own beds. Mum brought me a cup of honey and ginger tea and I watched the Glastonbury highlights on BBC iPlayer, whilst crying and throwing up into a bin.

## How many flights can you get for the price of one?

It was time to head back to Australia. Like my last long-haul flight, I didn't like the idea of going from one corner of the globe to the other without stopping anywhere. I set myself the challenge of seeing how many flights I could get for the price of a direct. I made notes on potential routes, cheap one-way flights and famous landmarks worth seeing. The result:

Leeds – Amsterdam – Seoul – Tokyo – Hong Kong – Kuala Lumpur – Sydney

Travelling for a total of £1,200, I made it my goal to do as much as possible in each place (minus Amsterdam and Kuala Lumpur which were short layovers). Stupidly, the night before leaving, I played six-a-side football and broke my ribs. The pain was excruciating. I couldn't put my seatbelt on after the game and didn't sleep a wink. I spent the night scrolling through Facebook trying to find friends who might be in the layover cities. I'd forgotten Joe Costello (who I met in Indonesia) was studying in South Korea with his girlfriend. I sent him a message and he offered to travel to Seoul to meet me. Despite only having 24 hours, we did as much as we could. I sampled local food (Dak Galbi) and experienced the towering heights of Namsan Tower, which offers a 360-degree view of the city.

Little reminder I was walking around Seoul with a broken rib – in case you forgot.

Send sympathy to @coryeveryday_ – thanks.

Every hotel was fully booked that night. The only available place was a brothel on the outskirts of the city. You know the furry wall in Get Him To The Greek? It was like that

everywhere. After checking in, Joe led me down the red-lit corridor to our room, and I'm not going to lie, I started questioning whether there was more to Joe than I'd first realised - especially as the room only had a double bed. In the end it was fine, Joe didn't want to have sex with me in a Korean brothel. We joked about the situation over a few beers and got an early night. Before my flight to Tokyo, Joe suggested climbing Seoul's highest peak in time for sunrise – clearly with zero consideration for my ribs.

It felt like a rib was piercing a hole in my lungs every time I inhaled. I winced every step of the three-hour hike up to Baegundae (836m). It was bad enough, but what was another dagger to the chest (excuse the pun) was that when we reached the top, we were greeted by a thick fog. The whole point of the trek was to see a view of the city at sunrise, but we couldn't see a thing. Whilst all this was happening, I received a reply from Takashi in Tokyo (from the Everest Base Camp trek). He was keen to meet and offered to collect me from the airport. In one of his messages, he proposed climbing Mount Fuji. I explained my rib situation and told him I couldn't but that I was looking forward to seeing the city. After hobbling down the mountain, Joe dropped me at the train station and we said our farewells.

It's always strange saying goodbye like that because you have no idea when you're going to see each other again. It's like the guys we met in South America. I didn't catch up with Emil and Anders for another seven years until I was road tripping Denmark with my friend Molly. It was the same with Michael and Shane who I trekked Machu Picchu with. I didn't see them again until I was visiting family in Brisbane in 2017.

There are certain people you share a moment with who become friends for life.

## Takashi's dream

It was early evening when I landed in Tokyo. Takashi greeted me near a small restaurant where we had spicy noodles. He's a man of few words, but I could tell he wanted to say something. Other than the occasional noodle slurp, it was complete silence until he announced, 'We will climb Mount Fuji!' It put me in an awkward position. 'I'm sorry but as I mentioned, I'm struggling to walk, never mind hike. My ribs are broken!' He didn't seem too impressed. 'I think we can try.' I was drawn to his persistency.

When a challenge is presented to me, it's like an irrepressible wave of adrenalin that I can't control. I don't find climbing Mount Fuji that stimulating, but if you say, 'You have to climb Mount Fuji with a broken rib' then I'm intrigued!

Before accepting his proposition, I asked for clarification. 'How long will it take?' He responded confidently, 'Five hours, maximum.' I pondered the task at hand. I'd managed three hours in Seoul and knew it would be special standing on top of one of the most iconic active volcanoes in the world. At that moment I discovered Takashi's impressive sales skills. He began telling me how his lifelong dream was to stand on top of Mount Fuji. He'd attempted to summit three times but had to turn back each time. I felt an added responsibility to ensure he reached the top this time.

Whilst being mindful of my ribs, I climbed delicately into his Toyota Pixis Mega. The Japanese car had a front nose like a UFC fighter and zero leg room. On the backseat, there was a tent, two sleeping bags, camping food and hiking gear. It was always Takashi's plan to take me to Mount Fuji and there was clearly no talking him out of it! It was a three-hour drive so to break the journey up we drove through the lights of Tokyo's city centre. It was like the movies, neon lights everywhere! I witnessed robots with neon-lit eyes strolling down the path and four life-size Mario Karts racing through the streets – with, you guessed it … neon lights.

It was 11pm by the time we arrived at the foot of Mount Fuji, and I was under the impression we were camping and climbing in the morning. We parked in a car park beside the forest and, without saying a word, Takashi began loading his bags with food and supplies. He didn't grab the tent though. 'What's going on?' I asked. 'We're ready, let's go!' 'We're climbing now?' 'Yes. If we go now, we should arrive for sunrise.' Before I had a chance to respond, he set off walking into the forest. I threw the rucksack over my shoulder and received a shooting pain where my perfectly aligned rib cage used to be.

I swore a lot on this trip. And to think I had the option to take a direct flight to Australia rather than partake in this ridiculous, unnecessary tour of mountains and volcanoes with a broken rib.

'Sometimes, the experience is worth the pain.' Cory McLeod

It was approaching midnight as we wandered through the spooky forest. It was unsettling as I could hear rustling in the bushes and large insects were landing on my neck. Asian black bears can be found in these woods so that was also in the back of my mind.

Takashi wasn't talking so I could hear every movement or sound. Eventually, we made it out of the woodland, revealing an incredible view over the horizon. Both Venus and Mars were visible as Takashi shouted, 'Look! Shooting stars!' The meteoric spectacle lit up the night sky for the best part of an hour. I'd never seen anything like it! I couldn't have been in a more special place to witness it, stood on Mount Fuji, in the middle of the night, with a random guy I barely knew.

We were taking forever to ascend. I was having to shuffle slowly due to my ribs and Takashi was stopping every five minutes due to the pain in his knees. We weren't the best expedition team ever, but at least we were determined. When we reached the halfway stage we took a selfie to mark the occasion. I'm not usually one for being realistic, but I didn't think we were going to make it at that point. Looking up was so intimidating. The steepness made the mountain look like it was coming back on itself.

Six hours in, the sun burst through the layer of clouds below. I felt like I was in a dream going from shooting stars to that sunrise. We smiled at each other and sat down to enjoy the show.

As the intensity of the sun increased, we began slowing down further. My ribs hadn't got any better and Takashi's knees were wearing him down. I was battling through the pain but every time I looked back Takashi was sat down. I was trying not to become frustrated, I knew it wasn't his fault. I played the meteor shower and sunrise back in my mind, then envisioned Takashi summitting and fulfilling his life-long dream. He looked defeated so I hobbled back down and sat beside him on the wall. 'Together, we are going to do this … whatever it takes!'

What we thought would take five hours took 16. We used every ounce of will and grit in our bodies to pull ourselves up that mountain. The final stretch was brutal and I was wincing with every step. Takashi was facing demons of his own so insisted I went ahead. When I eventually made it to the top, I was so dizzy. The altitude sickness hit me like

a Japanese bullet train. I stumbled to the nearest shop and downed two sugary drinks (before even paying for them). I felt horrendous but made my way back to the top of the path so I could look out for my friend.

I could see Takashi at the bottom of the path and encouraged him to keep moving. He waved up to me, got his head down and didn't look up again until he reached the top. I embraced him with a hug – it was emotional! We went through so much together in one night, it's hard to put into words. I felt privileged to be a part of his journey, finally achieving his dream of standing on top of Mount Fuji.

I slept the whole way back to Tokyo. For my final hour in Japan, I walked across the Shibuya Crossing and ate local street food under the neon lights. It was an intense 24 hours. Takashi dropped me back at the airport and waved me off as if I was his son heading to college.

## Typhoon

Hong Kong didn't go as planned … not that I did any planning! I was hoping to take a ferry to Macau and leap off the highest bungy jump in the world. My dreams were shattered when a typhoon hit Hong Kong, disrupting all ferries for the subsequent two days. Thankfully, there was plenty more things to do. I climbed up to the Sky Terrace 428 viewpoint and witnessed the tame but cute 'Symphony of Lights'. It was pre-season for football teams across Europe and, as luck would have it, Liverpool were playing Leicester City in Hong Kong. Tom Joel, a friend-of-a-friend from Harrogate, was a sport scientist for Leicester. I messaged and he replied back saying to meet them at a bar later on. I was so exhausted that I passed out and missed my opportunity to party with Leicester's Jamie Vardy.

I had a short stop in Kuala Lumpur before my connecting flight to Sydney. Thankfully, this time, it was a Xanax-free experience.

## The steaks are high

I was thrilled to be back in Sydney but knew there was a possibility I wouldn't be there much longer. Sam Hodson, Tom Higham and myself had been discussing plans to start a DJ company in Dubai. We'd been floating the idea around ever since Tom visited, but now it had some real traction. Whilst I'd been away, Kylie had jumped ship to manage a new steakhouse in Double Bay – Mr G's. I knew nothing about different types of steaks and ways to cook them, but apparently the tips were good so I signed up. I wasn't overly impressed, I had to wear a wooden bow tie and apron. I felt like I'd taken a step back in my illustrious hospitality career. I had become accustomed to the Aussie slang and chilled vibes at Watsons, but now I was serving the rich elite of Double Bay, one of Sydney's wealthiest suburbs.

I spent most of my shifts brainstorming a name for our new company in Dubai. Kylie would catch me scribbling on beer mats and customer receipts. I didn't want to leave Sydney but the lure of starting my own company took over. There were negatives of Dubai (like all places), but there was nowhere else in the world I could set up my own company so easily. I could in the UK, but I'd never DJ celebrity and billionaire's boat and villa parties – soon to be my new life.

## Leap of faith

With the plans for the company set, agreed and in motion, I booked my flight to Dubai for the end of September. Our company name … The Mixer. The name Sam and I had originally come up with when DJing that New Year's Eve party. What a waste of beer mats! With my time in Australia running out, I realised I hadn't really left Sydney. I'm not counting the Carl Cox night in Melbourne! I had family in Brisbane, Charles was in New Zealand and some Harrogate friends were travelling the east coast.

With that in mind, I joined Charles in Queenstown for three nights. A week before leaving, I was drunk on a night out and booked the 134m bungy jump. When I woke up, it became clear I'd booked it a week early by mistake and was due to jump in two hours' time. I explained to their customer service team that I was in Sydney with a McDonald's en route. Thankfully, they found the funny side and changed the date free of charge.

Queenstown is a thrill-seeker's paradise. In summer, Charles said he spent his free time doing water sports on Lake Wakatipu, and in winter he'd head to The Remarkables, a nearby ski resort. Instead of paragliding, white-water rafting or ziplining, the first place Charles took me was Fergburger. The restaurant is widely regarded as serving the world's

best burger. It was delicious but bloody massive. I woke up with meat sweats but the bathroom was literally too cold to take a shower. A few sprays of deodorant and aftershave later and I was on the bus to the bungy jump. The nerves were kicking in, but I was looking forward to leaping from one of the highest bungy platforms in the world. These experiences are what I live for and what keeps me alive.

When we arrived at the pod, dangling 134m above a ravine, it became apparent there weren't many volunteers to go first. Thankfully, I'd watched YouTube clips of bungy jumps 'gone wrong' so I knew what not to do. I was up first so the last thing I wanted to do was fuck it up. It all happened so quickly. Within seconds, I was strapped up and standing on the ledge. The countdown came soon after and that was it … all there was left to do was leap as far as I could and look as elegant as possible.

I nailed it! I looked more confident than I actually was, swan-diving with both arms out and a big grin on my face. As I plummeted towards the ground, a noise came out of me that I've never heard come out of me before. It was a squeal that sounded like a wounded goat falling down a mountain. 8.5 seconds of freefalling felt like a lifetime and it was pure relief when they finally yanked me back up. My mum cried when she watched the video. She said I looked like I had died. I'd never felt an adrenalin rush like it. I wanted that feeling again so I booked the Nevis Swing and they let me start in the harness upside down. I was in love with Queenstown. Everyone was so chilled and it was a good vibe wherever you went. Charles's housemate worked at the Skyline Luge and gave us free tickets. The gravity adventure experience overlooks Lake Wakatipu and involves tiny cars

that travel (at speed) down the mountain, through tunnels and sharp bends. It's good fun – even for two fully grown adults!

That night, we bought a bottle of Veuve (as you do) and went on a bar crawl. Queenstown nights out reminded me of university – lots of young, intoxicated people stumbling from bar to bar. Oddly, I bumped into university friend Matt Brady. We had a flaming sambuca together, and I haven't seen him since.

The following day was much more relaxing. We visited one of the world's most famous trees, 'That Wanaka Tree', got lost in the Wanaka maze and enjoyed some wine tasting, which had one of the best backdrops I've ever seen! The scenery was out of this world. No wonder Lord of the Rings was filmed there!

# 26

## Unwinding

After completing my final two weeks at work, I booked a five-day trip to the east coast. Harrogate friends Joe Collinge, Dan Mezzela and George Pike were backpacking around Australia. They were driving from Sunshine Coast to Byron Bay, so I joined them for a road trip. Sean Harris (also from Harrogate) was working in Sunshine so we had a mini reunion before setting off. One of the highlights was stopping at Nimbin – Australia's

most notorious hippie town. It's a cool spot, hidden away in the hills and a great place to unwind – in more ways than one! We wandered through the woodland and came across a shack covered in graffiti. Two old-timers were lighting up a joint on the steps. It was a nice vibe and so far removed from the hustle and bustle of Sydney.

I was expecting similar things from Byron Bay. My mates claimed it was the coolest place to hang out in Australia. Unfortunately, for us, it was overcast and the beach didn't look quite as Instagrammable as I'd hoped. We walked to the lighthouse on the hill and luckily the clouds dispersed to reveal a sunset of vibrant yellows, orange, pinks and purples.

## THE MIXER

I returned to Dubai with a new sense of drive and determination. Travelling and partying was a thing of the past and I was ready to become a legit, legally factual businessman and company owner. Together, with Tom, Sam and his girlfriend Daisy, we hired a lavish apartment on the 80th floor of Princess Tower in Dubai Marina – mistake number one. As a treat to ourselves for starting a company, we began our journey in luxury, wasting all our money on rent. In fairness, we were riding a wave of enthusiasm and things did start moving quick. Tom built the website and converted my logo design from scribble to graphic. Sam managed the finances and looked for deals on equipment. Using my contacts, I began networking and launched the social media pages. Our first purchase was the decks and speakers – the foundations of any successful DJ company!

# THE MIXER
## EVENTS & ENTERTAINMENT COMPANY

We were so excited that we set up our new equipment on the dining table and threw a party that night. We didn't invite anyone, it was just us three behind the decks and Daisy raving hard in front of us with a gin and tonic. It was a special moment. The boys didn't know each other well so it was the perfect bonding session. The following day we signed the trade licence and became an official company. I was 34 per cent majority stakeholder, with Sam and Tom both 33 per cent. It felt great. I immediately changed my Tinder bio to managing director and founder of The Mixer.

Through our friend Sally, we landed our first job – a 'Pimps and Hoes' villa party – in Dubai, I know! As well as DJs, they requested an LED dancefloor, lighting around the entire garden, karaoke and a projector screen. All this on our first event! It felt way over our heads but the money was fantastic so we said YES! The Dubai malls are expensive so we had to do some digging around the outskirts of the city. It called for a trip to Dragon Mart, a huge, indoor marketplace filled with rows and rows of stuff – lots of stuff! From bedding, to robots, to fridges, to bouncy castles, you name it, it's in there! I get lost every time but find some absolute bargains and the quality is good for the price. We bought uplights for the garden and hired the dancefloor. Ideally, we would've bought the dancefloor, but we had no storage other than our living room.

Due to licencing issues, it was hard to find a karaoke with good quality songs and most of the software was ancient. Eventually, we came across a Filipino karaoke set. The software wasn't too bad but the songs were all out of tune. We took the risk and bought it in the hope that guests would be so drunk they wouldn't realise. We paid what we rented it out for. Any sales after would be pure profit. Spoiler alert – we never sold the karaoke again.

For the projector, we found a company that would hire it out for a discounted rate – if we set it up ourselves. It sounded straightforward. Embarrassingly, whilst setting up, a strong wind passed through the neighbourhood, knocking the projector over. Tom suggested finding some rocks to use as a weight for the legs. The client's garden consisted of a pool, a jacuzzi and artificial grass so we had to try elsewhere. After driving around the community aimlessly we reached the main road. As we approached the roundabout to come back on ourselves, we noticed a pile of the finest mini boulders you're ever likely

to come across. We jumped out of the car and started loading the boot. It was peak-time traffic and everyone was looking at us like we had something wrong with us.

It was chaotic and disorganised, but we managed to deliver a successful first event. The pimps and hoes had a great night and there was plenty of dirty dancing. We learnt a lot of lessons by throwing ourselves in at the deep end, and the next few events became a breeze. Most parties were simple DJ set-ups with party lighting and uplights for the villas. As we entered busy season in November and December, we started making good money. Life was good. My parents were visiting at Christmas so I was eager to treat them. My plan was to pay for everything while they were in Dubai. I could finally start giving back after everything they'd done for me.

The Abu Dhabi Formula One was the biggest weekend of the year in the UAE and a great opportunity to make a name for ourselves, securing a slot on one of the VIP yachts by the track. As we were a new company with little experience, we struggled to find a yacht that would book us. To ensure I made money that weekend, I signed up as a bartender. During my first shift, I overheard the owners of the boat talking about hiring a DJ for the weekend. They had a guy lined up but I thought it's now or never and interrupted their conversation: 'I run a DJ company in Dubai and our best DJ, Tom, is available this weekend. He's played all over the world and supported big names, including Steve Angello and Claptone.' They asked how much we'd charge and on the spot I came out with 9,000 … per day! Our bookings were averaging 3,000 dirhams, so I tripled it as it was F1 weekend and last minute. Money clearly wasn't an issue for them. 'That works. Bring your guy tomorrow and he can play.' I was proud of myself, what a sale!

Sam drove Tom and the equipment to Abu Dhabi the following day. In addition to our normal speaker set-up, we had to hire subwoofers: firstly, due to how loud the Formula One cars are, and secondly, there are 50+ yachts all blasting out music, so it's a competition of who can be the loudest. They crammed everything they could into our little-rent-a-car and the rest travelled in my cousin's catering van. I was working on the yacht from sunrise to sunset so couldn't help with the equipment. From what they told me, it was a nightmare! It took them five trips from the car park to the yacht – a long way in the sweltering heat!

## Silver lining

On the very last trip, exhausted and carrying four bags each, they stumbled across the one and only Carl Cox. I was still upset with Carl for not replying to my tweet in Melbourne. Carl noticed Tom and Sam carrying DJ equipment and said hello. From then on, nothing

phased them, their weekend was made. Tom DJ'd all night and the crowd went wild, officially getting in the mixer! Although the client was impressed, their DJ friend wanted to play the remaining two days. All in all, it was a great experience and we made valuable contacts.

## Sky die've

For the first time in my life, I was making decent money. I wanted to spend it wisely … so booked a skydive. It was expensive but arguably boasts the best view of any skydive in the world. As you plummet from 13,000ft, you can see the Palm Jumeirah, World Islands, Burj Al Arab and even Burj Khalifa in the distance. As confident as I may have been, I discovered I still had breathing issues. I had asthma growing up but hadn't used an inhaler in years. For the entire free-fall, I couldn't inhale and my lungs felt like they were going to pop. The cameraman was gesturing to do a 'Superman' pose for the video but I was more concerned about the exploding veins on my forehead. I was seconds away from passing out when the parachute released and jolted me back into the sky. The release of pressure allowed me to take a big, deep breath and the remaining five minutes was pure bliss as we soared above the marina.

## Ho Ho Ho! Yo Ho Yo Ho!

For Christmas, Tom, Sam and I bought 'The Mixer' branded T-shirts for each other, to wear at events for brand awareness. I wore them every day, even sometimes to bed. My parents arrived Christmas Eve so we celebrated with a few drinks and went go-karting. Mum cried all the way around as people kept bashing into her. Ryan and Ben were due to skydive on Christmas Day but Ryan injured his back (at work, not go-karting). He asked if I wanted to take

his place and jump again. Before I could say yes, my dad (aged 61) interrupted: 'I'll do it!' Everyone laughed, but he was being deadly serious. He jumped the following morning dressed as Santa Claus and arrived at Christmas dinner with a big grin on his face.

Dad's love for adrenalin definitely rubbed off on me as a kid. During a holiday to Chile, I remember him jumping from Aunty Lis's roof into her pool. I thought he was so cool but Mum was furious at him for being a bad influence. A few years later, we were camping in the Yorkshire Dales with their friends. The other kids were playing on a tree swing over an ice-cold river but jumping back onto the muddy bank. When I had a go, I took a big run up, swung as far as I could and bombed into the water. As well as freezing, the currents were deceptively strong. Dad cursed and ran towards the water, but I remained calm and swam to shore.

It's good to do things that scare you.

As a special treat for my parents, I organised a pirate-themed yacht party. My cousin's catering company provided the food, our Venezuelan friend, Enrique, provided the pirate cocktails – and of course The Mixer provided the music. 32 friends signed up for the party and I collected 300 dirhams from each person to cover food, drinks and boat hire (the DJs played for free). We received funny looks from onlookers as I blasted 'He's a Pirate' leaving the marina. With a rum in hand, I looked like a less-good-looking Jack Sparrow behind the decks. It was one of the best yacht parties I'd been on and the party continued in a bar until the early hours. Stupidly, I had all the boat party cash on me and my friends believe someone took off with my wallet. I lost thousands.

## One of the most stressful weeks of my life

As you can imagine, it was one hell of a hangover. I called the yacht company, the taxi company, the bar, I couldn't find it anywhere. As well as The Mixer events, I'd been working extra hours with the catering company so I could spoil my parents. I went from hero to zero in a matter of rums.

For New Year's Eve, we had three events booked. Tom was DJing in a restaurant, Sam was DJing a villa party and I was DJing an Australian wedding in the desert. DJing a wedding in the desert sounds amazing but it was a logistical nightmare! A few weeks before the special day, I met the bride for a coffee. We discussed the vision for the music and set-up arrangements. The plan was for me to DJ on top of a sand dune for the ceremony and later move to a desert camp where they would host the evening party.

Family and friends had travelled from all over the world to be there, so I had to nail it. In hindsight, all three of us should've been there to deliver the event, but at the time we thought three incomes were better than one. There were two DJ set-ups, 12 lights, eight speakers and a projector screen to play background movies. I was freaking out the night before the event. There was so much to think about and the movies I'd downloaded weren't working. To make matters worse, I had to collect my friend Jess from the airport as she lent me her car. The stress was building so much that I had the most intense stress attack of my life. There was too much that could go wrong and I couldn't handle the thought of ruining their wedding day.

Thankfully, Sam supported me for the set-up in the morning before heading to his event. Our car wasn't built for sand so we transferred equipment to an off-road 4x4. Everything was on track as we arrived to the first location. For the ceremony, we hired an additional DJ controller as our main controller was being used for the evening party. The bastard thing wasn't working and we only had an hour to fix it until the first guests arrived. Thirty minutes after that, the bride would be arriving by camel, and if we didn't fix it by then I would've honestly let Sam bury me in the sand until I suffocated.

We tried everything to fix it but nothing was working. We were receiving feedback faintly from one speaker but the other wasn't working at all. The groom and groomsmen arrived early to greet the guests. Thankfully, they stood by the working speaker! The other

speaker was by the front of the ceremony so it was vital we fixed it. The guests started to arrive and take their seats. I was starting to panic and the fact it was 30 degrees in the middle of the desert and I was in a business shirt and trousers wasn't helping!

As we received the two-minute signal that the bride was coming over the dunes, Sam pressed something and both speakers kicked in. He grabbed me by the head with both hands and looked me dead in the eyes. 'Don't touch anything!' He was running late for his event so ran off into the distance. I DJ'd for the next 12 hours. Early on, I played cool chill-out music, including the likes of Air, 'La Femme d'Argent' and Groove Armada, 'At The River' (which references sand dunes). See, I'm clever like that.

We pulled it off and the ceremony was a success! It was a picturesque setting and I must say the music was on point, even the camel was gurning. The guests were being transferred by off-road cars to the desert camp venue (1km away). Once I'd packed down, I looked up to discover I'd been left – in the middle of the desert! I waited for ten minutes but nobody returned. I was left with only one option. I removed my shoes, gathered my belongings and ran across the desert. One kilometre, in wedding attire, in 30 degrees. Now that's what you call going the extra mile … or kilometre.

I arrived at the venue drenched with sweat and my tongue was stuck to the roof of my mouth. The set-up looked awesome, it was just lacking music! The guests hadn't taken their seats so thankfully it wasn't a big issue I was late. I played background music during the dinner which allowed me time to prepare the party music for later. The best man approached me and asked if I had David Bowie, 'Let's Dance'. He'd planned to

play the intro to the song before every joke he told during the speech. Luckily, I had it but some notice would've been nice! The waiters supplied me with a constant flow of canapés and beers which helped me settle into the evening. I had grandparents twisting to Chubby Checker, aunties and uncles twirling to Van Morrison and parents rocking to The Rolling Stones. As much as it wasn't my jam, I even had kids dancing to Taylor Swift and Bruno Mars.

As it struck midnight, the bride and groom were on their friend's shoulders and the guests held up sparklers as I played Kanye West, 'All Of The Lights'. I was dancing as much as they were – mainly in celebration of how I'd pulled it off! In the end, it couldn't have gone any better. Everyone came up to me and said how good it was. It was a huge relief! It was 3am by the time I arrived back to Dubai. My friends, Ahian and Pippa were still awake so I joined them for drinks to wind down. I'd been so busy I forgot to call my parents. We met for brunch the following day to celebrate the new year (they paid).

## Your set is on fire

It was a hectic end to the year, but I was glad my parents were finally able to experience Dubai. Most people have a negative misconception about Dubai – either saying it's fake or has no history. What I say is … it's making history! The DJ bookings continued rolling in. On 4 January, we were hired to DJ a luxury villa party in the Al Barari neighbourhood. We were playing for Dubai's elite and there was even a celebrity singer attending from one of Kygo's hit songs. As the party started taking shape and people began dancing, one guy decided to pour gasoline into the firepit. It exploded onto a group of people and set them on fire. One guest fell to the floor in agony, whilst the others sprinted towards the pool and dived in, head first. It was lit.

The guy rolling on the floor was attended to and taken to hospital. We were instructed to keep the music playing by the client – it was a weird vibe! The guests stayed but no one felt like dancing. We stuck to chilled disco, which kept people tapping their feet without causing offence. At the end of the night, the client thanked us for keeping the party going and apologised for the chaos. The guy survived, we got paid, all was good!

## Radioactive

Fabian was one of my best mates in Australia and had been inviting me to Germany for a while. It was the perfect opportunity to face my fears and go back to Time Warp Festival. Maybe it was careless after such an horrendous experience last time, but I wanted to prove to myself I'd become healthier and I wasn't going to let anxiety win. This is how my brain works.

As ever, I searched Skyscanner for the cheapest route. Dubai – Kyiv – Frankfurt. Next job was to find things to do in Kyiv. The top search result was 'Visit Chernobyl'. I didn't even know you could visit Chernobyl. Dark tourism has always been more appealing to me than nice beaches and museums. The thought of a site like that, left untouched for so many years, really piqued my curiosity. I knew I had to go.

I faced difficulties outside Boryspil International Airport trying to figure out which bus would take me to the city. A guy in a beaten-up, yellow Volkswagen beeped his horn and shouted me over. It's natural to be pre-judgemental towards locals when visiting a foreign country. At first, I tried to ignore him and look the other way, but he kept persisting. I walked over and he offered to take me to the city for the same price as the bus. His car looked dodgy but he seemed genuine enough and was playing good music so I accepted his offer.

You can judge a lot by someone's music taste.

He turned out to be one of the funniest people I've ever met! He had me in stitches going on about how beautiful women were in Ukraine but how ugly he and his friends were. 'None of them want to fuck us! They all move abroad for good sex!' In fairness, the women really were beautiful. Even in McDonalds, it was like being at New York Fashion Week. Tall, slim (not fat shaming, I'm overweight as I type this) and beautiful eyes. I signed up to the Wi-Fi and searched for hostels in the area. Luckily there was one nearby, so after I finished my сирний бургер та картопля фрі, I walked down to check in.

Initially, I felt cautious and intimidated as I walked around. The sky was a moody grey and many of the local men were stocky builds with leather jackets and shaved heads. It was stupid really, every person I met in Ukraine was extremely friendly and just because the sky is grey doesn't mean you're going to get kidnapped. If that was the case, Manchester would have the highest kidnap rate in the world.

I selected a 12-bed dorm in the hope of meeting other people. Connor, a politics student from North Carolina, was also checking in. He seemed cool so we headed to a restaurant. We had a delicious beef and potato stew accompanied by a beer and it only came to £3 each! After the meal, I logged into Tinder to see if there were any locals who knew of somewhere good to go out drinking – that's all I was after I promise! I started talking to a girl and she invited me to one of her local bars. 'Is it okay if I bring my friend Connor?' It was a weird request on a 'first date' but I explained how we were in the same hostel. As the date was in a sports bar we began talking about football. Liverpool were in the semi-finals of the UEFA Champions League and had to get past AS Roma to reach the final, which was to be held in Kyiv's NSC Olimpiyskiy stadium.

I was rambling on about how much I love Liverpool and that I'd come back to Ukraine if we reached the final. In a fairly tranquil manner, she interrupted me. 'I work for UEFA.' My face dropped. 'What!? That's so cool! So you'll be working at the match?' 'Yeah! I will be looking after the VIPs in the hospitality lounge. I can't make any promises but I can ask around and see if there's anyone selling tickets closer to the time.' The date was a success! I now had a 1 per cent chance of getting a ticket. I felt bad for Connor as we'd been talking about soccer-ball the whole time.

Always choose hostels over hotels if you are travelling alone. You are more likely to meet like-minded people who you can travel with, share experiences with … and even share dates with!

Following breakfast, I made my way to the 'Chernobyl Tour' meeting point. I booked with the company that had the most imaginative name – Chernobyl Tour. It had a nice ring to it. They were a well-organised company and the Ukrainian tour guide was brilliant. She spoke fluent English and knew the entire history of Chernobyl, the city and also the events surrounding the disaster that occurred on Saturday, 26 April 1986. I was last on the bus and the only seat available was next to a Ukrainian woman. The first hour of the journey was complete silence until I broke the ice. 'Hey, so what made you visit?'

'I was born in Chernobyl and there the night of the disaster. We were evacuated and this is the first time I've been back.' I was stunned! 'It was too sad to return but now I am old enough and have the courage.' I didn't know what to say but tried to be comforting. I couldn't imagine what it must've been like to be evacuated from home, leaving all personal belongings and childhood memories behind.

At the entrance to the Exclusion Zone we were handed our Geiger counters. They were $10 to rent and provided radiation levels in the area. It was interesting seeing the levels fluctuate depending on which building or tree we were next to. As we stepped inside the first abandoned building, we noticed one of the bedrooms still had children's toys on the bed. It was eerie! The kitchen had plates, saucepans, cutlery and even bottles of vodka in the cupboard. It was surreal knowing there was once life in this place.

My Geiger counter was showing between 1 and 2 microSieverts during our first few stops. Those numbers weren't too high so I was fascinated to see what it could reach as we approached the city and the reactor. Before lunch, we had the opportunity to walk

through the iconic children's playground. Gaming fans will recognise it from one of the maps on Call of Duty. There's an 85ft Ferris wheel, abandoned bumper cars and swing boats. I remember the intro to the game: 'Fifty thousand people used to live here, now it's a ghost town.' It really was a ghost town. There was no life anywhere. The bumper cars were all rusty and covered in wilted leaves.

With the Ferris wheel being such a large metal structure, I decided to test my Geiger counter up close. It spiked from 1 microSieverts to 40 in a matter of seconds. I stepped back from fear I'd become infected and turn into a mutant Wolverine.

Despite the incalculable number of mammal and birds that died due to radiation, some life returned to the Exclusion Zone. Wild foxes, boars and even bears wander through the lush green forests surrounding the power plant. Thankfully, I only saw a fox. Although, it did have unnaturally bright blue, radioactive-looking eyes.

When they said lunch was included, I presumed it meant a sandwich and drink delivered from Kyiv. It turned out there was a restaurant overlooking the power plant. Aside from it looking like prison food, I was concerned about how radioactive it was. I scanned the meal with my Geiger counter and it showed 0.7 microSieverts. Surely the food you're ingesting should have zero radiation!? After learning about Chernobyl in school, I never thought I'd be sat opposite the power plant enjoying mince and gravy-covered mashed potato.

Before heading back to Kyiv, we took photos outside the nuclear reactor. The guide assured us it was safe as long as we weren't there too long. I'll let you know in a couple of years if I've grown any extra toes. It was an amazing experience and like no other place I'd been to. Walking through the abandoned classrooms, supermarkets and bedrooms will stay with me forever. I still have nightmares from the creepy dolls with no eyes that were left on children's beds.

## Facing my fears

I was facing my demons going back to Time Warp again but promised myself to take it easy. I spent the whole night dancing with Fabian, Janaína and Clara, which was great as I'd not seen them since Sydney, and I bumped into Alex Blakemore from Harrogate. Thanks to drinking water regularly and not drinking much alcohol, I lasted until 11am and didn't feel bad. It sounds stupid but I'm proud I went back and enjoyed myself without going too hard.

*Fabian and I, representing our old Sydney house, 'Manning Road'.*

## The golden ticket

A few weeks later, Liverpool secured their place in the Champions League final. I was at home in Dubai watching Netflix when I received a message from my Ukrainian Tinder date. 'I found you a Champions League final ticket!' I danced around the apartment, shouting and screaming. Her housemate secured a job working in the stadium so agreed to sell his ticket (face value) to me and they also let me stay in their house for a week. I couldn't believe it.

I'd recently joined the Dubai Reds Liverpool Supporters' Club. The chairman, Neil Briody, was boarding the same flight to Kyiv so we met for a pint and travelled over together. He was a die-hard Liverpool fan and had been to some of the biggest games in recent history. The Ukrainian people were fantastic. Many of the hotels bumped up the prices to extortionate amounts. In response, the locals made a Facebook group offering their houses for Liverpool and Real Madrid fans to stay in for free. It was a great example of how sport can bring people together. We dropped our bags at Neil's apartment, he changed into his Liverpool branded shoes (which he wears for good luck) and we hit the city. Neil ordered two pints of San Miguel. When the bill arrived, he had to double-check

his currency converter. 'Sixty-five pence!?' It was his first time in Ukraine. I've never seen a man so happy at the price of a beer.

The atmosphere at the fan zone was electric. Liverpool and Real Madrid fans were drinking together, singing songs and taking part in activities. At one end of the fan zone, they had a five-a-side pitch. Neil started laughing and pointed at one of the guys on the pitch: 'What on earth is he doing wearing jeans playing football!?' I looked closely. 'Because it's Cafu. He can do what he wants.' The former Brazilian international was amongst a bunch of celebrities playing the game, including Andriy Shevchenko and heavyweight boxers Vitali and Wladimir Klitschko. I signed up to play in one of the later games so I could say I've graced the same pitch as Cafu. I wasn't graceful though, I'd had ten 65p pints.

The party really started when the rest of the Dubai Reds arrived. Thirty of us singing and dancing with our flags and scarves. One of our flags read 'TAX DODGERS ON TOUR'. Live bands played in the day and DJs mixed into the night. It didn't matter which bar you went in, the majority of people in there were Liverpool fans. Whenever Madrid fans started singing a song we'd drown them out. It was all in good fun and I never saw violence or anger towards one another. Football fans get a lot of bad press, but that weekend fans showed their support in the right way – how it should be.

For match day, we met in Shevchenko Park, the Liverpool fan zone. As ever, Scousers packed out the venue. Beer was flowing … and flying everywhere! I was concerned about losing or dampening my ticket so hid it in the middle of my bag. It was the most valuable ticket in the world that day. Musician Jamie Webster and podcasting legends Redmen TV got the crowd going, singing Liverpool anthems. I bumped into Chris from Redmen TV in a bar before the match. It was cool to see him as I'd been watching all their build-up shows.

The walk to the stadium still gives me shivers. The sun was setting as thousands of fans marched down the street with their scarves raised high. I entered the turnstiles with Ryan Knowles (Dubai friend) half-expecting my ticket to flag up as fake. 480 million people tuned in for the match, and I was there! Unfortunately, my seat was in a neutral

section beside the Madrid fans. Abuse was directed at me and my red shirt as I walked down to watch the teams train. I was jealous of the Liverpool fans on the other side of the ground singing 'You'll Never Walk Alone' and 'Fields of Anfield Road' but I couldn't complain. Dua Lipa kicked things off with her performance of 'One Kiss'. Every person in the stadium was jumping and singing.

The first half of the match was nail-biting stuff, quite literally. There was nothing between the two sides, but the big talking point was Sergio Ramos's deliberate foul on Mohamed Salah. Salah went off injured, holding his head in his hands (mainly to hide the tears). We were all crying too … Salah was our star player and our main hope of winning the Champions League.

The second half was a rollercoaster of emotions. Our young goalkeeper, Loris Karius, messed up by throwing the ball to Karim Benzema, allowing him to score an open goal. Sadio Mane clawed one back for us to even the scoring at 1-1. I thought we were back in

with a chance until Welshman Gareth Bale scored arguably the greatest-ever Champions League final goal – an overhead kick into the top corner. Karius then spilled Bale's shot into the back of the net to make it 3-1. Being next to the Madrid fans was painful. We'd worked so hard to reach the final and lost due to two freak goals. As the final whistle blew, my side of the stadium erupted and the Madrid bench ran onto the pitch. Loris Karius was left alone with his face in the grass, crying his eyes out. As much as he was to blame, you can't imagine what he must have been feeling. Eventually, someone pulled him to his feet and he made his way to the Liverpool fans, raising his hands in apology. That took some guts.

We were deflated and heartbroken but still congratulated Madrid fans in the street and drank with them while they celebrated. My time in Kyiv was almost up. I said goodbye to my hosts and met up with my Ukrainian friend Ievgen, who I worked with in Dubai. He introduced me to Borscht soup (delicious) and showed me around the Holy Dormition Caves and the Motherland Monument (World War Two monument).

## You're crazy!

Back in Dubai, temperatures were soaring above 50 degrees celsius and events were drying up (quite literally). I returned to the UK for summer and made use of the free rent at my parents' house (I cleaned dishes and cooked occasionally, I promise). In the first week of being home, I broke my collarbone in a collision at football. I was up against a 6ft 5in midfielder so wanted to show him I was up for a battle. He went to control a throw-in and I dived headfirst to win the ball. He kicked me so hard in the face that I crashed to the ground, landing on my shoulder. The crack was so loud the referee stopped the game. In my confused state, I tried to play on but felt two bones moving under my skin and dropped back to my knees. I'm not much of a complainer and because you couldn't see the damage under my shirt, I don't think people realised how bad it was. Nobody helped me, it was weird. I walked myself off the pitch and to the hospital down the road.

The pain was as sharp as the broken rib I'd suffered 12 months before. After a week of agony in bed, I was eager to get out the house. The lads invited me on a country walk. 'That would be nice!' A leisurely walk, in fresh air, catching up with friends, having a pint in an old traditional pub. Exactly what I needed! It wasn't until I was in the car I discovered we were climbing Helvellyn, the third highest peak in England.

It wasn't quite Everest but there have been many injuries and even fatalities traversing the sharp-topped ridge. With vertical drops either side of the ridge, it usually requires all fours to climb across the boulders. I had a sling so it was all threes for me. People were giving me funny looks. 'You're crazy!' That only eggs me on though.

Work opportunities were hard to come by with one arm. I was desperate for cash so took a job in a chocolate factory. I didn't tell them my collarbone was broken and for two days kept my left hand gripped to my right shoulder for support. The job was to remove chocolates from the conveyor belt and place them into packaging. Sounds easy but I had to work twice as fast. By the end of each day my good arm was hurting more than the

broken one! Eventually, the manager noticed I was doing it one handed and took me to one side. It was clear I couldn't keep it up and I was back to being jobless.

## Against all clods

The only income I had for the following week was to come from the bowling green. Despite being in a sling, Dad and I qualified for the prestigious Harrogate Pairs Finals Day at Knaresborough. Sixteen pairs qualified and we were major underdogs. I had one arm and Dad rarely played competitively. Due to the scorching hot weather, the green quickened and Dad struggled to keep his bowls on the green. Knaresborough was one of my old home greens so I managed to bowl well enough to get us through the first round and into the last eight. For the next two games, Dad was unbelievable! He fine-tuned his delivery and delicately dropped them down the hill, onto the jack.

Growing up, whether it be on a bowling green or football pitch, Dad was always on the sideline supporting me. He dedicated his free time to ensure I was involved with sports and competition. It was special to have him with me for this one.

Despite how well we'd bowled to reach the final, my firing was all over the place. The sling was causing me to be off-balance when releasing the bowl at speed. In the final, we were up against brothers Jason and Paul Worsnop. They won the coin toss so Jason set a difficult mark that just crept over the crown. The grass dried up so much that the green was almost unplayable. We went 14-0 down. Dad managed to score one point and put us back in the game (sort of) at 14-1. With the jack in his hands, Dad could go anywhere he wanted. He chose the corner that served us so well in the previous games. Unfortunately, the surface was like glass and the jack flew off the green into the gutter. Jason took us back on his mark, and three ends later we were 20-1 down.

The Worsnops needed one more point to win the competition and Paul's last bowl was almost touching the jack. I had one bowl left to save us from complete embarrassment. In true Hollywood style (despite only 50 people watching), I ripped the sling off my shoulder, flung it into the air and announced to the crowd I was firing. I thought fuck it. I

threw it as hard as I could and smashed Paul's bowl off the green. The crowd were on their feet applauding, and laughing, because I threw the sling off. Unfortunately, the mountain was too high to climb and we bowed out the following end 21-2. I was proud of Dad and will cherish that day for the rest of my life. We walked away with £80 for our efforts – enough for an Indian takeaway and a crate of beers.

## It's coming home

The plus side of being stuck at home was the 2018 FIFA World Cup had kicked off in Russia. England were growing in confidence and playing well. As we reached the knockout stages, the whole country started to believe. For each game, Tom McGinness booked a private room for us in The Empress on the Stray – another pub his mother Sharon and husband Simon own. The atmosphere was amazing! I'd never seen the people of England so happy … usually everyone is depressed. We took the lead in the semi-final and, as pessimistic as I have been watching England over the years, I started to believe too. I should've known better. Two late goals from Croatia ruined the dreams of so many good, honest, pissed, little Englanders that night. I can't even imagine the scenes if we'd have made the final.

By the end of the World Cup, my collarbone had healed enough to apply for jobs again. I secured a short-term contract for a company that produced fly zappers and mouse traps. I shared a work station with a fellow temp called Sean. He was a few years younger but we had a laugh, playing silly games to pass the time. I knew I wasn't going to be there forever so appreciated it for the stress-free job it was.

Thanks to contributing to the killing of millions of flies over summer, I'd saved up enough money to fly back to Dubai. I even squeezed in a lads' trip to Bratislava and a few days in Budapest on the way. After a full day's bar crawl, Charles led us to Subclub, a nightclub situated in a soviet bunker under the Bratislava castle. When we arrived, there was a group of teenagers smoking outside. They said they were too young to go in but liked listening to the beat of the music. We followed the ludicrously fast beat down a long, dark tunnel. Charles forgot to warn us it was a psychedelic trance night. Six of us (dressed in shit-shirts) found ourselves on the dancefloor surrounded by Slovakia's biggest, hardcore psychedelic trance heads. I told Charles I needed something stronger than beer to get me through the night. He returned with a tray of absinthe. Fucking absinthe!

That's the end of the story because I don't remember anything after that. It was one of the worst hangovers of my life. Thanks Charles! I spent 24 hours in bed before boarding an 8 euro bus to Budapest to swim in the Szechenyi Baths.

# 27

## (13 September 2018 – 12 September 2019)

### Year two of The Mixer – Dubai's most successful company with a ridiculous name

We were back! We just had no money to fund the bloody thing. Sam and I were broke and homeless so moved into our friend's sister's family house – they offered! I'd been playing football in the expat league the previous season but wanted to challenge myself at a higher level. I spoke with Kevin Fairhurst who ran the league and he put me in touch with Kev and Cobby who managed Dubai Allstars in the DAFL League. Many ex-professionals and former academy players played in the DAFL. Allstars were an established club in the region and nearly as old as Dubai itself! I trialled with the fourth team and played a

near-perfect game so they bumped me up to the thirds. I was working hard on my fitness outside of football and cemented my place in central-midfield for the upcoming season. Despite being the third team, it was full of talented footballers who could've been playing semi-professionally back home.

Before the first game of the new season, the coaches were pulling out the new shirts from a box and throwing them randomly to each player. Of course, the one that landed on my lap was my lucky number – 64.

Running The Mixer was challenging and frustrating. We could have three events one weekend and make decent money, then go a month without another booking. To support the business (and ourselves) we continued to take extra shifts with the catering company. We'd feel like giving the business up, then all of a sudden we'd land a crazy gig in a huge villa, with super rich people and models, and be like ah fuck it, this is the life! One of our bookings was for a famous model and former Big Brother housemate. Events like that provided the motivation to keep pushing.

## Meeting the girl of my dreams

I was done with serving canapés to rich people, especially as I was now a business owner and senior supervisor of events. However, I had to put my ego to one side when my cousin asked me to work for an A-list celebrity on a yacht. They told us it was a 'VVVVVVVVIP' but we didn't know who until they arrived. My first task was to manage the guest list and tick people's names as they embarked. Fifteen people checked in and I didn't recognise anyone. The VIP names read 'H +1'. I was thinking, Really? Ian Watkins from the 90s pop group Steps? That would've been a bit of an anti-climax (no offence Ian). Eventually, a posh car turned up … and out stepped Rihanna.

Play it cool Cory, play it cool. I tried saying hello but couldn't even manage those five letters. I exhaled something like 'Hweho'. She was elegant and cool, saying hello to everyone she passed. The 'H' she arrived with was her then-boyfriend, a Saudi billionaire businessman. In fairness, he was cool too … I was just jealous! They were in Dubai celebrating his birthday. I had seven hours on a private yacht with Rihanna – living the dream! I was hoping paparazzi would ride by in a speedboat so we'd get papped together. Unfortunately, our phones were confiscated!

Champagne was flowing, the sun was shining and 'Ri-Ri' was dancing in a glistening, golden dress. Eventually, I overcame the nerves and relaxed into the experience, helping her with drink orders. Not many people get to say they partied *worked with Rihanna. She approached me before going to the bathroom. 'Hey, can I give you this?' As she passed her half-empty drink to me, my colleague noticed her lipstick on the straw. His eyes lit up and he nodded in slow motion for me to drink it. I shook my head and took the drink to the clearance area. As I lowered it into the crate, I paused, and thought … Fuck it!

The following night, they booked us for a private dinner in a luxurious beach house. The interior was like a jungle, with trees and a stream running through the middle. We served welcome canapés before a civilised sit-down dinner. Everything seemed under control and security were patrolling the premises. I expected things to fizzle out after the dinner but they prepared a dancefloor. In the words of Lil Jon, 'Shots! Shots! Shots! Shots! Shots! Shots!' Enrique (bartender) asked me to cover him on the bar while he went to the toilet. Rihanna was 'lit' – whatever that means. She stumbled up to the bar and requested 'Five tequilas please!' (She was always polite). By the time I'd finished pouring the fifth one, she forgot she'd ordered them and wandered off. Moments later there was a huge bang. Someone fell onto the glass table and it smashed everywhere. That signified the end of the night and it was the last time I saw Rihanna. Still to this day, she's the friendliest and most genuine celebrity I've met.

## Highs and lows

December was a successful month for the business. I was ballin'. The following month, Kelly and Ryan were getting married in Melbourne, Australia. They'd asked Sam and I to DJ so it was a relief knowing I could afford to go. For New Year's Eve, we DJ'd a rooftop party for a British billionaire. Every firework display in Dubai was visible from the top and it had a jacuzzi and cocktail bar. We wanted to make a good impression to the client so we agreed not to drink much. The more the hosts drank, the more they encouraged us to drink with them. I lost count of how many Café Patron shots we had. They were a lovely, welcoming family and wanted us to enjoy the New Year celebrations as much as them. Everyone was wasted and we partied through till sunrise. It was an unbelievable night. Although, I probably shouldn't have made out with the billionaire's daughter and jumped in the jacuzzi fully clothed.

In general, Tom, Sam and I worked well together. Considering we were all new to running a business, we'd done a commendable job. We had a smart-looking website, an ever-growing social media following and we were building a reputation in Dubai. Due to increases in income and success, complications over money arose. We argued over profit distribution and what was fair. It wasn't pleasant at times. There were some awkward and tough conversations. Looking back, that was all part of the learning process and I took many valuable things away from those experiences.

Daisy had moved back to Australia and Sam was finding the long-distance relationship tough. During our final gig before flying to Melbourne, Sam broke the news. He'd booked a one-way flight to Australia with no plans to come back. This was a big blow as he was a vital part of the team. We were a tripod and we were losing one of our legs (insert sad emoji). Sam's final party was a rich 18-year-old's birthday. They emailed a brief of what music they wanted – we didn't have any of it! It was all this Mumble Crap/Rap malarkey. What are kids listening to these days!? I felt like such an old man. The lyrics to every song were like, 'Uh, yeh, fuckin' this, fuckin' that, uh, iddy, fiddy, biddy, tiddy.' They're giving rap a bad name. That's my take on it. Apologies if I've offended anyone in the mumble business.

## It's wedding season!

It was set to be the wedding of the year! Kelly and Ryan had become two of my best mates since cousin Danny introduced me to them in 2013. Whether it be offering their spare room or giving me advice, they've always been there for me. When Kelly asked us to DJ their wedding, we felt honoured and couldn't say no! They booked a three-storey house for the Dubai crew in the edgy suburb of Fitzroy. Graffiti art decorated the narrow alleys of the hip neighbourhood and there were vegan restaurants bloody everywhere. As a thank you for making the trip over, the happy couple (to-be) placed a bottle of champagne next to each of our beds. There was also an envelope containing a few lines… I promise it was just kind words! For our standards, it was a fairly civilised evening as we had the stag and hen party the following day.

Ryan's best mate Jaz (female) was the best man/woman and organised a trip to Melbourne Races. Just what I needed! I'd worked my ass off all season to blow the money on some horses running around in circles. I'm not sure what the girls were doing for the hen party – probably drinking cocktails out of mini-dick straws. For the first few races, we all lost money, but we didn't care. The boys (and Jaz) were all together, getting loose and celebrating Ryan's last day of freedom. As we were about to leave, Steve suggested we all bet on one final horse. None of us were keen to lose any more money, but in the name of love we agreed to do one more. It was the last race of the day and it bloody won! We went straight to the bar and bought a huge round of drinks. In the end, we didn't make any money (as we spent it all) but at least we made some memories.

Next up, was a taxi to the casino – to lose more money! We crowded around a roulette table in the middle of the hall and ordered a round of rum and cokes. As the others were too intoxicated, Steve and I organised a team pot and any profits we made would be split evenly. It couldn't have gone any better. As the ball span around the wheel, we'd cheer it on and when it landed, we'd erupt into celebrations. We kept winning, over and over again! Every time we won, we'd order another round of drinks. Maybe that was our downfall, otherwise we'd have walked out with an obscene amount of cash. Nonetheless, I'd been out all day and not spent a dollar!

To finish the night in style, we headed to the local strip club – to lose more money! This is where the night really took off. I'll save Ryan the embarrassment, but, long story short, he dressed up as a gimp and was whipped by a dominatrix to the point of bleeding. To finish, he had to crawl naked across the stage 'meowing' like a cat – naked, because the dominatrix wedgied him so hard his boxers ripped off. Like all great stag parties, they're ruined by the girlfriends turning up. The lad's faces as the girls rocked up mid-lap dance was a sight to behold. At first, it was awkward, but eventually everyone laughed about it and even the girls had lap dances.

We had six days to kill before the wedding and I'd always wanted to visit the Great Barrier Reef. Sally, Westy, Sam, Daisy and Mel agreed to join and we flew out to Cairns the following morning. We swam with exotic fish, hiked through the Daintree Rainforest

during a storm, sunbathed in Port Douglas, fed wild crocodiles and Mel took part in a naked jelly wrestling match – and won! I had an amazing time but felt guilty for going to the Great Barrier Reef. As I snorkelled, I could see most of the coral was dead and colourless. I even witnessed tourists kicking it to boost them back to the surface.

We returned to Melbourne for the special day. A team of hair and makeup artists arrived to pamper the girls whilst the lads ironed their suits and gelled their hair. The girls were sipping champagne and the guys were doing vodka syringe shots. Whilst they were getting ready, Sam and I headed to the venue to prepare the music. The wedding was held at Melbourne Zoo and you could see the animals as part of the experience. The ceremony took place in the garden whilst monkeys were swinging in the trees. We played chill-out music with some cheesy romantic songs thrown in. Ryan wasn't too keen as he's a big metalhead, but you have to play to the majority … and the bride! Shamelessly, I bought Steve Madden, snake-skin shoes for the wedding. I saw them glistening in a shop window and they fit the theme – I couldn't not get them!

It was emotional watching Kelly and Ryan tie the knot. I'd actually never seen Ryan in anything other than a vest and shorts. Once we got all the I dos and love yous out the way, it was time to party! Danny was the MC and cracked a few jokes before the speeches. Unfortunately, we had issues with the equipment and couldn't access the wedding playlists we'd prepared. The evening party was a wing-job using a spare USB we had from an event, but everyone had a great time and the dancefloor remained full most the night.

I woke up at 3pm to the smell of cooking kangaroo. In all my time in Australia, I'd never tried one so I joined the BBQ downstairs. It was so tough that when I tried to tear it with my teeth, it flew out my mouth and landed on the floor. I gave up and went back to bed. Business was quiet in January so I had the flexibility to extend my stay in Australia. The following day, I booked a flight to Sydney to reunite with my old mates. I moved places every few days and caught up with almost everyone from Watson's Bay and Manning Road.

## Return to Sydney

Like the old days, Jack collected me from the airport and we went for burritos at our favourite restaurant. I spent a few days with Manda and treated her to ice cream at our favourite spot. Whilst staying with Débora and Gabi, I met their housemate Janaína. During a conversation at lunch, it became clear we shared a similar passion for travel. Janaína had also been to Everest Base Camp and favoured adventure holidays over lounging about in fancy hotels. She was planning to backpack South-East Asia later in the year and invited me to join. Initially, I said yes, but in truth, I didn't know where I would be or what money I would have. After two weeks of partying with old friends, it hit me how much I had missed Sydney. I don't usually live with regrets but I did feel like I'd left a place I truly loved prematurely.

The question was whether moving back to Dubai to further advance my career was the right move.

Shout-out to: Jack, Manda, Débora, Gabi, Bhea, Bastien, Fabian, Victor, Renata, Estel, Lucas, Mel, Paula, Rebecka, Emilia, Josefin, Camilla, Matteo, Sami, Ross, Julien and everyone who made those two weeks so good and looked after me!

## Heading west!

I felt satisfied with how much I'd done on the north, east and south coasts of Australia, so it was time to squeeze in a quick visit to the west. After the wedding, Daisy and Sam travelled to stay with Daisy's parents in Busselton (two hours south of Perth). Busselton boasts the southern hemisphere's longest jetty (1.8km long) and is the gateway to one of my parents' favourite wine regions – Margaret River. Sam, Daisy and her brother Luke arranged to pick me up from Perth in the evening and take me to the Big Bash League game between Perth Scorchers and Melbourne Stars (Australia's version of Twenty-20 cricket). I had a few hours to kill so took a train to Fremantle as I heard the port city was famous for fish and chips. A bar overflowing with people was offering free beer tastings. I felt inclined to sign up. The waitress must've misheard me as she delivered ten beers to my table. Ten! I was on my own so there was only one thing to do … I drank them all one by one and reviewed them on my Instagram story, @coryeveryday_.

When I returned to Perth, Sam suggested meeting at a bar close to the train station. More beers! I couldn't wait to return to Dubai and start my rehabilitation. I was never a fan of cricket – probably because I sucked at it. Chris Hooper invited me down a few times to help his team when they were short. I couldn't bowl or bat but I was decent at catching so they put me at the back of the field to prevent sixes. Thinking back, they probably just wanted me as far away from the game as possible. I was pleasantly surprised at how fun the Big Bash cricket was! Fireworks were popping off everywhere and fans were raving to the music in the intervals.

The next morning, we followed the coastline down to Busselton via some spectacular beaches. Due to my fear of sharks, I was content admiring the gorgeous blue water and not actually going in. Daisy's phone pinged: 'Ooo! Dad says he's going to take you two out in his fishing boat tomorrow!' I wasn't impressed. I responded with a less than convincing 'Great!' I had no intention of paddling in great white shark-infested waters, never mind floating in the abyss, inside a small, 20-year-old, rusty fishing boat. I'd met Kathy and Peter (Daisy's parents) briefly once before, but I really got to know them that evening when we played Cards Against Humanity. I can't believe we played that around the dinner table. Daisy's parents lived on a farm and their house was surrounded by wild kangaroos. After dinner we went out to see them. Some of them were built like heavyweight boxers so

I kept my distance. When I looked up, I saw a sky as clear as the one I saw in the Atacama Desert. They went to bed and left me gazing in the garden. I couldn't stop looking up. It brought back the same goosebumps I experienced before. Sometimes you have to leave the city to see how beautiful the world is.

We were up early to help Pete load the car. Kathy made us a big breakfast to keep us going until we returned home. *If we returned home. The sharks were playing on my mind. What if we capsized? As we left the harbour and headed out to sea, we noticed a large cruise ship in the distance. It was the Queen Elizabeth! The 294-metre long, $530 million luxury cruise ship was making a 38-day voyage from Southampton (UK) to Melbourne. As we circumnavigated the ship we received whistles and waves from the people on the terrace. The difference in size was frightening.

It was a nice distraction from the dangerous (or what I perceived to be dangerous) waters we were in. Pete said he'd never seen a shark whilst out in his boat. That didn't make me feel any more relaxed though. I suspected he was only saying that to make us feel better. Once we travelled far enough, Pete handed us two fishing rods. The goal was to catch some food for the BBQ that night. This was before watching the Seaspiracy documentary! With the girls waiting at home, I felt an added responsibility to ensure they didn't go the night hungry. Pete said there was tuna fish in abundance and we shouldn't go home with anything less. We were out in the sun for hours and with our pale skin, it looked like the only thing the girls were getting that night were two overcooked lobsters.

Fishing requires patience. It was late afternoon when a school of tuna fish bolted past the boat. 'Now!' shouted Pete. We threw both lines and within seconds we could feel a tug. 'Reel them in!' It was that much of a tussle I thought I had a shark! I was using all my strength and it was barely tightening up. Finally, after two minutes, this giant tuna reached the surface. I was ecstatic, in pure amazement, I'd managed to catch one on my first fishing trip. Seconds later, Sam pulled another tuna out. It was equal in size and we had enough food to feed the entire town. Pete threw one back in the ocean and gutted the other, placing it in ice. Despite coming back heroes and providing dinner for the family, I was caught in two minds as to whether I could end an animal's life again.

Before flying back to the sandpit, we sampled wine in Margaret River and tubed down the Wellington Dam rapids. I was upset to be leaving Australia (again), but knew it wouldn't be my last time.

## New beginnings

I was back to square one: homeless, jobless and moneyless. Kelly and Ryan let me crash at their place until I figured things out. In the meantime, I worked a few shifts with the catering company and DJ'd a Valentine's Day party. The Mixer wasn't providing enough stability and Tom was leaving in April to DJ in Mallorca. I was at a crossroads in my life. I didn't know whether to stay in Dubai, move back to the UK or try somewhere new, like Canada … or Mars. Out of nowhere, I received a call from Valeriya, an old work colleague. She'd been the catering manager at a healthy food company for the past year but was looking for a new challenge. Valeriya recommended me as a replacement and asked if I could go in for an interview the following week.

I saw it as a great opportunity. I had nothing else going for me and to have 'manager' in my title appealed to me. I bought new shoes, new jeans, a new white shirt and wore my favourite blue jacket. And of course, I got my hair did. I went into the interview with a relaxed, care-free attitude. If I didn't get it, I would leave Dubai, and if I got it I would give it everything. The CEO was immediately impressed by my hospitality background. When I told her I also owned a company that sealed the deal. Despite interviewing five others they called me back the following day to offer me the job.

Even if starting my own company was a risk and may not be classed as an overall success, at least I took a chance. Through all the experiences and lessons I learnt running The Mixer, I was able to land a manager role with a big company.

The day before starting my new job, I was going through the menus when Dario, my assistant manager at Dubai Allstars, called: 'Can you get to Jebel Ali in 30 minutes for a game?' 'I guess. Who are we playing?' 'You're not playing. I need you to be a linesman for England versus Scotland legends match. I'm the referee and one of the linesmen dropped out.' I arrived at the changing room in 25 minutes and was on the pitch in my officiating uniform in 30. I was horrified when I saw the line-ups. I'd never been a referee or linesman in my life. Kevin Phillips, Ally McCoist, Colin Hendry, Lee Hendrie, all these legends of the game and I was calling their offsides. I felt so vulnerable with my pathetic little flag on the sideline. To make it worse, all the Scotland fans were drinking in a large group next to me.

I thought it would only be the Scots giving me abuse, but it turned out both teams despised me (as a linesman). I was called a twat by Kevin Phillips (a hero of mine), and Colin Hendry, one of the scariest people in football, made me feel like a three-year-old child being told off by his war veteran grandad. I got distracted by the action and completely missed an offside. An England player was five yards offside and tapped the ball in but I'd not raised my flag so stuck with my decision. Despite it being a charity game, Colin Hendry stormed across the pitch and managed to fit in about 35 swearwords in a 10-second rant towards me. It was horrible but I appreciated his passion. Still that will to win so many years after his retirement was impressive. I couldn't wait for the half-time whistle to blow. The second half was as bad as the first, and I can safely say I will never do that ever again.

Kevin Phillips shook my hand at the end and said, 'Well done mate but you were a bit dodgy early on!' Although he called me a twat (which was deserved), that cheered me up and made me appreciate the whole experience.

For the first two weeks, Valeriya was on hand to train me before she left. I couldn't believe how much work was involved. I was noticing early signs of why she was leaving. Luckily, I had catering supervisor Sam Katende to support me. Sam was from Uganda but a lifelong Liverpool fan. When we weren't talking about work, we'd be talking about Liverpool. My catering team also consisted of Jerry and Joe from the Philippines and

Manoj from India. They were great guys and worked hard under difficult circumstances. I hit the ground running and started smashing the sales targets. I was working 16-hour days and landing some big deals in the process. It became evident we needed to expand the team to cope with the demand.

## Liverpool four, Barcelona nil

Liverpool were on another fine run in European football. However, after the first leg of the Champions League semi-final they were trailing 3-0 to Messi-inspired Barcelona. There must have been 99 per cent of people alive that day who had already accepted Liverpool were out. The other one per cent were Liverpool fans. The players used the spirit of the Anfield crowd and scored an early goal through Divock Origi. That unsettled Barcelona and gave us hope, but you knew at any moment, Messi could beat five players and score. Early in the second half, Georginio Wijnaldum scored two goals to level the score at 3-3. I was screaming at the top of my lungs! Barcelona, with their two ex-Liverpool players, Suárez and Coutinho, looked shell-shocked going into the final stages of the game.

One of the most iconic moments in football happened in the 79th minute. Liverpool won a corner on the right-hand side. Quick thinking from 14-year-old ball boy Oakley Cannonier allowed Trent Alexander-Arnold to assist Divock Origi, who scored the winning goal to send Liverpool into the final. Nobody knew what had happened – the people watching at home, the people in the stadium and especially the Barcelona defence. The commentator became an internet sensation overnight with his words, 'Corner taken quickly … Origi!' before the ball smashed into the net, sending Liverpool into dreamlands. My flatmates thought I was having a fit. I went straight to Skyscanner and booked a flight from Dubai to Madrid so I could go to the final.

## Island life

Part of the deal of me accepting the job was that my employers would have to let me go to the Philippines with Janaína in May, and also Glastonbury Festival in June. I'm not sure how I got away with that … maybe that English charm! I'd been in touch with Janaína regularly whilst she'd been travelling through South-East Asia. We agreed two weeks in the Philippines would be the best opportunity to meet up. Sam covered me whilst I was away but I had to be available by WhatsApp or email in case of any issues.

We began our journey on the island of Palawan. Carol (Sydney housemate) was living in Port Barton with her boyfriend and newborn son, so we headed there first. By chance, Fabian and his girlfriend Renata were on their way out of Palawan the day we arrived so we managed to catch them for lunch. Janaína and I boarded an uncomfortably hot four-hour bus from Puerto Princesa to Port Barton. We passed out for the entire journey, apart from waking up each time we hit a pothole. Carol greeted us at her restaurant, Gorgonzola, which was close to the bus station. I was amazed by how big the pizzas were at their place. Carol's partner explained they were the reason their restaurant was always full. People walk past, see the pizzas, think they have to try one and end up buying drinks at the bar all night. Clever!

Up until COVID-19, they'd been seeing more and more tourists arriving in Port Barton every year. It's a quiet fishing village, home to beautiful, white-sand beaches and very few people. Due to its close proximity to El Nido, more and more people are discovering the hidden paradise. Unfortunately, we missed the sunset. Carol said the best sunsets are in Port Barton so I was looking forward to witnessing one the following evening.

Despite the peaceful, hippie vibe we managed to arrive during their biggest party of the year – they even advertised it as 'The World's Best Party.' They were hosting a full moon beach party, similar to the one in Thailand. I say 'similar' with a pinch of salt. It was a tiny cornered-off area at the end of the beach with a stack of four mouldy speakers. It was our first night on holiday so we couldn't say no and joined in on the fun. By the end of the night, we were five buckets down, covered in UV paint and even had a wrestling match in the sand. We stayed up talking on the beach until the sun came up.

Many of the bars and cafés were promoting sustainability and using eco-friendly products, such as metal straws. It was nice to see the locals looking after their own land. It's a shame the rest of the world weren't following suit! We joined Carol for breakfast at her friend's vegan café. It was up a treehouse, overlooking the beach. I was in love with the place. After breakfast, we spent a few hours at Carol's house with her son. He's without doubt the happiest kid I've ever met. Carol believes it's down to living in nature, breathing in fresh air and eating nutritious food. It makes sense when you think about it! She continued to say that her own mental state has improved dramatically since moving away from cities in Brazil and Australia.

For the remainder of the day we relaxed by the beach. I was so content but wondered whether I could live in a place like that all year round. It took one sunset for me to change my mind.

I'd seen some special sunsets on my travels but this one surpassed them all. As the sun dipped behind the mountains, silhouettes of fishing boats gently swayed on the liquid gold water.

Before heading to El Nido, we spent the next morning snorkelling with giant sea turtles in crystal clear waters. For lunch, we stopped on a small island. As I was serving myself rice, an incredibly long and thin snake, as turquoise as the water we were swimming in, dropped down from the roof and hissed. Before it could wrap itself around my neck, I slowly moved back. The guide assured me it wouldn't attack and to enjoy my lunch. I'd lost my appetite though.

I don't mind touristy places if there's a good reason they're touristy. El Nido is one of those places. The white-sand beaches might have been full of tourists, but I found myself distracted by the remarkable limestone cliffs towering above. They were reminiscent of the cliffs I'd seen in Thailand. On the first night, we hiked up to Taraw Cliff for a bird's eye view of another fiery sunset. It was an easy climb and involved crossing a suspension bridge through the middle of the forest.

We were advised to island hop around the Bacuit Archipelago – a great place for scuba diving and snorkelling. Including ourselves, there were 14 people from all over the world who booked the 7am tour. Despite the language barrier, everyone smiled and waved. The 14th person was incredibly late. We were about to set off until we heard screams from a man in his 30s sprinting across the beach. It was Marcus, a crazy Brazilian who'd been blogging his way around the world, under the travel alias Viajando Com Marcus. He was high on adrenalin from missing his alarm and sprinting barefoot, two kilometres across the beach. Through making people laugh, Marcus got everyone on the boat talking to each other. It was also nice for Janaína as she could speak Portuguese again. We navigated between lagoons and reefs, kayaking and snorkelling with some of the most amazing, colourful fish I'd ever seen. I saw more fish than the Great Barrier Reef and the coral was much healthier.

Marcus joined us for the remainder of the week. First, we moved to the island of Coron, where we swam through Japanese shipwrecks from World War II and dived

into the mysterious Barracuda Lake. The freshwater lake was unique because the water temperature differed by up to 10 degrees celsius depending on where we swam.

In the evening, we climbed more than 700 steps up Mount Tapyas for a panoramic view of Coron. We'd been drinking beer all day so it wasn't easy! At the top, there's a Hollywood-like C-O-R-O-N sign and cross, which can be seen for miles.

Next activity was canyoneering through jungle trails at Kawasan Falls in Cebu. I was excited as some of the rock jumps were from obscene heights. With our Go-Pro's at the ready, we travelled downstream, jumping in lagoons and sliding down waterfalls.

The jumps grew in size, starting with six metres, then eight, then ten. Eventually, it reached the point where we were standing over a 16m drop.

I didn't have a fear of heights until I stood there. Without a cord it felt more intimidating than the bungy. I was psyching myself up when the guide shouted, 'Hey, you want to jump even higher? Climb the tree for an extra three metres!' Girls were watching so I had to do it. Janaína shouted, 'Go on migo! I can film you!' Oh great, like that helps! All of a sudden, I was standing on a flimsy branch drooping over the cliff. Before bottling it, I took a deep breath and jumped. That same noise that came out of me in New Zealand came out of me again as I submersed into the lagoon (for what felt like an eternity). We felt like celebrating life when we returned to the village. Rums were on special offer – equivalent of $1 per rum. Although everyone in the bar was enjoying a quiet, relaxing drink, we managed to turn the place into a club and persuaded everyone to dance.

Unfortunately, Janaína was feeling sick the following day (not due to alcohol). Our plan was to head to Oslob to swim with the whale sharks. I didn't want to leave her but Marcus had already been so offered to stay and then they'd travel the following day.

## Travelling is the best kind of education

The main reason backpackers head to Oslob is to swim with the whale sharks. Whether right or wrong, many locals rely on the tourism it brings. The dark reality of what it's really like only hit me once I entered the water. Maybe some people are more educated than me (they probably are) and wouldn't consider it in the first place, but I was naïve and didn't see anything wrong with it when I booked it. I was sharing a dormitory with a German guy and he'd booked the same boat trip. It was the first of the day, leaving at 6am, so we had one beer and an early night.

I was still guilt-free as we made our way down to the beach. It wasn't until the sun rose that I noticed the sheer volume of people queuing and how many boats were being prepared. Sixteen of us crammed on the first fishing boat. We were only 100m from the shoreline and fishermen were throwing endless amounts of bait into the shallow waters to attract the whale sharks. Luckily, we were the first boat of the day so it wasn't too crowded under the water. The actual experience of being in the water with these mammoth beings was incredible. Although us tiny land-based humans looked so

*'Travelling is the best kind of education.' – Cory McLeod*

inferior, I never felt intimidated by the gentle giants. After 15 minutes in the water, we returned to shore. More boats arrived, circling around the whale sharks, clearly making them feel claustrophobic. I felt awful. Despite feeling I shouldn't have participated, by doing it, it made me aware of the problem and now I can educate others. Oslob is a beautiful place and there's many more reasons to visit, such as their beaches, waterfalls and rainforest.

## 6 hour bus. 2 motorbikes. 4 flights. 56 hour journey from Cebu to Madrid done. Let's bring it home Reds! (@coryeveryday_ Instagram post, 1 June 2019)

It was my final day in the Philippines and I still hadn't told work that I was planning to go to the Champions League Final versus Tottenham Hotspur. I had a flight booked that was leaving Dubai for Madrid two hours after arriving back from Manila. I spent four hours in a Filipino coffee shop drafting the perfect email. I used a mixture of the sales techniques I'd learnt and some sympathy about how my team never reach any finals and it was a once-in-a-lifetime opportunity. Three Frappuccinos later, I received the greenlight. 'Yes!' I high-fived the waiter I'd befriended and ran to the airport. I couldn't believe they'd let me extend my trip. My email must have been well-written!

Two hours to get from one plane to another in the same airport shouldn't be that difficult, but when you land an hour late and find out the connecting flight is in a different terminal … well, then you're fucked! After landing in Dubai, I ran to collect my suitcase and asked the airport staff to help me get to the next terminal. They advised me to get a taxi. That meant one unfortunate taxi driver, who'd waited several hours in the taxi line, only had a three-minute drive to the next terminal. When I broke the news to him, he started shouting and throwing his arms in the air. I felt bad so paid extra to soften the blow. I made the check-in desk with seconds to spare.

Thirty Liverpool shirt-wearing fans were on the same flight via Lebanon. Unfortunately, I was still yet to find a ticket. The prices on the re-sale websites were extortionate and every contact I had said they couldn't even find themselves a ticket. Thomas 'Peds' Peden, who at the time was just a lad from football, was also arriving in Madrid around the same time (he's now a very good mate of mine). He flew via Istanbul and Prague and spent a few nights in each place. After all the drama rushing for my connecting flight, everything began to run like clockwork. Peds landed 20 minutes after me. Neither of us had a hotel booked but I was talking to Raul, one of my close mates from the techno parties in Dubai. He was back living in Madrid and said, 'Fuck it, you two can crash at my place!' Five minutes later, after asking him questions about public transport, he said, 'Fuck it, I'll come and pick you up!'

Raul once hosted a 'Techno Paella' house party for his birthday. Fifty people showed up and Raul, wearing only an apron, cooked a giant paella for everyone and had ten DJs play throughout the day – including Sam and myself.

We accepted we'd have to settle for watching the game in a pub. Thousands of ticketless fans travelled to Madrid for the game so we were anticipating a great atmosphere wherever we ended up. Despite being a lifelong Real Madrid fan, Raul agreed to wear a Liverpool shirt for the day to get involved in festivities. Almost 100,000 supporters attended the fan zone in Plaza Felipe II. Jordi, my other Spanish-techno-party-friend, had also landed in Madrid and managed to find us in the crowd. We partied until it was time to watch the game. Finding somewhere for the match was harder than we anticipated. Every pub was full. Jordi and Raul called some friends and between them they managed to find a place outside the city centre.

When we arrived, the first person we saw outside was another 'lad from football', Paul 'Borgy' Borg. He'd experienced the same issues and looked at pubs further out. Unfortunately, he's a Tottenham fan, but we had a laugh about the match and stood together for the game. What surprised me the most about my time in Madrid that day was how all the English fans got on together so well. The Spanish locals were expecting brawls, broken glass and broken teeth, but it was anything but!

As the game kicked off, it was a battle between which supporters could sing the loudest. Borgy was directing chants at Peds and I, but after two minutes Salah converted a penalty to silence him. Tottenham began taking control in the game so I was relieved when I heard the half-time whistle. We ordered a round of shots to calm us down. The second half was as tense as the first. After the longest 42 minutes of my life, Origi scored to win us the Champions League. It was more relief than joy. We'd come so close to winning the big prizes in recent years that it took a while to sink in. The heartbreak in Kyiv became a distant memory. When the final whistle blew, it was time to celebrate. The pub erupted into Liverpool songs and to be fair to the Spurs fans they stuck around and congratulated us.

In amongst the mayhem that evening, I lost Peds and Raul and ended up in a nightclub with Jordi until six in the morning. Understandably, the lads were passed out when I arrived home and not answering their phones. I spent two hours on the front doorstep of the apartment until Tom woke up, then gathered my belongings and left for the airport. It was one hell of a trip travelling from Cebu in the Philippines all the way to Madrid (via Dubai and Lebanon). On the way back, I had a layover in Istanbul, before landing in Dubai at 8am.

I went straight to the office and did a full day at work. Commitment.

## Things never go to plan. If they did, life would be boring.

I had two weeks back at work before returning to Glastonbury Festival. I was surprising myself at how much I was improving at sales. Of course, I had to sell 'the product' (catering), but I was focusing on being genuine and trying to build strong relationships with clients. Although I rarely met them, we became good friends over the phone. See, you don't have to have a loud Essex accent and glistening white teeth to earn commission in Dubai! The night before I left, we won the EFA Cup Final (in 44 degree heat). I scored the penultimate penalty before our keeper Gareth saved the penalty that won us the game.

Charles, the hero on so many occasions, volunteered to drive me and his uni friend Steve down to Somerset. Tatters and his mate Danny were driving down later so we collected the four-man tent from his house. The drive down south flew by (mainly because me and Steve were drinking). We'd seen a post on the 'Glasto Chat' Facebook group: 'If you want to avoid queues, arrive in the afternoon on the Wednesday.' Their thinking was if you arrived at 'peak time' it wouldn't be busy because everyone would be avoiding it.

After what happened to us in 2017, we were keen to try anything! We arrived at 2pm in the afternoon and, much to our elation, there was no queue!

Steve had a one-man pop-up tent so his was up in a matter of seconds. Charles and I unpacked the four-man tent whilst Steve cracked open a beer. Our home for the next five nights was laid out on the grass. Charles, with mud on his knees, reached into the tent bag, then quickly turned to me with a straight face … 'There's no pegs… or poles!' Tatters was an hour away from the festival. He was livid when we told him he had to buy a new tent, but it was his fault! The nearest outdoor shop was Weston-super-Mare, a seaside town on the west coast of England. The boys arrived with a new tent three hours later.

As we did the previous Glasto, we spent the Wednesday evening wandering around the festival drinking beer and cider. We knew the next four nights were going to be chaos so we took it fairly easy (about 20 cans). Like 2017, the Thursday night was wild. I dressed-up in a shark onesie and had four-ecstasy-pills-too-many watching Ross From Friends and Jayda G. I was reaching the dizzying heights of euphoria like the old days – it was great! I was in such a happy place during Jayda G's set. Everywhere I looked, people were smiling, high-fiving and enjoying being alive. Best tracks: Funk Force Project – 'Funk in NJ', Terrence Parker's remix of Loleatta Holloway's 'Dreamin', Gary's Wallace Presents Ecstasy – 'Gotta Have You' and River Ocean's 'Love and Happiness'.

I included these tracks in some of my mixes – www.soundcloud.com/cloddj (If I fail as an author, DJing is my back-up plan).

As you do when you're high and loving life, you start talking to strangers. I ended up partying with some in the Naughty Corner until 4am. On the long walk back to the campsite, a girl approached me who was not in the best state. She was having difficulty finding her tent. I was exhausted but felt bad leaving her and agreed to help. THREE HOURS LATER we still couldn't find it! She knew it was orange and that was about it. I was frustrated and coming down from the high. The longer the endeavour went on, the worse I felt. From my experiences and troubles with anxiety (Yes Sharon ... I know, I shouldn't have taken Class A drugs), I've learnt if I have a big night out I need to go to bed as soon as I start feeling shit. We didn't have much space in our tent so I made her a bed in the porch and tried to sleep in a camping chair.

I'd clearly been awake too long and received confirmation that I had indeed had four pills too many. I was getting heart palpitations and feeling faint. I shook Tatters awake and he recommended drinking water. After no signs of improvement, he walked me to the welfare tent where volunteers and medics had a fire burning. I was dressed in a shark onesie, shivering in front of a burning steel bin, with three other guys who were also a bit too fucked. It was comforting knowing I wasn't the only one.

I appreciate the work the volunteers do. They aren't judgemental and work through the night to ensure everyone is safe. They kept checking on us and providing us with hot tea. I felt ashamed at the time, but I'm sure they're used to it. Actually ... I'm still pretty ashamed. The sun was coming up and most people were back in their tents. Despite this, I did follow one figure all the way from the bottom of the hill. She wasn't veering off the path or stumbling so I was intrigued. She was the first sober person I'd seen all night (aside from the welfare volunteers). The closer she got, the more I recognised her. It was festival director Emily Eavis – the owner of the land I was currently on. I thought 'brilliant!' A genuine hero of mine and she's going to see me trembling by a fire at the welfare tent, dressed as a giant fish with sharp teeth. We made eye contact as she walked past and her reaction was a mix of disappointment and confusion.

I said my goodbyes and thank yous and made the shameful walk back to the tent. It was 11am and our guest was still in the porch, fast asleep inside my sleeping bag. The lads weren't too impressed. I was forced to wake her up and we laughed about the previous night. She had no idea what I went through from the moment I met her. I was glad she was okay and wished her luck for round two of the tent hunt. Each festival we choose a 'wild card' – one pick of a DJ/Band that we all have to go to. It works well as we discover new music through each other's recommendations. My pick was Morcheeba. Along with French electronic group Air, they were my favourite chill-out band growing up. The average age in the Avalon Tent when Morcheeba performed was around 45. There was only a handful of people in their 20s. They must've all been at George Ezra listening to his nursery rhymes for adults. I don't know if it was the comedown or the fact I was so overjoyed to finally see them live, but I was tearing up when lead singer, Skye Edwards sung 'The Sea'. The lads enjoyed them too, which was a bonus.

Friday's headliners were Stormzy on the Pyramid Stage, Tame Impala on the Other Stage and Jon Hopkins on the West Holts Stage. I wasn't a huge listener of any of them but an old school friend invited me to Tame Impala. I always thought it was a bit of a weird, almost psychedelic, experience listening to Tame Impala. I was right. After a heavy night on ecstasy, I was keen to avoid a repeat. The Chemical Brothers and Leftfield were also DJing the following night. Unfortunately, the person beside me had some ketamine.

You know when you're in the wrong place at the wrong time? I had one microscopic sniff and the whole set became a distorted blur. I spent the entire time looking at my feet. The colours from the lasers were nice though. I remember lots of pinks and blues. I started coming around for the last song – 'New Person, Same Old Mistakes'. I was definitely a new person after that experience, but still making the same old mistakes.

Saturday was the return of the shark. He could smell the blood of a big night out. We started with Charles's wild card: Gerry Cinnamon. Half of Scotland were there so we had to make do with a spot outside the tent. It was only him, his guitar and loop pedal but he had the place bouncing. Being in a shark onesie was a good opportunity to get on TV. Halfway through Liam Gallagher's set on the Pyramid Stage I jumped on Tatters's shoulders. I had no idea I'd made it onto the big screen until I received messages from friends and family who'd seen me.

Understandably, Tatters, Charles and Danny were staying at the Pyramid Stage for The Killers. I'd seen them twice and they were superb. However, The Chemical Brothers were more my thing and I'd still never seen them. Steve was also keen and joined me on my mission to the front of the crowd. The electronic duo from Manchester were known for putting on a show … but we were seriously in for a treat that night!

3D animations of dancing robots, superheroes and mummies accompanied hypnotic strobes and lasers, and flares were going off everywhere! It almost looked like a war zone, but instead it was thousands of pilled-up ravers. It was one of those *I was there* moments. I still get tingles thinking about when they dropped 'Hey Boy Hey Girl'. At the time, I had tingles of another sort – I was dying for a piss! We had such a good spot at the front so there was no way I was leaving. My saviour was a badly beaten and trodden bottle of water.

*Mum and Dad dressing up as Siouxsie Sioux and Keith Flint in the 90s.*

I unfolded it and revived it with oxygen. I was wary of pissing on people's legs so placed the Evian bottle inside my onesie. I was also wary of Clod Jnr getting stuck inside the bottle so tried my best to aim. It sprayed fucking everywhere! After the first few seconds, I'd missed so much that I just let it go. I accepted I had to abandon my ego and piss on myself, inside the onesie.

In a classy touch, The Chemical Brothers displayed 'In memory of Keith Flint 1969 – 2019' on the big screen at the end of their show. They'd taken the headline spot from The Prodigy after Keith's passing – and done him proud.

It was another memorable weekend at Glastonbury. The festival brings so many people together from all walks of life and all different age groups. Real life (traffic jams, work deadlines, paying bills) loses significance and for a few days of the year we get to enjoy Glastonbury as real life. Long may it continue!

'Thank you very much to Mr Michael Eavis (and Emily). Still running the best festival that exists, despite everything.' – Thom Yorke during Radiohead's headline set in 2003.

## Real-life grand theft auto

I've said it before and I'll say it again – Stay in touch with the people you meet! I decided enough was enough and I was ready to invest in a car. I'd been renting bangers for years. Either the windows didn't work, the speakers were blown or the air conditioning only blew hot air. Sonny (from Football) had been posting about his company Expat Motors. They were a dealership in the UAE with reasonably priced cars. When I arrived at their office, I was greeted by Sonny and his colleague Sean. They presented the available cars and gave their opinion on each. Eventually, I narrowed it down to a seven-seater Mitsubishi Pajero or 2014 Dodge Challenger.

In truth, I was more swayed by the Pajero. They're reliable cars and I was visualising camping trips in the desert with friends. As I pondered, Sean turned to me. 'What car

would you rather see in your driveway when you head to work in the morning?' And that was it … sold! 'You won't be able to get a car like the Challenger when you have a wife and kids … so enjoy it while you can!' He was right and I felt a rush of adrenalin as I signed the papers. I couldn't wait to test the speed of the car on the Dubai roads. I'd gone from jacking the car on Grand Theft Auto on the PlayStation, to actually owning one! Expat Motors added a friend's discount which was the icing on the cake!

## Becoming an athlete

This next story was not part of the script. I was dog sitting at Kelly and Ryan's whilst they were on holiday. I'd cracked open a beer and was scrolling through Netflix and YouTube trying to find a documentary to watch. One that stood out was The Barkley Marathons: The Race That Eats Its Young. It documents one of the most difficult foot races in the world – a race that's only had ten 'finishers' in the first 25 years! People travel from all around the world to test their physical and mental endurance against race director Lazarus Lake's brutal imagination.

Welcome to the world of ultramarathons.

I was hooked. I searched 'Ultramarathons in Dubai' (bear in mind I'd never even entered a 5km race). The result: 'World's Longest Desert Ultra Marathon – 300km across Dubai's sand dunes.' I closed the tab and switched over to something else on Netflix. It was too big of a jump from beers on the sofa. As the beer cans stacked up, I started shaking my head. I knew what was coming. I'd zoned out of the painfully bad Rom-Com and all I was thinking about was that race. Could I do it? What's the point of life if I don't challenge myself? From that moment, I didn't drink another alcoholic beverage for four months.

Kelly and Ryan arrived back a few days later. 'There's no way you can do that!' That was all I needed. On 29 July, I posted an announcement on my Instagram @coryeveryday_, that I would be entering the 300km desert ultramarathon. The thinking was, if everyone knew about it, then there was no going back. I had to hold myself accountable. Of course, everyone thought I'd lost my mind. 10km races, half marathons and marathons had never appealed to me. I preferred the idea of seeing if I could go from 0 to 100, pushing my body to its limits. I also announced I'd be raising money for a mental health charity. I wanted to raise £10 for every kilometre I ran in the race.

I had no real plan, only that I would increase the running distance each week. It was Dubai summer and temperatures were reaching 50 degrees celsius. Although I could only manage 2.5km runs in the first week, I was teaching my mind and body the discipline of being out there every day. After three weeks, I'd completed one half marathon and lots of 2.5km/5kms/10kms. The furthest I'd ever run was 21km (aside from running down from Everest). I completed it in two hours and 45 minutes. I felt I was ready to give a marathon a go. Remember, this was a fast-track ultramarathon training course!

I searched 'Indoor running tracks in Dubai.' It was impossible to do one outside in summer so I had to find a track with air-con. The advertisement said, 'Run on a state of the art 400m indoor running track at Dubai World Trade Centre!' The casual trainers I'd been using had holes in so I picked up some semi-expensive running shoes on the way. I was pumped and ready to go! My body wasn't, but my mind was. I'd seen the Joe Rogan podcast with Courtney Dauwalter where she talks about her win at the Moab 240 – a 240-mile race across the desert in Utah. She won the race in two days, nine hours and 59 minutes, and beat the runner-up by over ten hours. Courtney was a full-time high school teacher until 2017 when she realised she had an ability for long-distance running.

It baffles me people like Courtney, Alex Honnold (who free-soloed El Capitan) and Spencer Seabrooke (who broke the world record for the longest free solo slackline) aren't more highly regarded. For me, they're some of the best athletes on the planet.

I walked into the leisure complex psyched. My heart rate was high, but I was in control. What I wasn't in control of was that the running track had been removed to allow space for trampolines and badminton courts. Talk about false advertisement! Before losing all my energy, I thought, If I don't do it now, then when would I do it!? The staff told me there was a running track ten minutes away. It was outside in 40 degree heat.

It wasn't a running track, it was a busy footpath looping around Dubai Mall and the Burj Khalifa. I pulled into the car park and paid for four hours, which was optimistic to say the least! As I set off, it felt like the opening scene of a horror movie. The sky transitioned from bright blue to dark grey and a sandstorm swept through downtown. Through the training, I'd developed persistence and was determined to get the job done regardless. As I wiped sand from my mouth and eyes, a middle-aged woman (who was running for cover) yelled in disbelief, 'What are you doing running in this!?' Getting it done!

I knew if I completed the training marathon, in these conditions, then I had the grit to get the 300km done. After a few laps, my new trainers were proving to be too narrow and blisters formed on the sides of my feet. By the half marathon stage, I was in excruciating pain and muttering to myself, 'You idiot! Why did you use a brand new pair of trainers for a marathon, after three weeks training? Idiot!'

My knowledge about calorie intake was minimal. In fact, I didn't bring any food at all! The only option was to head into Dubai Mall. Don't hate on me but the smell of Kentucky Fried Chicken was hard to resist! Yes, I went into KFC halfway through a marathon and ordered chicken tenders, fries and a coke (for energy). The salty food was a welcome break from the taste of sand. After 30 kilometres, it was pitch black and I'd lost the ability to run. I couldn't put pressure on my left foot. Doubt was starting to creep in but I'd told everyone I was going to do it so opted to risk further damage. At kilometre 35, my groin packed in. I can't imagine what people must've thought seeing me hop around, groaning in agony. At 22:22, my Apple Watch registered a marathon time of 6 hours, 9 minutes and 48 seconds. That's what you call 'getting it done!'

I couldn't walk for the next two weeks. I self-diagnosed plantar fasciitis, which is an intense pain around the heel and arch of the foot. It became apparent that if I didn't recover quickly, I wouldn't be able to enter the ultramarathon. In desperation, I searched

'How to fix plantar fasciitis?' I agree with you, the next part sounds like bullshit! I came across a Canadian doctor's amateur, home-made video. He advised to lie on your front and get someone to bash the back of your heel with something sturdy five times. I didn't have anyone with me so positioned myself where I could hit the back of my heel … five times. I don't know what happened or how, but I was instantly relieved of all the pain and could walk normally again. And more importantly, I could run again.

The race directors began organising weekly build-up runs in the desert to help local competitors get accustomed to running on the sand. My alarm was set for 4am every Friday. This allowed enough time to drive to Al Qudra (desert meeting place) and be ready

to run at 5:30am. I only expected a few people to turn up on my first visit, but there were 20! It was comforting to know I wasn't the only crazy person. There were three races people were training for: 50km, 110km and 300km. I met Tamer in the first build-up run. He was an Egyptian guy with a similar story to me. He was unfit, had never entered a race before, but wanted a challenge.

As we were the only amateurs attempting the 300km, we stuck together – usually at the back of the group! Every Saturday, Tamer and I met in the desert for extra training. I stuck to my original plan of building the kilometres up every week, but running the Friday and Saturday in the desert. Through the week, I'd run down a flat beach road. The hardcore

desert training included times we'd drive to Al Qudra on a Thursday evening, run 25kms, sleep in the car for a few hours, then run 30kms at the crack of dawn. Training was tough, but necessary.

It's easy to get lost in the desert. The further you go, the more everything looks the same and the ever-shifting dunes make it easy to lose track of your surroundings.

On two occasions, I lost the rest of the group and ended up in the middle of nowhere without water. There's no over-dramatising, it was fucking scary! One time, I was attempting to complete my first 42kms across sand dunes. Despite struggling at the back of the group, I kept raising my thumb to the people ahead. Eventually, the hazy silhouettes in the distance disappeared altogether. I was on my own and had 12kms left before returning to base. I slurped (with the limited energy I had) from the hydration tube but nothing came out. 'Holy shit!' It was 43 degrees, I had no water and I was lost! I was heading in the general direction, but going slightly off track could mean potentially life-threatening time spent in the sun.

My tongue was stuck to the roof of my mouth, my phone had died and I was becoming delirious. It was another mental battle I had to overcome. I believe suffering with anxiety helped in some way. The self-assured voice which I'd developed in my head over the years kept repeating 'Just keep moving. You can do it!' Two hours later, I stumbled back into the car park. I downed two litres of water and sat under the cold shower until my normal body temperature returned.

My CEO put me in touch with her nutritionist Rawan, who examined my diet and body composition. Based on the not-so-healthy results, she designed a meal plan that was best suited to my training. Rawan had never worked with an ultramarathon runner before so was enthusiastic about being part of the team that would (hopefully) get me to the finish line. I was overweight and only had four weeks to get in shape before I was due back for a follow-up assessment. I had to cut out the late-night snacks! During the training, I thought I was smart substituting my usual chocolate and ice cream for bananas and raisins, but Rawan shouted at me (in a caring way) saying it was still spiking my insulin levels before bed.

# 28

(13 September 2019 – 12 September 2020)

## Breakdown

'Absolutely gutted. Found out the Al Marmoom Ultra Marathon has been postponed or cancelled. The reason why hasn't been released yet and there is going to be an update and hopefully a new date released in January 2020. I'm not even sure I can make the new date and not sure I can keep up this training. It's been 20-hour days working and running at times.

Can't even begin to explain how much work and sacrifice I've put into the training. Going from never running to actually thinking I can pull it off. Hours in the heat, up and down dunes and sleeping in the car running back-to-back or overnight in the desert. Just spent £250 on supplements for the race, ordered a load of equipment etc so it's been really hard to take.

Still very much focused on raising the £3,000 for Mind Mental Health Charity so hopefully I can make the new date or find another challenge to raise money for. Really appreciate everyone who has donated so far to the charity and to the companies who have helped me enter the race, and big thanks to the group down at the weekly runs who kept me motivated.

There's a 50km mountain trail run in two weeks I'm going to enter for now to keep me going and then I'll hopefully have an update on what's next.' – Posted on my Instagram (@coryeveryday_), 14 November 2019

I had a breakdown at the office when I heard the news. I sat in the toilet cubicle with my head in my hands, playing everything over in my head. All the times I'd driven out to the desert, slept in my car, ran through exhaustion, and even all the birthdays and parties I'd missed. Colleagues tried speaking to me in the canteen afterwards but I was blank, I didn't know what to say. All the hard work, stress and sacrifice had gone to waste. Of course, it hadn't gone to waste but it took me a while to get over it. I was still fit and in good shape so refocused my energy on the 50km race that was in two weeks' time. I owed it to all my friends and family who had supported me.

Still to this day, I don't know why the race was cancelled.

## Refocusing my energy

29 November was race day. The 50km desert/mountain ultra (organised by Urban Ultra and Adventure HQ) was a two-hour drive out of Dubai, with a 6am start time. I was so nervous that I didn't sleep at all. Dubai Allstars' Christmas social was in the evening and providing the required motivation. I was so unprepared and incompetent that I downed a protein shake before setting off (worst idea ever) and was still attaching my race number as they shot the gun. It was pitch black and I started questioning what the fuck I was doing. In order to see the markers we had to wear head torches for the first hour.

The very first thing we had to do at 6:01am was climb the biggest, baddest, steepest sand dune I'd ever seen! I was sinking into the soft sand and the protein shake was sloshing around in my stomach. People were scrambling on all fours and it felt like forever until we

*Photo credit – Urban-Ultra.*

*Aid stations – a checkpoint where food, liquids and medical support is provided for athletes.*

reached the top. I was buggered, but what a view! The sun was coming up from behind the mountains and a red mist hovered over the remaining sand dunes, which thankfully weren't as challenging as the first one! After 5kms of dunes we ascended into the mountains. I found myself in the top five or six places. At 28, I was the youngest competitor in the race, but that means nothing in the ultra world. Some of the world's best ultramarathon athletes are well into their 50s.

20 kilometres and two aid stations later, I was starting to fatigue and my lack of competitive experience was showing. I went too fast too early and people started overtaking. However, it was never about what place I finished, I just wanted to leave knowing I'd put everything into it. We followed these tiny orange markers for guidance but sometimes they were so hard to see and I missed two turnings, costing me about ten minutes in total.

The next part of the course wasn't mentioned in the pre-race briefing. The track led us through dense shrubland that looked like my parents' back garden. We hacked through spikey bushes, climbed over walls and crossed streams. I wondered if I'd signed up to a parkour competition by mistake. The most brutal part of the race came soon after escaping the jungle. It was a painfully long, straight path, exposed in the baking hot sun, and it only seemed to go up and up. The heat was draining everything out of me to the point I couldn't even run anymore. I promised myself that when I reached the top I'd run the remaining kilometres to the next (and final) aid station. The final aid station was at kilometre 40. I hadn't seen another competitor for hours until Joao Rebelo (Spain) arrived at the aid station moments later. He looked legit. Expensive gear, cool shades and a dark tan, suggesting he'd spent a lot of time running outside.

Joao had recently competed in Marathon des Sables in Morocco, regarded as the toughest foot race on Earth.

The arrival of competition was the boost I needed. I ate two energy bars, downed an electrolyte-mixed-water and raced ahead. It was almost as fast as a Formula One pit stop. Joao was hot on my tail the whole way. Every time I looked back, he was there, gradually getting closer. I made it my mission (the final mission of many missions that day) to not let him pass. I felt like Gandalf in Lord of the Rings. The final three kilometres were agonising. My knees were in immense pain, I was burnt to a crisp, and I was cursing and stumbling with every step. On the final bend, I looked back and Joao was right behind me. The finish line was in sight. I didn't want to be seen hobbling down the final stretch, so I toughened up and ran through the pain, crossing the line with a huge grin on my face. I did it!

**I finished the race in six hours and 20 minutes.**

And somehow, against all odds, I made the top ten males in my first ever ultramarathon. In fact, in my first ever race full stop.

Big thanks to my sponsors:
The Empress on the Stray
Brown and Blond
Hēisè Deluxe
Expat Motors
Right Bite
Eco Ocean Supplies

## We're proud of you

Sometimes, I don't think parents realise how powerful and fulfilling it is to hear the words 'We're proud of you'. I only remember my dad saying he's proud of me twice. He rarely opens up, but after achieving ten GCSE's and passing my driving test first time, I could see the emotion in his eyes when he told me. The last time my mum told me she was proud of me was after the ultramarathon. She couldn't believe I'd done it. Knowing you've made them proud at something makes you want to keep doing it.

Don't get me wrong, I've disappointed them plenty of times too!

## Sheikkkkhhhhh!

As a treat for finishing tenth place in the ultramarathon (and for everything I put myself through over the four months), I booked a trip to Jordan with India and Nathan. Ever since watching Indiana Jones and The Last Crusade, I'd always wanted to visit Petra. The scene where Harrison Ford faces three challenges to find the Holy Grail is one of my all-time favourites. Karl Pilkington from An Idiot Abroad also made me want to visit. He stayed in a cave for one night opposite the wonder and famously said, 'You're better off living in the hole, looking at the palace, than living in the palace, looking at the hole.' In a way, he was right!

Entering the Lost City of Petra felt like arriving back in Jesus' times. To reach the ancient tombs, we followed a passage deep into the canyon. The walkway was narrow so we had to move out the way regularly to allow horse and carts to pass. They were there, not because it was authentic, but because lots of lazy people couldn't be arsed walking. We wanted to embrace the culture so purchased a headscarf and abaya from a local shop – of

course I went for the most flamboyant choice. Eventually, the passage opened out to reveal the majestic Treasury engraved into the rock face. Two influencers trotted past on a camel, blocking my view just as I was taking a photo! The reflection from their fake teeth nearly broke my camera. I was causing a scene with the locals. They kept pointing at me and shouting 'Sheikkkkhhhhh!' I had no idea what was going on. One of the shopkeepers asked me for a photo and explained I was wearing the Saudi king's kandura.

The locals informed us of a special candlelit show with live music that evening so we returned after dinner. Blessed with a clear night sky, we sat in the dirt drinking Jordanian tea, in front of the famous doorway. I felt a rush of euphoria when I looked up at the twinkling stars above. When the show started, they lit up the Treasury in a series of colours that alternated every few seconds. They looked just like the uplights we used for The Mixer!

The following day, we travelled to Wadi Rum where The Martian and Lawrence of Arabia were filmed. During our Jeep tour of the red desert, we witnessed many prehistoric inscriptions and archaeological sites. Thanks to Nathan and India's organisation, we had the privilege of staying the night in a Bedouin camp (otherwise I'd have booked a cheap hostel). We shared a three-bedroom hut. The inside wasn't impressive, but when you opened the door it revealed what can only be described as a settlement on Mars.

The row of huts were surrounded by giant red rocks, similar in colour, shape and size to Uluru in Alice Springs, Australia. I sat on a bench outside our room until the sun went down. It was so peaceful. As the twinkling stars returned, the local Bedouins prepared our evening meal. The Zarb, which is a traditional Arabian oven, was lowered

into a pit and covered in sand. After several hours of cooking, the Zarb was reclaimed from the depths of the Arabian desert and we were presented with a delicious local barbeque.

After dinner, the Bedouins organised a circle so everyone could introduce themselves. There was a Japanese couple who lived in the countryside, three German girls who grew up in the city, then the Bedouins who lived in the harsh desert, riding camels to collect food and water. When it came to my go, Nathan interrupted and pulled out his phone to show the '21 Years' video. The Bedouins found it hilarious. 'This is you! This is you!' It was surreal seeing these traditionally nomadic guys enjoying my YouTube video, in the middle of the desert, on perfectly good Wi-Fi.

Now, I have a history with Jesus. I used to always faint in church and have no idea why. Maybe I was a devil-child. I even fainted at a funeral at the age of 19. My parents instilled a make-your-own-choices-and-beliefs method of thinking into me. It's an upbringing I'm grateful for. I wasn't forced to go to church or any other place of worship. I used to be made fun of at school for my beliefs (or lack of them) and, of course, I didn't originally make it into the good secondary school because I didn't have enough 'church points'. Despite my differences with Jesus and the church, I was still fascinated by the story of Jesus's baptism site and looking forward to visiting the historic place, set on the east bank of the River Jordan.

The crazy thing is, out of all the kids I went to school with (mainly Christians), I'm probably the first person to actually visit the baptism site – 35 church points please! My kids should be safe getting into the good school now.

As we approached the river, two members of Jordan's military were bearing arms. I thought it was a bit excessive for a place of worship, but looked over to the other side of the river and noticed two more officers with guns. It was the Israeli military. There's a conflict on the Jordan River over who has ownership of the official baptism site and where exactly John the Baptist baptised Jesus. A large group of Americans were taking it in turns to get baptised on the Israeli side. Our guide permitted us to step into the holy water but urged us not to cross the halfway line as we would be shot. I was intrigued by the baptisms and, as I never had a chance to as a kid, I enquired. Unfortunately, the priest had no more slots available. I was slightly disappointed. There's not many better places in the world to get baptised!

I began that whole experience not knowing if a man named Jesus ever existed, but after spending some time reading the history of the baptism site and listening to the guides, I now believe there was a man named Jesus. I reckon he was a healer of some sort, a doctor maybe, and people worshipped him for that reason.

Following an enlightening day, we headed to the lowest point on Earth – the Dead Sea! I'd read articles and watched documentaries but was still unsure what to expect. To fully immerse ourselves into the experience, we covered ourselves head-to-toe in mud, cleansing our skin before entering the water. Nathan went first. India and I were expecting him to fall back into the water but he was too scared. He didn't know whether he'd sink or float. Three boys started pointing at Nathan and laughing in a high-pitched voice. To save him from further embarrassment, me and India ran into the water and pushed him in. He bounced straight back up! I joined Nathan in the water and, with all my might, I couldn't get my body under the surface. Maybe Jesus really did walk on water.

When we booked Jordan, I didn't realise how close it was to the Syrian border. We were only 250km from Damascus. The closer we drove to the border, the more tents and refugees we spotted down the side of the road. Families and whole communities were finding any empty space outside the warzones to take shelter. Whether it be a petrol station, a mall, a hotel, military would use under vehicle search mirrors to check for

LOWEST POINT ON EARTH
SEA LEVEL -398 M

bombs when we pulled over. As we were driving down the road adjacent to the Dead Sea, we noticed a large convoy up ahead. A military van was being escorted by four police cars. It was eerie as each of the four cars were pointing assault rifles at the van. God knows who was inside! Nathan and I were assessing the situation, making sure we weren't under any threat. When we looked at India, she was on Snapchat filming it all! 'India! What are you doing!? You're going to get us shot!'

## A very cold Christmas

After returning from Jordan, I flew to the UK for Christmas. This always involves a trip to visit my mum's side in Middlesbrough. This particular year was the 50th anniversary of The Boxing Day Dip: a tradition, where thousands of locals brave the North Sea, running from the beach into the ice-cold water. Many participants dress up in funny costumes, raising money for charity in the process. Every Christmas I've said I'll do it, but end up bottling it. Either I've been too hungover or overdosed on turkey and cranberry sauce.

After completing the ultramarathon, I was feeling up to the challenge. I wish I'd had a fancy dress costume to keep me warm, but unfortunately I only had my boxers. It was nippy – in both senses! When the starting pistol blew, I found myself at the front of the pack, sprinting towards the sea. Despite the freezing temperatures, our family and friends were cheering us on … in their winter coats, hats, gloves and scarves. As we approached the crashing waves, I

glanced back to see a stampede behind me. There was no chance of stopping! I dived headfirst into the water and had a mini heart attack. I knew it was going to be cold, but not that cold! I staggered out of the water, gasping for air and searching for warmth that wasn't there. Eventually, my guardian-angel-mother appeared from the crowds and handed me a towel to dry off and begin my recovery. It was time to head back to the heat of Dubai.

## COVID-19

My parents were heading to Dubai as news broke of COVID-19 sweeping through Asia. It was to be another week full of activities. There was no pirate yacht party or skydive this

time, but Dad did book a zipline through Dubai Marina. At that time, we had no idea about the severity of the looming pandemic.

The night before my parents arrived, my friends organised a desert party and asked me to DJ. I took a moment to climb the dunes and appreciate what was on my doorstep.

It was cool to have my parents back in Dubai. I loved how they weren't keen on coming the first time but ended up loving it. At the start of the holiday, both my mum and India fell sick. Looking back, it could've been COVID-19 but there was no news of it being in Dubai at that time. As well as flying across the marina on a zipline, they visited the Sheikh Zayed Grand Mosque and Louvre museum in Abu Dhabi, watched sunset from the Dubai Frame and sang karaoke songs in Mr Miyagi's bar.

In that same week, I left my catering manager role and reunited with Danny, Kelly and Ryan. They were aware of my impressive sales numbers and hired me as business development manager for their sister company. It felt like the perfect career progression. I signed the papers and made it clear the next title I wanted was general manager. I just had to prove myself first.

## Lockdown

Things escalated fast, especially in Dubai! Days after my parents left, it became compulsory to wear masks and we had to apply for permits to leave the house. Oh, and work cut our salaries! It was a big shock to the system. I was living in a small room on the 29th floor of a high-riser in Dubai Marina. Thankfully, I had a balcony so at least there was access to fresh air. One of the positive (excuse the pun) take-aways from COVID-19 was how it brought a lot of people together. I became really close with my football team. We organised games of poker on Zoom and spent hours together, laughing and getting to know each other. As money was dwindling (from salary cuts, not poker), Dario, Mike and Cobby offered their places to stay. Although I didn't take up on the offers, I really appreciated them reaching out. Thanks to making the final two in poker with Dan Fahy (on multiple occasions), we discovered we had a curiously similar music taste. He was also a big fan of Jeff Buckley, Elliot Smith and Radiohead, among others.

With so much time off work, it provided the motivation to try new activities, record new DJ mixes and finish the book I'd been meaning to write. My old Swedish housemate Jennie suggested learning yoga and meditation. Trying yoga for the first time when you're not flexible is one of the most painful things you'll ever experience. I enjoyed the challenge but I couldn't even do the downward-facing dog position so I didn't have much hope. The meditation was a good way to wind down on an evening before bed but it didn't quite click with me. I found it difficult to focus and my mind has been known to wander. I believe meditation is a valuable tool and works for a lot of people, but for me, listening to a good piece of music can do so much more. For example, 'La Femme D'Argent' by Air, '8 Ball' by Underworld, 'Porcelain' by Moby, 'The Sea' by Morcheeba and 'In The Waiting Line' by Zero 7 all send me into a deep state of relaxation.

I was happy with the new mixes I'd recorded. It was nice to have more time to dig for tracks.

DJ mixes – www.soundcloud.com/cloddj.

After my chaotic journey to Everest Base Camp, I released an eight-part blog. I'd considered developing it into a book, but it wasn't until lockdown that I had the spare hours to do it. Each day, I'd wake up, work out in my room then open my laptop and start writing. By the time I moved out (May 2020), I'd finished the first draft. Due to cash flow, the company reduced our salaries even further. It reached the point where I couldn't afford my rent and had to move back home until things eased up.

Due to UK restrictions, I had to quarantine for two weeks before moving back in with my parents. After living abroad for so long it was nice to spend some quality time with them. Dad kept me fit by taking me on runs and Mum and I played Scrabble almost every day. One of my new lockdown hobbies was tennis. Josh, Charles, Tom, Sam, Daisy and I would go to Valley Gardens twice a week and play doubles. After the initial disappointment of lockdown, it seemed people were looking to make the most of their time off.

## If only my old English teachers could see me now!

When I left school, if you'd have told my teachers I'd be releasing a book ten years later, they would've laughed. I was decent at English but didn't apply myself. I finished with Bs in English Language and English Media. I spent more time playing hangman than dissecting Shakespeare – just ask Mr Pocock!

During the writing process of my Everest book, I'd been going back and forth with local author David Ayre. He helped me format and publish the book through his publishing company. I knew him from my time playing for Knaresborough Bowling Club. We actually won a pairs competition together 12 years earlier. Ryan's mum Gwenda was an English teacher in Australia and offered to help edit the book (free of charge). She highlighted several instances where I'd crossed over into different tenses by mistake. I've probably done it several times in this book too! Gwenda removed all the swearwords and Yorkshire slang from the book. There were too many swearwords but it was a shock for an Aussie to remove all the slang, especially when they're renowned for their extensive catalogue of made-up words.

When the book was published on Amazon on 19 June 2020, neither I nor my mates could believe it. I was inundated with messages of support and congratulations. Due to so many people buying the book in the first few weeks, it started to rise high in the rankings. It reached the top 500 in travel and tourism books and top 10,000 overall. Seven days later, there were more reasons to celebrate. Liverpool Football Club, after a 30-year wait, were announced as champions of England. I'd been through so many ups and downs following them over the years. It was unbelievable to finally get our hands on the trophy! But despite some good things happening to me in 2020, the world was still a very strange place. People were arguing on social media and fighting over toilet roll in supermarkets.

We had to meet our Doncaster-based family (Dave, Maggie and Kirsty) in a car park to exchange birthday presents (after sanitising them). We forgot what it was like to have human contact. Fist bumps became the new norm and hugging was a thing of the past.

Despite our struggles with the new reality, we had friends and family in healthcare who were suffering much worse conditions, working day and night to save lives. Shoutout to my doctor friend Chris who was living in Canada but flew back to help in our local hospital. Every week, the British public showed their appreciation of the NHS staff by clapping in the street. Liverpool captain Jordan Henderson created the 'Players Together' initiative, encouraging professional footballers to donate some of their wages to the NHS. Captain Thomas Moore, a 99-year-old war veteran, raised over £15 million for the NHS by walking 100 laps of his garden.

## Return to normality (hopefully)

With some restrictions being lifted in Dubai, it was time to head back and prepare for the busy season. It was a wise decision as the UK were set to have a miserable winter with even stricter lockdown measures. I was optimistic Dubai would be one of the first places to reopen. Unfortunately, a few weeks into my return, new measures were introduced. This affected both our business and social life. With most offices remaining shut and private gatherings banned, it was becoming increasingly difficult to sell catering for events. For my birthday, I'd hired a yacht to celebrate. Two days before the party, they banned any type of live music. It would've been pointless without a DJ so I cancelled. Local authorities then announced 11-a-side football would be postponed until further notice. I was gutted as I'd been working hard to get fit. Football was my escapism from the mounting stress and depression caused by the pandemic.

I understand the complexities prioritising certain things during a pandemic, but I do feel people suffering with mental health issues were neglected. You need some freedoms to maintain a healthy mind and being locked up isn't one of them. The feeling of being trapped and there being no sign of it ending took its toll. It blows my mind that politicians weren't advising people to eat healthy, exercise every day, boost vitamin D levels etc. Every second advert on television should've been about that.

# 29

## (13 September 2020 – 12 September 2021)

### A COVID Christmas

After a few tedious months working in a lifeless Dubai, we had our first big booking of the season. Jamie Jones (who I'd seen DJ many times) was headlining an exclusive event on a beach in Ras Al Khaimah and we were catering. All guests and staff had to show proof of a negative PCR test to enter. Some of the tables were up to 100,000 AED so I felt lucky being there. I was supervising the event but spent most of the time by the dancefloor enjoying the music. The success of the event was evidence that parties could resume safely.

Although it was a 'COVID Christmas', I was glad to be flying back to the UK to see my family. As we could only spend Christmas Day with our own household and one support bubble, there was me, my parents, Nana Mavis and Uncle Martin. It was confusing and awkward. We didn't know if we could hug, we kept a distance at the dinner table and I was worried about spreading something to Nana who was vulnerable. Despite this, we still played games, watched Christmas movies and drank too much Baileys. I was grateful I could even see my family at all.

### Takashi's new year message

Takashi was the first person to wish me a Happy New Year in 2021.

'2020 has been a year of unprecedented challenges, but also one of strength, resilience and progress. As we approach 2021, we remain committed to move our life forward for the best of all. Happy New Year!!'

### Got got by COVID

I thought I was invincible. After a full year of the pandemic, I still hadn't contracted the virus. In January 2021 that changed. I've no idea where I got it. In the days running up to the result, I'd been in the office, at work events and in a bar with three friends. I was feeling run-down at work with a bit of a headache. I usually feel like that after the weekend

anyway so didn't take much notice. It was when I was at home changing for football that I realised something was up. I'd packed my bag and was about to leave when I made the smart decision to message my manager Cobby and take a PCR test. Thankfully I did as I could've spread it to the entire team.

For the first four days, I was bedbound with flu symptoms. I was living in a shared apartment so had to stay in my room the entire time, which was claustrophobic! I ordered meals from Deliveroo and collected the items wearing a mask and gloves. By the end of the week, only a mild headache remained. I believed I was on the mend until I ate a spicy curry that had no smell or taste. A second wave of illness arrived, causing me to sneeze more than the first week. The strength of the virus, on me, a relatively fit, 29-year-old, made me

appreciate how rough it must've been for the elderly and people with underlying health conditions. Whatever was inside me felt powerful. After a few days, my state improved dramatically. I went from feeling dreadful to back to normal in one good night's sleep. My smell and taste returned and I felt fit to work again.

It wasn't only work I was hoping to be fit for. Conor McGregor was fighting Dustin Poirier at UFC's Fight Island in Abu Dhabi. A negative COVID result was required to cross the border from Dubai and enter the arena. Thankfully, I received the greenlight and booked my ticket. The only downside of being negative was that I had to work until midnight. I couldn't refuse to work if I was going to the UFC. I persuaded Dubai Allstars teammate Nick Michaels to join me and we set off at 2am. To make the fight accessible for fans in America, it was held at stupid o'clock UAE time. Selfish, as we all had to go to work in the morning!

The return of spectators saw 2,000 fight fans attend the rematch. As always with the Irish fans, the atmosphere was electric and you would've thought every seat had been allocated, given the noise. Not many were giving Dustin a chance but as he entered the cage with his famed walkout song, 'The Boss' by James Brown, you had the impression he was a fighter with a lot more belief this time around. Last time they faced each other, Conor outclassed him in both the fight and the trash talking. Despite an encouraging start from Conor, Dustin 'The Diamond' Poirier dominated the fight, finishing with an onslaught of hard-hitting punches. Dana White and the UFC led the way in showing the world how to put on a sporting event safely.

After two weeks in bed, I was desperate to play football again. Peds invited me for a game with his new seven-a-side team 'Elite DXB.' The team was founded by Elite Sport

Performance owner Chris Bowman and, due to their work training professional and ex-professional footballers, I ended up playing alongside former Manchester United FC and France international legend Mikael Silvestre. Thankfully, I started on the bench so had limited time to embarrass myself in front of him. When Chris asked me where I wanted to play, I politely said anywhere. What I wasn't anticipating was Chris putting me on in defence, alongside Mikael. Right before I went on, I repeated to myself 'Don't do anything stupid. Don't do anything stupid.'

I started strongly, playing nice, short, carefully picked-out passes, making good interceptions and most importantly, not fucking up in front of Mikael. It was the first game of a knockout tournament – meaning if we lost, we were out. With one minute remaining and the score tied at 1-1, I'd built up enough confidence to take the ball out from the back and travel up the field. I took it past one player and tried to play a ball out to the left wing. Blinded by the floodlights (my excuse), an opposing player intercepted it, ran the length of the field and scored the winner. I wanted to crawl up into a ball and die. Mikael looked at me with disgust and walked off the pitch.

Thankfully, in the following weeks, I was moved into a more attacking position and my performance levels improved. I was linking up with Mikael better than he linked up with Rooney. Nearly all my goals came from a Silvestre assist. At 43, he was still winning his battles, had the vision to make a good pass and could still bomb down the wing to deliver a cross. I treated him like any normal guy but really it was an honour to play with him (despite my Liverpool affiliation).

## Couch-with-COVID to 50km in six weeks

Whilst battling COVID, I came up with the idea to enter the Al Marmoom 50km Desert Ultramarathon. It was a reason to get fit again but also a challenge to see if I could complete it so soon after having the virus. I had six weeks to prepare for it (not long for an ultramarathon). My training plan was similar to the last ultramarathon, but even more fast-track. I ran every day and lost a lot of weight in a short amount of time. Saying that … I still looked more like a shot-putter than ultramarathon runner. After all the hours of dedication training for an ultramarathon for a second time, the race was cancelled – again! Two days before the race! New COVID restrictions were announced and race organisers had no choice but to reschedule.

I didn't want to waste everything I'd done, so ran 50km anyway on my own, with no aid stations or support crew. I set off from Dubai Marina at 4:36am in a bid to run some of the distance without the torture of the sun. Despite the lack of training, I was feeling okay as I ran through Jumeirah and towards Burj Khalifa in Downtown. By the halfway stage my legs were aching. I was posting video updates to Instagram and the messages of support I was receiving from friends and family were helping me power through.

The heat of the sun was draining everything out of me. I was burnt, dehydrated and sweating copious amounts. At the marathon mark (42km), I hit a wall, a wall more intense

than anything I'd experienced in my first ultramarathon. I convinced myself I could finish under the six-hour mark and began speeding up. Bad idea! I crashed hard and could barely string two strides together (never mind words). I stumbled for the next few kilometres and found myself standing by a fridge in a supermarket. I'd become delirious. I couldn't remember making the decision to go inside the shop. I already had drinks and food in my bag. My body must've put me on autopilot to find cool air. I cooled down for a few minutes before heading back out in the 35-degree heat to finish the job. I arrived back at 10:51am - six hours and 15 minutes after I'd started. I burned a total of 4,478 calories – and it looked like it! I left the house fat and returned thin. To celebrate, I ordered a McDonald's and went to the pub!

## The Best Man (virtually)

This was a tough one. I was so proud when Balley asked me to be his Best Man. Who would've known, almost three years later, I wouldn't be able to attend the wedding. Due to the pandemic and the ever-changing UK restrictions (thanks Boris), the wedding was postponed several times, before eventually settling on 12 April 2021. Due to the extortionate quarantine hotel prices set by the UK government (thanks Boris) and the

amount of holiday I would've had to take, it just wasn't feasible. Balley's brother Martyn did a fine job stepping in for me and read out a short speech I'd written. Due to limited capacity at the wedding, Emma and Balley announced they were having another celebration that everyone could attend in September 2022. It was for this reason I decided to save all the embarrassing stories for the proper speech. Thanks to Stevie's (usher) efforts, all the guests who couldn't attend were able to watch via his Facebook live stream. It was in 240p video quality and buffering a lot, but it was lovely to be able to watch their special day.

## Sunwaves

As we were approaching summer and the end of the season, work told us to take some holiday before 'Expo 2020' commenced in September. I was at the airport two days later. Due to restrictions in Romania, Sunwaves Festival moved to Zanzibar for a one-off party. There was so much paperwork to enter the country and I had to book two PCR tests (one in Dubai and one in Zanzibar before returning).

Although I was travelling alone, Justin from Dubai Allstars and Mattia, a long-time friend from Dubai, were also going. I always thought Zanzibar was an expensive place, similar to Maldives or Mauritius, but was pleasantly surprised at how cheap the whole

trip was. The return flydubai flight was a reasonable 1,800 dirhams. The only downside was the limited leg room and the woman beside me having an anxiety attack during turbulence. 'Oh my god, oh my god, we're all going to die!' She was on her way to get married so maybe that was freaking her out too.

I can confirm we didn't die and after landing (safely), I booked six nights with Shamba Village in Paje. It was a new hotel and only 900 dirhams for the week. Tucked away inside a small jungle and only a five-minute walk from the beach, it was home to two pools, a poolside bar and incredibly friendly staff. I had a huge private room with an en suite bathroom. It was the perfect place to relax, party … and also write this book in the downtime.

Since Peggy Gou DJ'd at Soho Garden in Dubai, February 2020, I hadn't danced properly once (apart from in the shower). Sunwaves Festival was a return to freedom. Apart from the airport, I didn't see one person wearing a mask. I asked my taxi driver, 'Has Zanzibar had any problems with COVID?' He replied, 'No, COVID finished.' Within ten minutes of arriving at the festival, Mattia spotted me in the crowd. Mattia was at Raul's

techno paella party that time. After watching Herodot together, I went to see Loco Dice with Justin. He was with a big group and we partied till sunrise.

Although I'd planned to attend the festival every day, I realised I wouldn't be able to see the rest of the island if I was constantly hungover or pissed. With that in mind, I decided to take a few days off and hire a scooter to explore. In my opinion, it's the best way to travel – the wind in your hair (unless you're bald) and going wherever you want, discovering the unknown. Following a recommendation from the hotel manager, Abdul, I visited Kuza Cave. The cave is believed to be a spiritual healing pool and you can swim in the fresh water. I was on my own so just took a few photos and made my way back to the exit. As I loaded my scooter, the guide invited me for a drum lesson. His female friend joined us and they sang together whilst I attempted to match the drumbeat. Then he stopped banging the drum and asked me to sing solo. I apologised for my inability to hit any kind of note, gave my thanks, tipped for their time and scootered off into the distance.

Following my failed music attempt, I headed north to The Rock. The picturesque restaurant is situated on Michamvi Beach and surrounded by turquoise blue water. You can take a boat or walk when the tide is out. I strolled through the shallow waters and sat on a sandbar to take in the views and appreciate the paradise I was in. Dubai can be a stressful place so it was incredibly satisfying to be in the middle of the sea, with the waves crashing around me and no work. I was clearly enjoying heaven too much as it was dark by the time I returned to my scooter. I stopped at some villages on the way home and the locals were so friendly and welcoming. Usually you'd be cautious walking around a new

place at night, but I didn't feel under any threat whatsoever – although, a few kids did ask me if I wanted some pot.

I had one more night at the festival (seeing Dubfire and Ricardo Villalobos) before travelling to Makunduchi for a PCR test in the morning. The COVID centre was 20km south of Paje and located in a small wooded area on the edge of the town. I was joined by other party people and we were instructed to sit on white plastic chairs until our names were called out. I knew they were ravers because they had hippie clothes, multi-coloured braids and were tapping their feet to a beat from the night before. Unfortunately, the price of the test was $80. It was excessive but worth it to experience Zanzibar.

The next stop on my itinerary was Stone Town. Admittedly, the reason I booked one night there was because Freddie Mercury grew up there. Of course, there's more history to the town than that. I learned about the Zanzibar Revolution in 1964, when more than 20,000 people were killed, and the dark times during the slave trade in the 18th and 19th centuries. It's believed more than one million slaves passed through Zanzibar, either to work on plantations or be sold to buyers in other continents. Zanzibar was one of the last legally running slave markets in the world and it was distressing standing by the memorials thinking back to the atrocities that had occurred.

I found it easy to get lost as I wandered through the narrow coral stone alleyways. However, not all who wander are lost! Getting lost led me to the Africa House Hotel where they were serving ice-cold draught beer and had incredibly fast Wi-Fi. The bartender told me their balcony was the best place to watch the sunset. Their beers were expensive so

I headed to the Baboo Beach Café downstairs. They were selling much more affordable drinks, also with a view of the sunset, and I could still connect to the strong Wi-Fi above. Hashtag travel hacks.

My dad's friend, Chris Smith was in the band 'Smile' – which would later become Queen. Chris was one of the people to introduce Freddie to the band. After years of trying to launch his own career, Freddie was invited to join after their lead singer left. The rest is history. I had the pleasure of meeting Chris at one of his gigs in Otley (West Yorkshire) when I was a kid. He's still touring now!

## Travelling during a pandemic

I wasn't sure of my next plan so I flew back to Dubai and stayed with my friend Rachel for a few days. Travel had become complicated. Certain countries weren't accepting tourists, some were but with PCR tests (which get expensive), and some were only accepting double-vaccinated tourists. There were also online forms to fill in to be accepted into each country. Every website I checked for information seemed to say conflicting things. Eventually, I ended up on a flight to Tbilisi, Georgia. I knew nothing about the country but I was excited to try somewhere new!

Although it's good to travel to new places, it also helps if you do a bit of research first. I wasn't well-educated on the conflict between Azerbaijan and Armenia. On the way to the hotel, I was explaining to the taxi driver (who turned out to be from Armenia) that I was hoping to visit Azerbaijan and asked if it was nice there. He said, 'It is not a good country. We have been in a war with them. You should visit Armenia instead!' I replied in my dumb-tourist-accent, 'Oh right. Sorry … I didn't realise!' I kept my mouth shut after that. The journey from the airport was 30 minutes, but after 20, I could see he was getting fidgety. He asked if I wanted a cigarette. I politely declined as it was nine o'clock in the morning. He then asked, 'Is it okay if I smoke in the car?' 'Of course, go ahead!' 'Wow, you are a good man. Thank you!' His mood lifted instantly and he didn't stop talking for the remainder of the journey.

Borgy had recently been to Tbilisi and gave me a few tips of what to do in the city. I booked five nights with Hotel Kalanga, close to the centre of Tbilisi. The hotel was run by a lovely local family who lived in the building. I couldn't believe how lucky I was with the hospitality (once again). The lady who managed the bookings kept bringing gifts to my room. First, it was her father's Chacha, a locally brewed brandy that she presented in a swanky glass bottle. Local food, wines and even a homemade tiramisu arrived in my room in the following days. The family advised me to try Khinkali (a Georgian dumpling that became popular following the Mongolian invasion) at Machakhela, a popular restaurant in the heart of Tbilisi.

I followed the old cobbled streets leading to the restaurant and took a seat by the entrance. The entrance is important so you can imagine how many people were coming in and out – witnessing how miserably I was failing at eating their pride-and-joy-dumplings.

The twisted knobs of dough are typically stuffed with meat, potato or cheese. I was starving so ordered six pieces – which is a lot considering how filling they are. I didn't realise until after that there was a method to eating them. You're meant to pinch the hard end, bite a small hole so you can suck the liquid, then eat the contents. Also, the hard end should be left on the plate so you can see how many you've eaten. I was biting into the dumplings without a care in the world, spilling the liquid all over the plate, the table and my chin. I also got indigestion from eating all six of the hard ends.

During his stay in Tbilisi, Borgy met a lovely local girl named Anna when he was watching a EURO 2020 game in Maclaren's Irish Pub. He put me in touch and she agreed to meet me for one of the matches. Anna helped plan my week in Georgia and even booked some of the tours. I explained my struggles eating the Khinkali dumplings and she started giggling. 'In Georgia, you're seen as a bad kisser if you spill any liquid!' The restaurant staff were probably laughing when they saw how much liquid I'd spilt. I also met Pavel in the pub, who was born to Uzbekistani and Russian parents. He'd spent a lot of time in Georgia and knew the history of the country, which was great for me as I knew nothing! He offered to take me up the funicular (not an innuendo) the following evening and watch the sunset from Mtatsminda viewpoint (the best view of the city). Many locals spend their evenings up there as it's a nice, romantic spot and has a theme park for the kids.

The next morning, I booked the Viator (tour company) group trip to Kazbegi. We stopped at the Ananuri Fortress, the Russia-Georgia Friendship Monument and the Gergeti Monastery. The view from the Gergeti Trinity Church (20kms from the Russian border) was voted one of the best views in Europe.

There's so many lovely old ladies in Georgia. So lovely that you frequently fall victim to their sweetness. For the second time (in only a few days), I was heavily ripped off by an old lady who was selling me something. On the first day, I paid ten times the amount for a watermelon juice on the street. At the Russia-Georgia Friendship Monument, a lady sold me some hot Lays-crisps-on-a-stick for the price of a meal in a restaurant. Thankfully, the ketchup I covered them in was complimentary. I feel like I'm streetwise when I'm

travelling but sometimes I get mixed up with the exchange rates … and I have a history of being seduced by sweet old ladies.

I bought a Euro 2020 ticket for Denmark versus Czech Republic in Baku, Azerbaijan, but couldn't enter the country due to new COVID restrictions. I soon found myself back on Skyscanner looking for alternative, cheap flights. This led me to Athens, Greece. I'd only been to Zakynthos on a lads' holiday when I was 19 (which doesn't count), so I was keen to experience some real Greek history.

For my final meal in Georgia, I went back to the same restaurant to eat the dumplings properly and prove to everyone I was actually a good kisser.

## Greek Clod

I'd learnt so much about Athens in school so I was excited to see it first-hand. As accommodation was expensive everywhere, I settled for Athens Studios hostel. I'm approaching the age that I'm too old for bunk beds, but on this occasion I had to save the money. Sharing my room was a Dutch girl in her 30s and a Chinese girl in her 20s. The Chinese girl wore noise-cancelling headphones for the entire time, but she was nice whenever she did speak. Whilst I was unpacking my bags, the Dutch girl was patiently waiting for the Chinese girl to finish in the bathroom. When she eventually came out 20 minutes later, the Dutch girl asked if it was okay to use the bathroom. The Chinese girl replied, 'Sorry, you need to wait three minutes. I pooped.' At least she was honest!

I always imagined the ruins to be in the middle of nowhere so it was fascinating to discover everything was central. The Acropolis of Athens is the main tourist attraction and sits proudly above the city. The entry fee was 20 euros, but worth every cent. It was like

walking through a school history lesson as I ambled across the ancient temples of Athena Nike and the Parthenon. The Acropolis is one of the highest points in the city so you can see for miles from the top. Opposite, there is Areopagus Hill which is free to enter and most people take a seat there to watch the sunset.

I had one more day in Athens to see the Panathenaic Stadium before taking a 15 euro flight to Vienna. The Panathenaic Stadium was the world's first Olympic Games stadium and is the finishing point for the Athens Classic Marathon. Although it was

empty (without the 50,000 people who used to be in attendance), it was impressive and I spent several hours walking around trying to imagine the scenes that used to take place there all those years ago.

## New favourite building

Whilst boarding the flight to Vienna, I found another 15 euro flight leaving the day after to Montenegro. I could've ended up anywhere! I considered Kosovo, Hungary, North Macedonia and Albania. This left me with 24 hours to experience the home of Mozart and Beethoven. Vienna had never been at the top of my list of places to visit, but Josh did say it was his favourite city in Europe. For obvious reasons, Vienna is famous for its music, but it was the architecture that stood out for me. Whichever street I walked down, it seemed to be a mix of styles, both old and new. I found my new favourite building whilst wandering the streets: The Hundertwasserhaus. It's a quirky, colourful building which is built into apartments and came from the mind of Austrian artist Friedensreich Hundertwasser. It looks like no other and was the best 'attraction' I saw in Vienna. Vienna is blessed with lots of cafés, bakeries and restaurants. I had five coffees, three large meals and three desserts in one day. I left Vienna full and content.

## A pleasant surprise

I knew nothing about Montenegro. I couldn't even name one person who had been. I didn't know what their currency was, whether they spoke English, what the attractions

were, nothing! I was in for a treat because it was so much more than I was expecting. Soon after landing, I learned that not many locals speak English. It was challenging at times, but all part of the experience! My Swedish friend Rebecka saw my Instagram story whilst out drinking with her friend Elma. Elma was born in Montenegro and gave me some recommendations. Technically, we were still in a pandemic but she said Budva was the party place so that seemed like a good starting point.

The bus to Budva was hot and full of passengers. Thankfully, I had a window seat to enjoy the spectacular views. For the entire 90-minute journey, we were surrounded by lush, green mountains. There are 50 peaks over 2,000 metres in Montenegro. I ran out of data and had to guess where my hotel was. After jumping off at the wrong stop, I flagged down a taxi. None of the drivers spoke English so I was unsure if they knew where I needed to go. Thankfully, the staff at a nearby hotel knew the road I was looking for and helped me order a taxi. I booked a room with a 'sea view' in the Villa Imperija Guesthouse. There was a tiny bit of water visible through a gap between two buildings. I didn't complain as it was luxurious for 20 euros per night. Even the hotel manager didn't speak English. I couldn't remember the last place I struggled to converse with someone. It was a nice change and felt like proper travelling again. I say 'proper,' it's not like I was in a hammock in the jungle – I had a king size bed with an en suite bathroom … oh, and a sea view!

The marina looked stunning as the sun came down over the medieval walled streets. I'm aware it's next door but it had a lot of similarities to Croatia. I wondered why so many people visit Croatia and not Montenegro. COVID-19 may have been the reason, but I didn't meet one British person. My maturity was finally showing as I opted for an early night so I could explore the neighbouring town of Kotor in the morning. I wanted to hire a scooter but had to be in Serbia the following day for Exit Festival – I didn't want to risk anything going wrong! The bus to Kotor proved to be a stress-free alternative and not as busy as the previous day. The picturesque, waterside town is the gateway to the Adriatic Sea and borders Croatia and Bosnia and Herzegovina. Despite burning to a crisp, the highlight of Kotor was hiking up to San Giovanni Fortress. The view of Church of Our Lady of Remedy, Kotor Old Town and the bay was incredible.

## Come on England!

That same evening was the EURO 2020 semi-final between England and Denmark. Once I returned to Budva, I was desperate to find somewhere with an atmosphere, and, most importantly, somewhere that had fellow England fans. I left the hotel three hours before kick-off to hunt for people to share a beer with. I tried every bar in Budva and didn't find one England fan. It was astonishing, usually England fans are everywhere! I found an empty seafood restaurant which had a table perfectly placed in front of a big TV.

Typically, in restaurants and bars, you imagine to be served by young people. Montenegro is the opposite! All the waiters were old men. I was assigned the oldest guy in there. He was a lovely man who didn't speak English but very helpful and friendly. I pointed at the meals and drinks I wanted on the menu and that seemed to work. The service was excellent. He helped me find the channel to watch the England game and even started raising his fists in the air, chanting 'Come on England! Come on England!' I sent a video to Rebecka. Elma recognised him from her childhood. 'I know that man!' The waiter and I laughed over the coincidence. England won the semi-final in extra-time and although I would've loved to be in a busy pub in England with all my mates, I'll remember that match for the friend I made in the restaurant.

## Karma

Thanks to the UAE's relationship with certain countries, I was able to travel to these places using only a vaccination certificate – saving a lot of money on PCR tests! As much as I'd enjoyed the previous few weeks, I was most excited for Serbia and Exit Festival. Borgy and I snapped up some last-minute tickets. I hadn't been to an outdoor festival outside the UK since Tomorrowland 2015. I was also reuniting with the Americans who stayed in my Ultra Europe hotel room in 2013. They returned the favour and allowed Borgy and myself to crash in their place.

I never got around to washing my clothes or having my hair cut the entire trip, so that was my first task in Serbia. Thankfully, my Serbian colleague, Olga, was visiting home and able to help. Her mother worked in a laundrette and her best friend was a hairdresser. Sometimes, things just fall into place! Olga's house was in Novi Sad, 15 minutes from the festival site. After my haircut, she showed me around and took me to meet my friends. It felt like the world was back to normal. There was a good vibe wherever you went, with thousands of young festival goers packing out the bars and restaurants. Face masks seemed to be a thing of the past – even people in their 60s and 70s weren't wearing one! EJ, James and Cornelia met me in the bar outside the hotel. Olga only came to drop me off but ended up staying for drinks and later dinner to meet the rest of the team. I reunited with Joe and Joseph and met their other friends from California and Arizona. They were all legends and I could tell I was in for an amazing weekend!

Usually at festivals, you arrive in the afternoon and party until midnight. Exit Festival is different as you arrive at midnight and party until morning. I had no expectations as I'd never looked into the festival and what the stages were like. We navigated through a maze of small stages with varying genres. The first stage we stopped at was a reggae stage. It's the first festival stage I've been to where everyone sits down (all stoned). I thought people in our group were only drinking, which I was fine with, but one of them pulled out a bar of chocolate shrooms and offered me some. I thought when in Rome (or Novi Sad), and my night took a sharp right before going to never-never land for the next eight hours.

Everyone in the group had VIP access, apart from me. I tried walking through the VIP gate without being seen but they stopped me when they saw my general admission band. The rest of the group had already gone through but it shows what type of people they are as they came back out. We walked all over the festival site trying to find one to buy but none were for sale. Without telling me, they all chipped in and paid one of the security guys to let me in. If that's not good karma for what happened in Croatia eight years earlier, I don't know what is! The shrooms were bloody intense as I arrived into VIP. The exclusive area was a platform above the crowd so you could see everything and there were no queues for the bar.

The dance arena was enormous and the sound system and laser show was insane! Also … there was so many people! After 16 months of avoiding people, it was good to be embracing strangers again and enjoying music. Amelie Lens's acid techno set sent me into a different dimension. I spent the majority of it with my mouth open, staring into the sky, in pure amazement at the colours I was seeing. Everything was moving so fast on shrooms. I convinced myself that one Indian guy was the messiah. He was wearing this cool sarong and I was captivated by his dancing. It looked like he was orchestrating the crowd and the music.

I went for the best piss of my life during that set. My urine entered a black hole and all the walls in the bathroom pulsated, morphing into different colours. I didn't want it to end! During Charlotte De Witte's set, Joe came up to me and started telling me how he was in love with his girlfriend and that he was going to propose. There were so many things going on (vibrating trees, clouds forming into Lego pieces, soldiers marching into battle) that I had no meaningful reply. The following day, he told me all I managed to get out of my mouth was, 'Sorry mate, I'm too deep.' He found it hilarious and was glad I had a good time. Cornelia tapped me on the shoulder around 7am and asked if I wanted to go back to the hotel. It was like Inception (movie) when you fall back on your chair to wake yourself up. As soon as she tapped my shoulder I came out of my trip and knew it was time for bed. Afterall, we had three more days of partying ahead!

Dax J and Kobosil played Alex Blakemore's (also known as 'Balrog') track in their closing set that night. Alex is an old work colleague from Harrogate.

Borgy arrived the following afternoon. Thankfully, he was tired from travelling so we slept until 10pm before making our way to the festival for day two. Me and Borgy love our 90s rave music and it's one of the reasons we started talking during a yacht party in Dubai. When Pan-Pot finished their set with one of our favourites, Awesome 3 – 'Don't Go', we absolutely lost it!

Despite the lack of English people in Serbia, it was our mission to find someone to watch the Euro 2020 final with. Halfway through Paul Van Dyke's set on day three, a bald guy, by the name of Adrian grabbed me out of nowhere. 'You're English aren't you!?' 'Yes!

Are you?' Adrian was from Leeds, 29 years old and went to the same university as me. We exchanged numbers and agreed to meet up for the match the following evening. Nina Kravis returned to the day three line-up after recovering from COVID and I remember saying, 'This is the best rave I've ever been to!' I was high when I said it though!

## Is it coming home?

Before we could think about day four of the festival, we had the matter of facing Italy in the final of Euro 2020. It was England's first final since 1966, so it was a BIG deal! Rather than the comfort of a hotel, Adrian opted to stay in a hostel for Exit Festival. This was a good thing as he had made a lot of friends in there who helped create an atmosphere in the pub. I was nervous but truly believed football was 'coming home'. It only took two minutes for England to settle any nerves with a great finish from Luke Shaw. The place erupted with beer flying everywhere! 'It's coming home, it's coming home!' echoed around the pub. Italy grew into the game and equalised in the second half. I could barely look at the screen as the match entered extra-time and penalties. Despite winning a penalty shootout in the 2018 World Cup, England are notorious for messing them up … and that we did! We lost 3-2 in the shootout. So close yet so far!

We were distraught but it was a hell of a performance and everyone was so proud of the team. Thankfully, we had the festival to distract us from the heartbreak. Day four was more of the same. Thousands of happy people embracing each other and enjoying life. Solomun closed out the festival, playing an extended set until ten in the morning. It felt like the first big celebration since the pandemic and it was emotional when it came to a close. Exit Festival blew me away and I can't wait to go back. Thank you Serbia!

## Family time

The traveller in me wanted to keep exploring new countries, but I knew how long it had been since I'd seen my family. Unfortunately, I was forced to pay £250 on four PCR tests to enter my country of birth, despite being double vaccinated. This included postage for one of the tests which was £35! It would've been cheaper to send a watermelon to Australia! How they got away with charging that much I will never know. After my home quarantine, I was able to see friends and travel to Middlesbrough and Doncaster to visit family.

I was having a nice, relaxing time back home so it was a shock when I had a near-death experience walking in the Yorkshire Dales. Mum was painting by a lake whilst me and Dad explored. After veering off the footpath, we ended up in boggy marsh on the other side of the lake, where there were five cows. We didn't think anything of it and walked around them to take photos of the lake. After returning the phone to my pocket, I noticed one of the cows glaring at us. I've never found cows intimidating but I could sense this particular cow was pissed off about us invading their space. The cow slowly approached us and began to charge. The other cows followed suit, leaving us trapped between a river and the lake. We ran towards a bush and hid inside but the cows rammed us from all angles. It was terrifying! We managed to find a spot they couldn't reach and once they backed off we made our way out of the bush.

We were horrified to discover they'd called backup and six of them came charging back at us. Everything happened so quickly. We didn't know whether it was best to jump in the water or try scare them. My dad started barking at them which didn't help. We managed to run to another bush and snap off some branches to use in self-defence.

Every time they approached, we pretended to hit them and eventually they dispersed. As we were lodged in by the river and the lake, our only option was to go back the way we came. The problem was that we didn't know where the cattle would be. We tried trudging through a nearby swamp but it was too dense. These cows looked possessed and would've trampled all over us if they managed to knock us to the ground. A teacher died in Yorkshire under similar circumstances the year before. Thankfully, the cows moved to the adjacent field, allowing us to jump over a fence and return to the footpath.

I spoke to friends and family about the ordeal when I returned home and three people said they knew someone who had died from a cow attack. Never underestimate cows. They have so much power and as soon as they get you to the ground, you'll be lucky to escape. It's common for cows to protect their calves and feel threatened, but as far as we're aware there were no calves in the area.

As my time in the UK came to a close, I was grateful to spend a few days with Nana Mavis. She was feeling lonely as she'd been struggling with an eye infection and been unable to leave the house. Every time I see her we go for a 'Lemon Top' at Pacittos Ice Cream Shop in Redcar. If you didn't know, it's the UK's best ice cream! As my dad told me in Chile all those years ago, life does go quicker the older you get. I feel guilty I don't spend enough time with my family. It plays on my mind a lot living abroad and I value each day I'm able to spend with them. As well as family, there are friends I'm able to reconnect with when I'm back in the UK. I met my old schoolfriends Chris and Dave during my time back home. I hadn't seen Chris for seven years! I also managed to squeeze in Cal Bolton's wedding the day before my flight. I spent so much of my childhood with him and he was even at my birth!

In the end, it was a great trip back home and I wouldn't have changed a thing … apart from maybe going off the footpath on that walk and nearly dying! Oh, and missing my flight back to Dubai, that was annoying. At the check-in desk at Birmingham Airport, I was informed I didn't have the correct PCR test. I had to pay to change my flight, book two nights' stay in the airport hotel and book another expensive PCR test. Brilliant!

## 29 Years and 364 days

That was a life lived **every day** for **30 Years.**

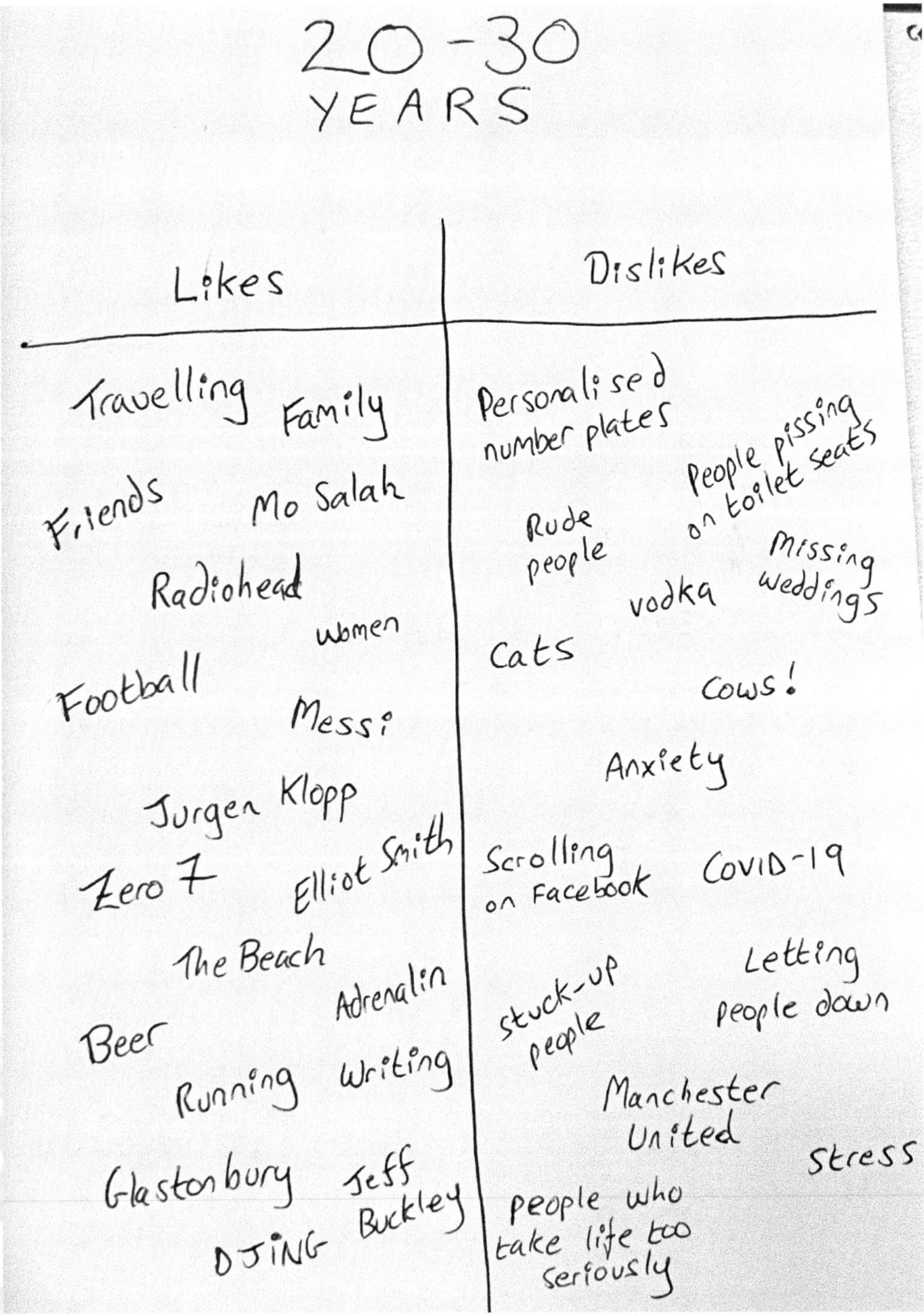

# 20-30
## YEARS

| Likes | Dislikes |
|---|---|

**Likes:**

Travelling    Family

Friends    Mo Salah

Radiohead

women

Football

Messi

Jurgen Klopp

Zero 7    Elliot Smith

The Beach

Adrenalin

Beer

Running    Writing

Glastonbury    Jeff Buckley

DJING

**Dislikes:**

Personalised number plates

People pissing on toilet seats

Rude people

vodka    Missing weddings

Cats

Cows!

Anxiety

Scrolling on Facebook    COVID-19

stuck-up people    Letting people down

Manchester United

stress

people who take life too seriously

*Can you believe that on my very last photo of the 30 Years project I had a cold sore? Typical!*

# 30

## (13 September 2021 – ?)

### The future

As I've arrived at the end of my first 30 Years and embarked on a new chapter in my life, I've started to wonder what my hopes and ambitions for the future are. Is it better to keep going as I'm going, making small steps forward in my career but having regrets, or is it better to dream big?

### Small dreams

Until the big dreams happen, I want to keep progressing in my career. My parents have always said not to take a job for granted, even if it's not your dream job. In the future, I'd love to own my own house, be a loving husband and a hero to my kids. My dad was 35 when he had me so I have a few years left before I need to settle down.

I hope my parents can retire soon and have free time to travel and tick off the remainder of their dreams. My parents were talented artists. I worry I was the reason for them stopping so I'd love to see them painting and drawing again. I want to help them build a website and social media following so they can sell their work. Another small dream is to see my parents back at Glastonbury Festival – only this time they'll have to buy a ticket and not jump over the fence!

I want to focus on my health more. That's not just a oh shit I'm getting older thing but I've never felt better than when I was doing the ultramarathon training (mentally and physically). I know I've written (typed) two books but I would love to read more. I've only read five, and two of them were my own. I know some people hate on him but listening to the Joe Rogan podcast has reignited my appetite to learn and discover new topics. Whether it's Graham Hancock talking about the mystery of the Amazon, Elon Musk revealing his plans to colonise the galaxy or Neil deGrasse Tyson explaining how Christopher Columbus was a dick, it's all been informative and compelling. At least now I have a reason to buy some books.

My navigation through life has led me to a somewhat corporate career. Although I'm proud of what I've achieved with work, I'd love to delve back into my creative side and return to drawing and art. DJing has also been something I've had to put to one side. It's something I love and if I did it full-time, playing the music I enjoy, I'd be so content. If I decide that's what I want, I just need to go out and get it!

I've talked in depth (maybe too much) about my love for partying. I just can't do it as much anymore because of commitments and health reasons. I've always loved ecstasy and mushrooms but never gone beyond that. Anxiety-allowing, I'd love to try acid … and maybe even ayahuasca in the Amazon! I still suffer from anxiety but I like to say I beat it because I'm in a much better place than the 2015–16 period. I'd love to help raise more awareness for mental health. It's being talked about more and more but we still have a long way to go!

Of course, I never made it as a footballer … even if I did play with Mikael Silvestre! Maybe I could try get my football coaching badges. My local club, Harrogate Town AFC are in League Two so, once I'm qualified, I might see if they have any vacancies.

## Big dreams

There's nothing wrong with dreaming big. Even if that dream never happens, it's fun chasing it and gives you a reason to work hard. I recently hit 50 countries and my big dream is to visit every country in the world before I die. It's a bit difficult when work is so hectic and the pandemic has restricted travel, but nevertheless I plan to get it done.

If I returned to my creative roots, I'd love to get back into film/television – but more so, as a writer. It would be a dream to write comedy with Ricky Gervais, send a feature-length script to Taika Waititi (in the hope he'd direct it) or maybe even be in front of the camera, acting in a Danny Boyle, Quentin Tarantino or Christopher Nolan movie. If I ever tried vlogging full-time it would be a dream to collaborate with the YouTube channel Yes Theory.

I like surrounding myself with inspiring and motivated people. It would be a big dream to work with Jesse Itzler. I love his way of thinking and I know I could learn a lot from him. He's also one of the best in the business at public speaking and that's something I'm not so great at. Maybe one day I could even do a TED talk! Jesse regularly competes in 100-mile races. After completing two 50km races, my next goal is 100km, followed by 100 miles.

I also have some pretty wild, but not impossible dreams:
- Play in a football match at Anfield.
- Help make Crown Green Bowling a global sport
- Climb to the summit of Mount Everest.
- Have a daily photo taken in Space.

Oh, and go for dinner with Jim Carrey.

## Regrets

I have a life full of regrets, but who doesn't? I could've worked harder at school so that I wasn't serving canapés to rich people … but on the flip side, I'd never have met Rihanna.

I believe I could've made it as a footballer with the right application but I didn't take it seriously enough. It still haunts me to this day that I forgot my boots for a Leeds United trial. I'm still learning how to be a better person – still a work in progress! As much as I don't regret partying (the music, the dancing, sharing a moment with complete strangers), maybe I could've partied a bit less.

My music taste at the age of 12 was questionable. Not learning an instrument bugs me. If I'd mastered the keyboard or piano, I could've applied that to music production and made a house record. I regret not starting the YouTube travel show I had the idea for in 2015. Yes Theory are doing exactly what I wanted to do. I'd be lying if I said I wasn't jealous but their content is so good – they've nailed it!

I regret not backing up my photos before my phone was stolen in Ibiza. It pains me to think I never saw Jeff Buckley or Elliot Smith live before their passing. I still kick myself for missing Air when they played on my birthday in 2017 at Sydney Opera House. I regret not seeing my parents or family enough due to living abroad.

## Proud

Although I don't like the word 'blessed,' I feel blessed to have such great, easy-going parents. They've influenced me to see the world and meet new people. They've taught me the importance of being laidback and down to earth.

I'm proud of playing football and ten-pin bowling to a good standard. In crown green bowling, I'm proud of being the youngest winner of a senior competition in Harrogate and becoming second in Britain at under-18 level.

I love my hometown Harrogate and the people in it. There truly isn't another town in the world like it! I don't see my old friends as much anymore but when I'm back for summer or Christmas we have the best reunions and nights out. I appreciate all the different friends I've made from around the world. I know I always have a place to stay wherever I go and they are always welcome at my place in Harrogate or Dubai.

I'm proud of backpacking South America at a young age (with my parents, aged one, and with Tom and Balley, aged 19). Looking back, reaching Everest Base Camp was probably the best day of my life. I was so proud to be there – especially under the circumstances! Helping Takashi reach his goal of standing on the summit of Mount Fuji on his fourth attempt was something I will never forget.

## Writing 30 years: a life lived every day

To be honest, it just kind of happened – almost in the same way my dad had the idea for the flick book in 1991! Rather than just see my face growing up in the 30 Years video, the idea came to me to write about all the stories in between the photos. Although some are nostalgic and have interesting backgrounds, it doesn't tell the full story.

It took me a while to figure out how to fit 30 Years into a book. What made it easier was breaking it down into years. I made a title for each year and if a story or memory came to me, I'd make a note and write the story into the correct year. It went from there and, in no particular order, I started assembling the book.

Of course, I had my doubts about whether anyone would be interested in reading this. I'm not a celebrity of any kind and don't have a newsworthy story to write in depth about. I thought it might be something different that people can relate to. I've done some amazing things that I'm grateful for, but I've done them with relatively limited means. For the most part, I've worked to afford the things I've done and to travel to the places I've been.

It's been difficult balancing a full-time job and writing. I'd arrive home from work knackered and find it hard to psych myself up. Sometimes, I'd have a free weekend to write and other times I'd have a work event or birthday to attend. Writing can be enjoyable and I've loved reminiscing, but it does take up so much time – and that's before the editing has started! It's funny, sometimes I'd find having a few drinks would provide inspiration and I could smash out thousands of words in a few hours. Other times, I'd find not drinking at all and planning a full day at my desk would work better. In the end, I realised there's no correct way to write a book, you've just got to go with the flow and write whenever you feel like it!

## Summary

It's been a hell of a ride. I've met so many great people and had so many unforgettable experiences. The majority of my best memories and experiences in these first 30 Years have been through travelling – so, get out there, see the world and meet new people! I believe that you learn so much about the world and different cultures through travelling, and, in time, the world is going to become a much better place. The recent pandemic is a reminder to live for the now. Don't spend so much time worrying about the future that you forget to enjoy the moment.

## The project

I will continue taking a photo every day and, who knows, maybe they will eventually master anti-ageing and the project never ends. I could even go backwards! #BenjaminButton. My dad is also continuing his project '60 to death' – morbid I know. You'll be able to find it on his 'cloddyclips' channel when he or I eventually upload it.

At the time of reading this, my next video '30 Years: A Photo of Cory Every Day' will be live on YouTube and other video platforms.

After being inspired by Beeple's 'Everydays' project, I launched my own NFT collection. There are 10,000 images in the collection and you can own part of the project by searching '30 Years: Cory Every Day' on OpenSea.

You can also find more content and information related to the project on my Instagram @coryeveryday_, TikTok @coryeveryday and www.linktr.ee/coryeveryday.

## Message to take home

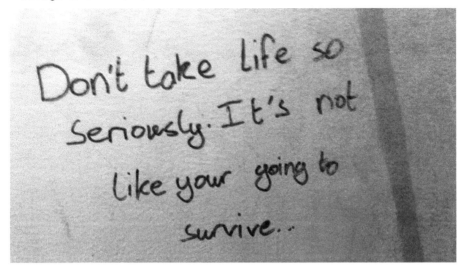

## Acknowledgements

Firstly, I want to thank my parents, Karen and Ian. They're private people and have allowed me to open up and reveal a lot of details about their life, as well as mine. They are the reason I'm here, they are the reason for the 30 Years project and they are the reason I am who I am (the good bits). The bad bits I get from my mates! I love you both so much and thank you for teaching me not to take life too seriously. You are legends!

Thank you to my family, my friends and all the people I've mentioned in this book who have been a part of the journey. I appreciate you all being in my life so much. I value the friendships and memories I have more than anything in the world.

Thanks to my grandparents Mavis, Bill, Cecilia and Ronnie for bringing my parents into the world and being so loving to me. Special mention for Ronnie who gifted my dad his brilliant journal. I discovered so many interesting stories about how our family came to be.

I would also like to say a special thanks to my old Sydney housemate Rebecka Davidsson. Rebecka offered to read through and critique the entire first draft. She improved the flow of the book and helped spot grammar mistakes – there was many. In fact, I don't even know if that should be 'there was many' or 'there were many.' I better not ask her for any more help… I'll leave that one.

Huge thanks to Dave Hall too! My lifelong friend, who allowed me to bounce ideas off him whenever I needed. He's one of the best writers I know and I've appreciated his advice along the way.

Finally, thank you to Donovan Murphy, who I met in Ibiza in 2015. He's a teacher and talented writer so I asked for his help. He filmed himself doing a 30-minute presentation explaining the past, present and future tenses. Now that is what you call dedication!

**Thank you to everyone who has read the book and here's to the next 30 Years!**

Tag me with a photo of you and the book on Instagram @coryeveryday_

ND - #0258 - 270225 - C0 - 234/156/19 - PB - 9781780916521 - Gloss Lamination